The Making of the Middle Ages

JOHN HAYWOOD

The Making of the Middle Ages

An Atlas of Europe

FOREWORD BY MICHAEL WOOD

With 193 illustrations

JOHN HAYWOOD was educated at the universities of Lancaster, Cambridge and Copenhagen. He is an expert on the history of early medieval Europe. His authorial credits include *Ocean: A History of the Atlantic Before Columbus*, *The Penguin Atlas of the Vikings* and *The Historical Atlas of the Celtic World*, also published by Thames & Hudson.

MICHAEL WOOD is a historian, filmmaker and broadcaster. Since 2013 he has been Professor of Public History at the University of Manchester. He is the author of many bestselling books, including *In Search of the Dark Ages*, *Domesday* and *In Search of England*.

COVER: A section of map from *The Western Roman Empire at the accession of Julius Nepos, 474*, taken from pages 72–3.

FRONTISPIECE: A 5th-century elephant ivory diptych depicting personifications of Rome (left) and Constantinople (right).

First published in the United Kingdom in 2026 by
Thames & Hudson Ltd, 6–24 Britannia Street, London WC1X 9JD

First published in the United States of America in 2026 by
Thames & Hudson Inc., 500 Fifth Avenue, New York, New York 10110

The Making of the Middle Ages: An Atlas of Europe © 2026 Thames & Hudson Ltd, London

Text and maps © 2026 John Haywood
Foreword © 2026 Michael Wood

Designed by Alice C. Woodward

All Rights Reserved. No part of this publication may be reproduced or transmitted in any form or by any means, electronic or mechanical, including photocopy, recording or any other information storage and retrieval system, without prior permission in writing from the publisher.

EU Authorized Representative: Interart S.A.R.L.
19 rue Charles Auray, 93500 Pantin, Paris, France
productsafety@thameshudson.co.uk interart.fr

A CIP catalogue record for this book is available from the British Library

Library of Congress Control Number 2025938783

ISBN 978-0-500-02980-0

01

Printed and bound in China by C&C Offset Printing Co. Ltd

Be the first to know about our new releases,
exclusive content and author events by visiting
thamesandhudson.com
thamesandhudsonusa.com
thamesandhudson.com.au

Contents

	Foreword	6
	Introduction: A Time of Darkness?	10
I	An Empire at Bay	16
II	Fall of the Roman Empire	38
III	A New Order	74
IV	Birth of Byzantium	100
V	Britannia	130
VI	Islamic Expansion	160
VII	The Rise of the Franks	186
VIII	The Age of Charlemagne	208
IX	Saints and Scholars	244
X	Trial By Fire	268
XI	Emerging Europe	308
	Epilogue: The Birth of the West	338
	Select Bibliography	342
	Sources of Illustrations	343
	Index	345

Foreword

'...it was as though the very world had shaken herself and cast off her old age, and were clothing herself everywhere in a white garment of churches.'

RALPH GLABER, ELEVENTH-CENTURY BENEDICTINE CHRONICLER

In recent years there has been much argument about the origins and identity of what has come to be known as the West. Is there a shared history? A common culture and civilizational values? As this book shows so graphically, the roots of Europe lie in what the historian Michael Wallace-Hadrill called – playfully but also seriously – the 'Barbarian West'. What he meant was that modern Europe is the creation of the Germanic tribes and kingdoms that settled in the territory of the Roman Empire after its fall and adopted Latin Christian civilization. They had not been part of the world of late antiquity, whose peoples lived along the welcoming shores of the Mediterranean 'like frogs around a pond', as Plato put it. They were outsiders, so-called barbarians, who had first come into the empire as economic migrants, guest workers and mercenaries, and later as invaders, conquerors and settlers. They had not shared in the cosmopolitan literate culture of the late Classical world, and after the fall of Rome, in many places written sources vanish (hence the old term used to describe this period, the 'Dark Ages'). Indeed, some former Roman colonies, where written culture had not been deeply rooted – the British Isles among them – almost drop off the map, with literacy and learning maintained only in the outer reaches, in Ireland and Wales, for example. The darkness, then, in the fifth and sixth centuries is real, if not everywhere, but out of that darkness a new world would emerge, which is the foundation of today's Europe.

FOREWORD

After the fall of Rome, the critical issue for leaders, thinkers and churchmen was how they could preserve and hand down the values of Classical culture. In the sixth century, writers in Italy in particular – for example, Boethius and Symmachus – were obsessed with the question of how the great cultural achievements of pagan Greece and Rome, the lifeblood of the Classical world for so many centuries, could be passed on in a Christian world threatened on all sides. Some, like the Roman statesman Cassiodorus, working for the Ostrogothic state in Ravenna, founded monasteries and assembled libraries to further the tradition of learning, pagan and Christian – his monastery of Vivarium in Calabria being the most famous.

It would take three successive renaissances, between the ninth and the fourteenth centuries, for European civilization to rise again. It is salutary to make comparisons; the very different trajectory, for example, in China, where the tradition of political unity went far back in time, reinforced by common language and script, administration, and even uniform weights and measures. Today's Chinese state is still the lineal successor of the Qin and the Han Empires over two thousand years ago, contemporaries of the Roman Republic and early Roman Empire.

This huge, complex and fascinating story is at the centre of this book, and is vital to our understanding of today's world, especially in such unstable times. And turning these pages, one wonders whether that story is most clearly readable in maps – maps of empires and wars, maps of states and kingdoms, maps of migrations and explorations, but also maps of the spread of religions and ideas. They tell the story of how western European societies emerged out of the breakdown of central authority and the formation of regional powers in the early Middle Ages, while still embracing the spiritual and cultural authority of Latin Christendom. All roads still led to and from Rome, and with them ideas, a vision of how society should be; the papacy, it is easy to forget, is the last surviving institution of the Roman Empire, as we witnessed so powerfully in the ceremonies for the funeral of Pope Francis in Rome in 2025.

There were, of course, many strands to the construction of a Western identity over the five centuries covered in this book. In the eighth century, the English scholar Alcuin, former librarian in York, who was headhunted to lead Charlemagne's court school in Aachen, narrowed them down to four dominant traditions: Latin Christian civilization, Judaeo-Christian religion, the wisdom of Greece and 'the light that came out of Africa'. By his time, prominent centres of learning such as Wearmouth and Jarrow, founded by the former barbarians in faraway Britain, had become powerhouses of culture in the new West, copying and spreading manuscripts across Europe.

How that chain of transmission worked in practice can be seen, for example, in England. In 597, Pope Gregory the Great sent a Roman mission to Kent to begin the conversion of the barbarian Angles and Saxons. Within fifty years a Northumbrian aristocrat, Benedict Biscop, would make five visits to Rome, bringing hundreds of books back home: manuscripts retrieved from the (by then dispersed) library of Vivarium; Greek books from the eastern Mediterranean rescued from the Arab invasions; books from North Africa that had come through Naples, the great centre of Greek culture and learning in southern Italy. A key link between Rome and England, in 669 Biscop would accompany Theodore of Tarsus to Britain, to become Archbishop of Canterbury, where he was joined by his friend and collaborator Abbot Hadrian 'the African'. Theodore was a Syriac- and Greek-speaking monk educated at Antioch; Hadrian is thought to have been from Cyrenaica in Libya. Together they formed the famous School of Canterbury, the greatest educational project in Britain before the sixteenth-century Renaissance. With the identification of their lecture notes in manuscripts in Britain and Europe, we can see clearly now how the wisdom of Italy, Greece, the Near East and North Africa was transmitted across Europe – biblical studies, grammar, cosmology, history, linguistics and medicine forming the foundation of the European cultural renaissance of the ninth century.

Theodore and Hadrian were later seen as progenitors in the story of the revival of European culture in the early Middle Ages. In the ninth century, Charlemagne and Louis the Pious would even hope to create a unified Christian culture in the West, a Europe-wide *imperium Christianum* – an ambition that proved beyond them.

Looking back from Auxerre in the late tenth century, a scholar called Gautbertus set out to write the intellectual family tree of the early West. He begins with Theodore and Hadrian, then their pupils Bede and Aldhelm, Alcuin in Charlemagne's Aachen, then in the next generations the renowned Carolingian teachers Hrabanus Maurus, John Scotus Eriugena, and Heiric and Remigius of Auxerre, the schoolmasters of the medieval West. He concludes with his tenth-century contemporaries, including Israel of Trier who worked in England in the court of King Athelstan and 'made Britannia famous through the world of the liberal arts. They furnished cups of nourishment for the faithful, and we still drink from their fountains today'.

By the time of Gautbertus, the wider world had changed forever. The Mediterranean was now a 'Muslim lake' and western Europe had been severed from much of its Classical heartland. The next age would look out to the Atlantic and a wider world beyond.

Our tale, then, is the rise of the Barbarian West: Franks, Visigoths, Ostrogoths, Lombards, Angles, Saxons and Jutes, the tribes that settled in the post-Roman world and founded their societies, imbibing the Latin Christian culture of late antiquity. By the year 1000 they had become the new Christendom, transformed by the Carolingian humanism of Europe's first renaissance, which shaped the character of the early western kingdoms, the French, the Spanish, Anglo-Saxon England and the German kingdom of Otto I, the First Reich. Such was the origin of the medieval and modern European countries and their Latin Christian culture.

It seems to me that this gives us a key to the grand narrative depicted so vividly in this book. In the culture wars of our time, the debate about the nature of 'the West' rages on. It has even been claimed that the identity of 'the West' is the retrospective construction of the Age of Enlightenment, or even later, the Age of Imperialism and colonization – the invention of a fictive ancestry in the Classical world. These elements no doubt played their part, but as the maps of this book show, they do not tell the fundamental story. The West, it is true, as Alcuin noted, had many influences, including Greece, the Near East and North Africa. But its roots lay in Germanic society, languages, culture, law and custom – including its characteristic assembly politics – over which were laid the rich strata of Latin Christianity and Hellenism. The five hundred years of the early Middle Ages were the crucible of the kingdoms and cultures of western Europe. The West was made by the peoples of the Barbarian West. This is the great adventure, no less exciting than the stories of India or China, that is so illuminatingly depicted in these pages.

MICHAEL WOOD

INTRODUCTION

A Time of Darkness?

Medieval western Europeans suffered from a lack of self-esteem: they felt that the ancient Greeks and Romans had done everything better. This was certainly how the Italian humanist scholar Petrarch (1304–1374) was feeling when he wrote in the 1330s that he believed that the fall of the Roman Empire had ushered in an 'age of darkness', one which had yet to end. Thanks to his revival of Classical Latin literary forms, later generations of scholars would see Petrarch as one of the figures who brought this age of darkness to an end by ushering in the Renaissance, and they rather liked the idea that they were bringing light to the world.

The term 'Dark Age' (in Latin *saeculum obscurum*) is often used to describe the early Middle Ages and was coined by another Italian, the ecclesiastical historian Caesar Baronius in 1602. By the end of the seventeenth century it had been adopted by English historians. During the eighteenth century, secularist and rationalist Enlightenment thinkers used the term 'Dark Ages' as a synonym for the whole of the Middle Ages (*c.* 476–*c.* 1492), a period that they regarded as being steeped in religious ignorance and superstition. In the nineteenth century, a more positive view of the Middle Ages developed and, by its end, the 'dark age' had been narrowed down to the five centuries following the collapse of the Western Roman Empire in the fifth century, for which there was a dearth of literary sources in comparison with the preceding and subsequent periods.

The Jelling Stone, from Jutland in Denmark – King Harald Bluetooth's memorial inscription to his parents, *c.* 983–85, also celebrates his conversion to Christianity (and therefore that of all Danes) in *c.* 960.

INTRODUCTION

The 'Dark Ages' has become a byword for ignorance, brutality and squalor. In everyday discourse, 'Dark Age' can be invoked to express disapproval of almost anything we find backward or irrational: it has become a value judgment as much as a historical term. It is because of these pejorative overtones that most historians and archaeologists are now reluctant to use the term, preferring to talk about the early Middle Ages instead (it is the term generally used in this book too). This isn't just academic pedantry.

It is all too common to judge the past by modern standards of behaviour and morality and to find it wanting. However, historians have a responsibility to be as objective about the past as possible, and do their best to understand it in its own terms. Ignorance, brutality and squalor there was aplenty in the early Middle Ages, but so too is there in our supposedly advanced modern world. Early Medieval Europe had its dark places and periods – Great Britain in the two centuries following the end of Roman rule in 410, for example – but Roman Britain produced no literary figure to compare with the Anglo-Saxon monk Bede. It was also the period when Ireland, Scandinavia and eastern Europe first emerged from prehistory into the light of recorded history.

However, it is a deeply inaccurate way to describe much of the world beyond Europe: the same period was one of major cultural achievements in India, China, the Middle East and Mesoamerica. Both the Dark Ages and the Middle Ages are very Eurocentric concepts.

It isn't just for its pejorative overtones that the term has fallen out of favour with historians and archaeologists: they can reasonably object too that, thanks to their efforts, the period is nowhere near as dark as it was when the term was first coined. After several centuries of intensive research in libraries and archives, it is unlikely that any major new documentary sources remain to be discovered, but since the late nineteenth century the increasingly scientific discipline of archaeology has unearthed vast amounts of material evidence from the period, shedding light on the everyday lives of early medieval people, their technology, arts and crafts, trade, diet, health and even personal mobility.

Information about the last three has come largely thanks to the still relatively new science of isotopic analysis of human remains, particularly bones and teeth. The different ratios of isotopes of

Scholar, pope and saint, Gregory I is depicted in this late 9th-century ivory carving seated at his writing desk, a symbol of clerical enlightenment in a time when the glory of the Roman Empire remained fresh in educated minds but was a fading folk memory.

INTRODUCTION

elements such as oxygen, strontium and calcium absorbed by bones from food and from drinking water reflect the underlying geology, whether diet was largely plant or meat based, and if it came mainly from terrestrial or maritime sources.

Bone is continuously replaced throughout life, so its chemical make-up reflects where the subject lived shortly before death. Tooth enamel, in contrast, is formed in childhood and never replaced, so its content reflects where the subject was born and brought up. Thanks to these techniques it was possible to determine that a young, high-status female buried *c.* 550 in a cemetery at the Anglo-Saxon royal stronghold of Bamburgh in Northumberland was born in Norway. Given her status, it is likely she came to Bamburgh for a diplomatic marriage, providing evidence for the existence of otherwise unrecorded political connections between England and Norway.

Another transformative science has been that of genetic analysis both related to modern populations and to ancient DNA (aDNA) recovered from human remains. This has allowed family relationships to be established among group burials, for example, but its greatest contribution has been to shed light on population movements in the early Middle Ages (and the rest of human history, of course). Primary sources from the period make much of invasions and migrations, but their exact nature has been much disputed. For much of the twentieth century, migration was the go-to explanation for archaeologists faced with evidence of cultural and technological change: new styles of pottery, jewelry, weapons and similar artefacts were almost always interpreted as evidence for the arrival of a new population.

However, bringing a more critical eye to the interpretation of primary sources, historians in the later twentieth century began increasingly to question this approach. Could there not be other causes of cultural change? For example, might not the considerable changes in material culture in England in the post-Roman period be the result of a small elite of aristocratic warriors invading, replacing the existing ruling class, and imposing their own cultural identity and language? Might not contemporary accounts of mass migration have been exaggerated? Historians had some justification in asking such questions: after all, the language of invasion is routinely used today by populist newspapers when covering immigration stories. However, as is so often the case with revisionists, they rushed to the opposite extreme, to the extent of denying any meaningful role for large-scale population movements in the history of the period. The evidence of aDNA has now brought welcome clarity to these issues. It is now possible to say that the early Middle Ages really was a period of considerable mobility, not only for individuals and elites but for large population groups as well.

Irrespective of what we choose to call this period, there is no disputing its crucial importance in European history. Lasting roughly from 400 to 1000, this period saw the fall of the Western Roman Empire, great migrations, the breakup of the culturally united Mediterranean world of Classical antiquity, the rise of Islam, the Christianization of northern and eastern Europe, the emergence of the distinct separate cultural identities of eastern and western Europe, the beginning of the shift of the economic centre of Europe from the Mediterranean to the southern North Sea, and the birth of many of the leading nations of modern Europe.

By the end of the period Europe's strongest states – the Greek Byzantine Empire and the German Holy Roman Empire – still harked back to the idealized unity represented by the Christian Roman Empire of Constantine the Great, though the outlines of modern Europe with its nation states was already becoming clear. Europe stood on the brink of a profound transformation as stability, prosperity and cultural life began a strong revival. In this way, the early Middle Ages represent nothing less than the birth of Europe.

The study of a period of such rapid mobility and transformational change can be greatly enhanced by a collection of good maps. As none exists at present, this is a need which the author hopes this book will supply.

I
An Empire at Bay

Beyond Rome's apogee

The Roman Empire of the early second century AD was an unrivalled superpower. Its borders were secure and it enjoyed political stability and economic prosperity. Any order other than Roman was becoming unimaginable, yet all was not well. On his deathbed, Emperor Augustus (r. 27 BC–AD 14) famously advised his successors against conquering new territory, but the Roman Empire continued to grow steadily throughout the first century AD, mainly through the annexation of client kingdoms such as Cappadocia in Asia Minor and Mauretania in North Africa. The conquest of Britain begun in AD 43 had not proved easy and the northern half of the island remained unsubdued.

Rome's last great conquering emperor was Spanish-born Trajan (r. 97–117), who annexed the mineral-rich Dacian kingdom in the Carpathians in 105 and humbled the Parthian Empire of Persia by occupying Mesopotamia and sacking its capital Ctesiphon in 115–16. Trajan died the following year, before his eastern conquests were fully consolidated, and his successor Hadrian (r. 117–38) immediately returned Mesopotamia to the Parthians in return for an advantageous peace treaty. He devoted much of his reign to fortifying the empire's frontiers: Hadrian recognized that it had reached the practical limits of its expansion. Rome could not maintain its existing frontiers and wage a long war of aggression in the east.

An early 4th-century Roman helmet from Berkasovo, Serbia, decorated with silver-gilt and glass gems. As the amount of silver-gilt and gems was determined by rank, this ornate helmet would have belonged to a high-ranking officer. A Greek inscription on the helmet reads: 'Dizzon, wear this in good health, Avitus'.

The Roman apogee under Trajan

I AN EMPIRE AT BAY

The end of territorial expansion presented a long-term economic problem. The main source of wealth in the empire was agriculture: some 95 per cent of the population worked as peasant farmers or as slaves on the *latifundia* (estates) of the wealthy. In pre-industrial societies, agricultural productivity depended mainly on the amount of labour available and could not easily be increased. As a result, the most efficient way the empire could increase its resources was by conquering new territories and taxing them. Now that opportunities for easy conquests were exhausted, the empire would have to live on a fixed budget.

Another problem was the imperial constitution. In theory, the emperor was 'first citizen', a glorified magistrate whose powers were granted by the Roman Senate and people. In practice, the emperorship had developed into a hereditary monarchy, though succession was no guarantee of ability and there was no constitutional way to depose a bad emperor. After the quintessential 'mad emperor' Nero was overthrown in 68, a civil war broke out as rival generals fought for power in the Year of the Four Emperors (69), which brought Vespasian and his Flavian dynasty to power. After the increasing tyranny of the third Flavian, Domitian, his successor Nerva (r. 96–98) restored stability to the imperial succession by adopting the experienced and able general Trajan as his son and successor. When Nerva died, Trajan's succession was uncontested. In the same way, Trajan chose his successor by adopting Hadrian. Succession by adoption provided the stability of hereditary dynastic succession and ensured that each future emperor had time to prove his suitability for office before he inherited power. Despite its success, the principle was abandoned by Marcus Aurelius (r. 161–80), for no obvious reason other than to favour his own family. He was followed by his deranged son Commodus, whose inevitable assassination in 192 was followed by another succession crisis and civil war.

Marcus Aurelius's reign saw another unwelcome development. In 166, while the Romans were distracted by a war with Parthia and the aftermath of a smallpox epidemic, a coalition of tribal peoples led by the Marcomanni broke through the Danube frontier and penetrated as far as northern Italy. It took Marcus fourteen years of hard campaigning to defeat the invaders. Large numbers of captive Marcomanni were granted land in the empire in return

Overleaf: Hadrian's Wall, begun in 122. The emperor Hadrian built this 117.5-km (73-mile) long wall from the Solway Firth in the west to the mouth of the River Tyne on the east to protect the romanized south of Britain from raids.

Marble bust of the emperor Hadrian (r. 117–38). Hadrian recognized that the Roman Empire had reached the practical limits of expansion and spent much of his reign fortifying its frontiers.

Trajan's Column was erected in Rome in 113 to celebrate the emperor Trajan's conquest of Dacia. In this scene legionary soldiers are portrayed building border fortifications.

for their military service; this would become an increasingly common practice in the centuries to come.

The Marcomanni had been defeated so comprehensively that they are seldom mentioned by later writers. However, their invasion was a symptom of profound social changes that were unfolding beyond the empire's frontiers on the Rhine and Danube. Recognizing that they spoke related languages and shared many beliefs and customs, the Romans collectively described the tribal peoples who lived in this region of central Europe as the Germani. Because the Germani lacked formal governments and did not live in cities, the essential attributes of civilized life in Roman eyes, they were also described in a more generalized way as barbarians (*barbari*, i.e. 'uncivilized'), a word they used also to describe other

tribal peoples outside the empire such as the Celts and the Huns. Though the Marcomannic confederation had been broken, new ones would form. Germanic pressure on the empire's northern frontier would become unrelenting.

The third-century crisis

The third century was one of the most difficult in Roman history. A combination of Germanic invasions, civil war and runaway inflation brought the empire to the brink of collapse. The battle of succession which followed Commodus's assassination was won by Septimius Severus (r. 193–211), a general who, like his defeated rivals, had been proclaimed emperor by his troops. Severus tried to re-establish stable dynastic rule by proclaiming his sons Caracalla and Geta as co-emperors while they were youths. Unfortunately, the brothers hated each other. Caracalla acted first and murdered Geta, seizing power for himself. His reign descended into despotism and in 217 he was murdered while campaigning in the east. Emperors began to come and go in rapid succession.

This chronic instability could not have come at a worse time for the empire. In Germania, formidable new tribal confederations were forming, the more effectively to wage war. In the east, the Parthians, discredited by too many defeats at Roman hands, were overthrown in 226 by the aggressive Sasanian dynasty. Until the 260s the Romans successfully defended their frontiers against these new threats, but the persistent pressure took its toll. In conditions of near permanent warfare, the army came to dominate political life. An emperor who proved to be a poor soldier, or a mean paymaster, would not rule for long.

As rival imperial candidates promoted by different legions battled one other for power, the frontiers were left open to invasion. Even when one claimant emerged supreme, he could not feel secure. Any new military crisis might provide the opportunity for one of his generals to attempt a coup, breeding a poisonous atmosphere of mutual suspicion. If a general felt that he was distrusted by the emperor, he might rebel simply to protect himself against a trumped-up treason charge and inevitable execution. Civil war and invasion were unceasing between 235 and 284. Of the twenty-six

THE THIRD-CENTURY CRISIS

Silver drachma of the Sasanian 'King of Kings' Shapur I (r. 240–270). Shapur took advantage of the instability of the Roman Empire to expand into Mesopotamia and Armenia. In 259 he humiliated the Romans by capturing their emperor, Valerian, at Edessa in Syria.

officially recognized emperors in this period, all but one died by violence. Dozens of usurpers died in battle, or were murdered or executed after unsuccessful bids for power. In desperate attempts to buy their soldiers' loyalty, emperors repeatedly debased the coinage to raise money, but this only added runaway inflation to the empire's problems.

The economic crisis, combined with the constant threat of invasion, caused a decline in town life, especially in western provinces. In Gaul, Hispania and Britannia, many towns shrank to a heavily defended administrative core. Economic problems were exacerbated by population decline caused by recurrent epidemic diseases. The empire's fortunes reached their nadir in 260 after Valerian (r. 253–60) was captured and killed by the Sasanians at Edessa (now Sanliurfa, Turkey). Septimius Odenathus, client king of Palmyra (d. 267), drove back the Sasanians but seceded from the empire, along with much of the east. In the west another usurper, Postumus (d. 269), founded an independent 'Gallic Empire' in 257. Valerian's official successor, his son Gallienus, controlled barely two-thirds of the empire and he was not secure even there. During his eight-year reign (260–68) he had to suppress eighteen usurpers, only to be murdered by his own officers. Gallienus deserved better, for his reform of the army proved key to Rome's survival.

During the first and second centuries, the Roman army had become a largely immobile garrison stationed on the empire's frontiers. When invaders broke through the frontiers, they could roam almost at will. To counter this weakness Gallienus created highly mobile field armies with a strong cavalry element that could operate independently. His military reforms were used to good effect by the succession of able, if short-lived, emperors who followed him. They all hailed from Illyria, a major recruiting ground for the army. Claudius II (r. 268–70) defeated the Goths, Aurelian (r. 270–75) reconquered Palmyra and the Gallic Empire, Probus (r. 276–82) defeated the Franks and Alamanni, and Carus (r. 282–83) drove back the Sasanians.

Apart from Dacia, lost to the Goths, and the Agri Decumates, taken by the Alamanni (both of them Germanic peoples), the empire survived the crisis with its territory intact, but internal stability seemed as far away as ever. Like so many of his predecessors, Carus was murdered and a new succession struggle broke out. The victor was another Illyrian general, Diocletian.

The third-century crisis

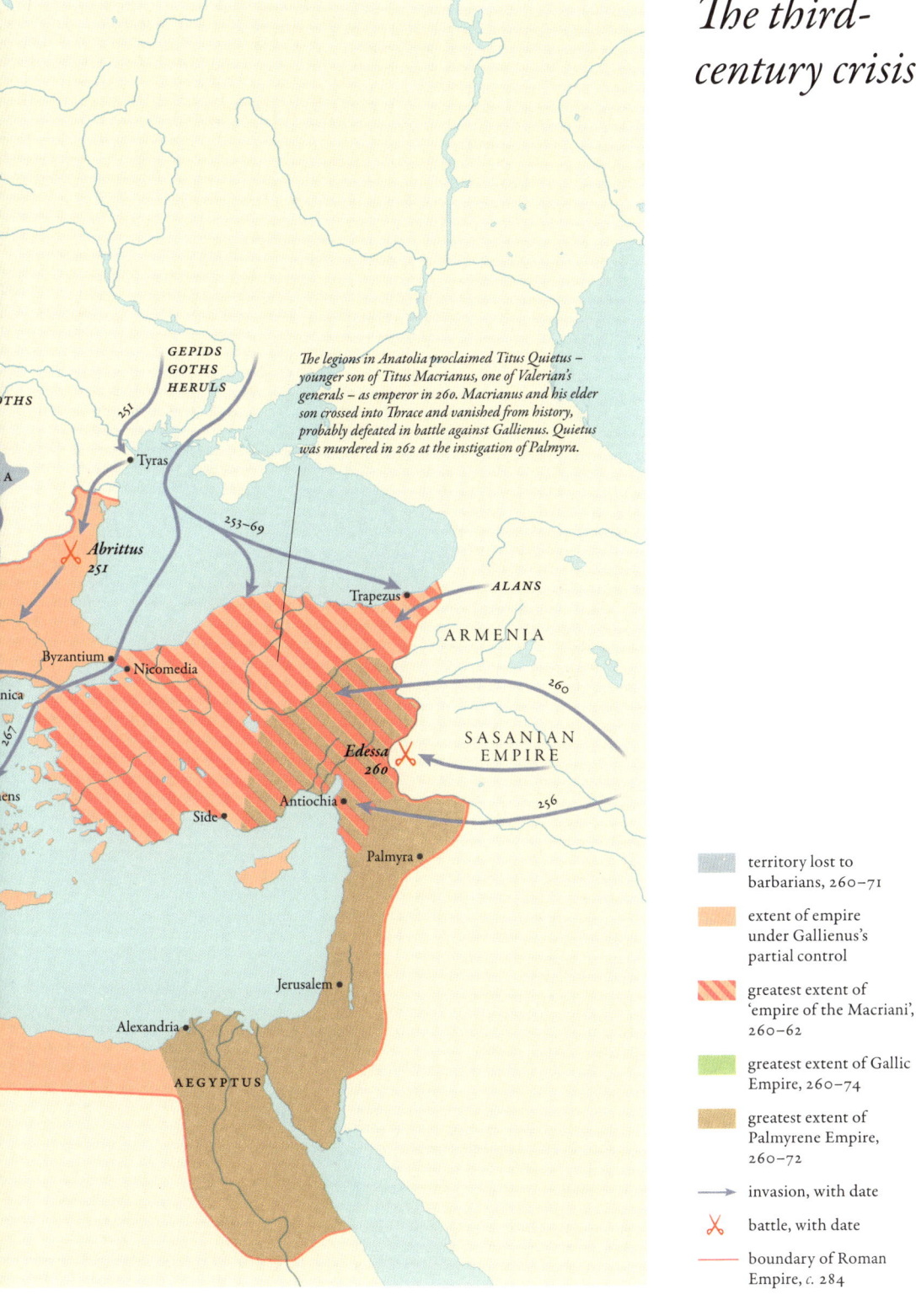

1 AN EMPIRE AT BAY

Reign of Diocletian

Diocletian's reign (284–305) was the longest enjoyed by any Roman emperor for 150 years. Diocletian realized that the empire needed fundamental reform if it was to survive. He succeeded so well that his system endured in the west for over 150 years and for almost twice that long in the east.

Many of the empire's problems stemmed from its sheer size. While the emperor was attending to problems on one frontier, others would be neglected and dissatisfied legions and ambitious generals could foment rebellion. Diocletian's solution was to share imperial authority in a tetrarchy, or rule of four. He first made a fellow Illyrian general called Maximian co-emperor, both of them taking the title Augustus. Seven years later he appointed two younger generals, Constantius (r. 305–06) and Galerius (r. 305–11), as junior emperors with the title Caesar. Each of the four emperors was given an area of command. Diocletian took the east; Maximian (r. 287–305) Italy, Hispania and North Africa; Galerius the Balkans; and Constantius ruled Britannia and Gaul.

The system was supposed to prevent succession disputes. Diocletian and Maximian would retire and be succeeded as Augusti by Constantius and Galerius, who would appoint two new Caesars who would in turn eventually become Augusti. It was not Diocletian's intention to break up the empire, but over the next century it became normal for the Augusti to split the empire between the east and the west. This division became permanent after the death of Theodosius I in 395.

Under the tetrarchy, Rome ceased to be the administrative capital of the empire: emperors henceforth chose bases closer to the threatened frontiers. To legitimize his position, Diocletian invoked the Roman state gods, claiming that he had become emperor by the will of the king of the gods, Jupiter. He ignored the Senate and abandoned the tired pretence, followed since Augustus's time, that the emperor was simply 'first citizen' (*princeps*), styling himself 'lord' (*dominus*). Christians who refused to sacrifice to the state gods were considered a threat to the empire's relationship with them so were persecuted. It is therefore ironic that Diocletian's doctrine of emperorship by divine will pointed the way to the Roman Empire's transformation into a theocratic state under the Christian emperors of the fourth century.

To improve security, Diocletian refortified the frontiers and greatly increased the size of the army, reforming the tax system to pay for it. To protect the state against the effects of inflation, much taxation was levied in kind rather than cash. To improve administrative efficiency, the number of provinces was doubled to one hundred, organized into twelve dioceses each under the supervision of a *vicarius* (deputy) with direct responsibility to an emperor. To keep civil and military authority separate, provincial governors were not allowed to hold military office. The secret service spied on everyone in a position of authority.

Diocletian also grappled with the empire's economic problems. Price regulation introduced to control inflation was only a partial success, because it drove goods off the market. Population decline had created labour shortages, so many key occupations such as bakers were already hereditary obligations. Diocletian extended this to the army and the peasantry who, in a precursor to medieval serfdom, became legally bound to the land. The heavy burden of taxation made the peasantry's lot even harder. Diocletian's reforms amounted to a remaking of the Roman Empire into an oppressive, bureaucratic, militaristic autocracy that taxed its subjects to the hilt and attempted to regulate their economic activity. However, there is no denying that he gave the tottering empire a new lease of life.

Diocletian's most serious failure was his plan for the succession. In 305 he abdicated and forced his reluctant co-Augustus, Maximian, to do the same. Galerius and Constantius succeeded as Augusti, and generals Maximinus and Severus were appointed Caesars. Unfortunately, Maximian's son Maxentius, and Constantius's son Constantine, had aspirations for imperial office and the support of the army, which favoured hereditary succession. Another civil war broke out. From this struggle Constantine emerged as Augustus of the west in 312 and sole emperor in 324.

The tetrarchs – Diocletian, Maximian, Constantius I Chlorus and Galerius – demonstrate their unity in this porphyry sculpture, which originally stood in Constantinople. Looted by the Venetians, during the sack of Constantinople in 1204, it is now part of the exterior of St Mark's cathedral in Venice.

Constantine and the Christian Empire

Constantine's (r. 306–37) conversion to Christianity paved the way for a cultural transformation of the late Roman world. Under his successors, Christianity became the empire's official religion (paganism was proscribed by Theodosius I in 391). Constantine converted because he believed that he had been aided by the Christian

Diocletian's reorganization of the empire

Division of responsibility for the dioceses listed below between the tetrarchs (indicated opposite by the vertical lines):

— Diocletian   — Maximian
— Galerius   — Constantius

...e declined in importance in the ...century as it was abandoned by ...mperors for bases closer to the ...atened frontiers. Diocletian only ...ed the city once, in 303, to ...rate twenty years on the throne.

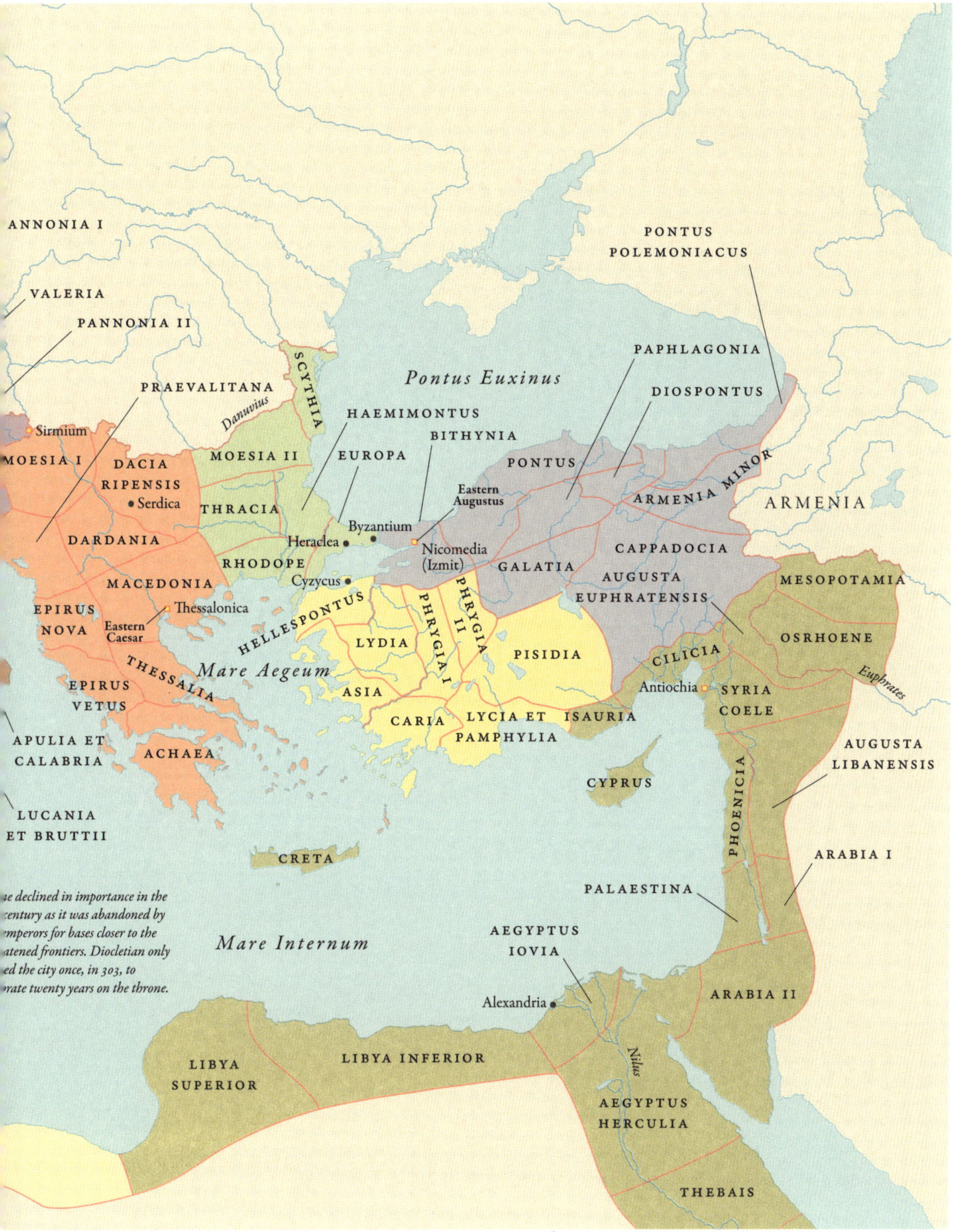

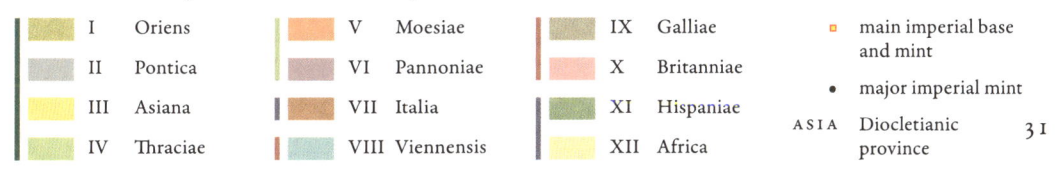

The twelve dioceses of Diocletian were numbered from the east:

I Oriens	V Moesiae	IX Galliae	▫ main imperial base and mint
II Pontica	VI Pannoniae	X Britanniae	• major imperial mint
III Asiana	VII Italia	XI Hispaniae	ASIA Diocletianic province
IV Thraciae	VIII Viennensis	XII Africa	

A 6th-century Byzantine mosaic from the Hagia Sophia in Istanbul showing the Virgin Mary and the Christ child flanked by the emperors Constantine the Great (right), the founder of Constantinople, and Justinian (left), the founder of the Hagia Sophia cathedral.

God in the decisive victory over his rival Maxentius (r. 306–12) at the Battle of Milvian Bridge, outside Rome, in 312. Before the battle Constantine apparently had a vision of a cross hovering above the sun, accompanied by the words 'Conquer with this'. Constantine ordered his outnumbered troops to paint the Christian *chi-rho* symbol on their shields, having seen this in a dream. One of Constantine's first acts after the battle was to issue the Edict of Milan (313), which granted toleration to Christians and ended their persecution. In return, grateful Christians called him 'Constantine the Great'.

Constantine's conversion was a decisive moment for the Christian Church. Christians were numerous in the empire, especially in the east, but nowhere were they a majority. Early Christianity was just one of a number of eastern mystery religions that were winning converts, and without imperial patronage it might have remained a minority cult. The sincerity of Constantine's conversion has been endlessly debated, but it is hard to see what he hoped to gain if his motives were purely political. Christianity was primarily a religion of the urban poor, with few converts in the politically influential upper classes. Roman emperors had always performed religious duties, and Constantine saw his own role no differently. Constantine believed that he had been appointed by God, giving him both the right and duty to intervene in matters of Church organization and doctrine.

In the second century the Church began to organize groups of churches under the supervision of bishops. By the fourth century bishoprics – or dioceses as they became known, from the name of Diocletian's secular administrative divisions – were organized into ecclesiastical provinces under archbishoprics. Church provinces were often based on secular ones. For historical or political reasons, a small number of archbishoprics – Jerusalem, Alexandria, Antioch, Rome and, from the fourth century, Constantinople – were bestowed with superior dignity and were known as patriarchates. Patriarchs did not, however, have authority outside their own provinces. Doctrinal controversies, of which there were many, were debated at Church councils, but the lack of central authority often made agreement difficult.

The greatest controversy of Constantine's day was over the nature of Christ. The orthodox doctrine of the Trinity, which maintains that God, Christ and the Holy Spirit are separate individuals but share the same substance and are therefore equal and eternal, was challenged by Arianism, a doctrine named after its creator, an Alexandrian priest called Arius (c. 255–336). The principal tenet of Arianism was that Christ clearly had a beginning and was not eternal but had been created by God and was therefore inferior to him. Apparently fearing that God would hold him responsible if the Christian Church split over this issue, Constantine called and presided over its first general council at Nicaea in 325. The council endorsed the orthodox doctrine, but Arianism regained influence under Constantine's son Constantius II (r. 337–61). Arianism was declared heretical in 381, but by that time it had won converts among the empire's Germanic neighbours, with far-reaching consequences.

One of the most important effects of Constantine's conversion was his decision to found a new capital for the Roman Empire free from associations with the pagan past. Constantine's choice was the small Greek port of Byzantium on the Bosporus. Begun in 324, the new city, named Constantinople after the emperor, was planned as a Christian city with no provision for pagan worship. The choice of site was an inspired one. Thanks to its strong defensive position

Christianity in the late Roman Empire, mid-fourth to fifth centuries

▨	main concentration of Christians in the 4th century	ASIA ecclesiastical diocese
Nicaea 325	early Church council, with date	IV diocese number
—	provincial boundary	▮ patriarchate

ⅱ	archbishopric
†	bishopric
—	division of the empire, 395

and excellent communications by land and sea, Constantinople became Christendom's chief bulwark in the east for the next thousand years.

The late Roman army

The legionary army that had created the Roman Empire was one of the chief casualties of the third-century crisis. In its place arose a more flexible, mobile army better suited to the needs of an empire that was now on the defensive. In the fourth century, the Roman army was divided into two types of unit: *limitanei*, or border garrisons; and mobile troops, both infantry and cavalry, called *comitatenses*. *Limitanei* lived in forts and were allocated land so they could grow their own food. As a result, they have often been described as a peasant militia but, though *limitanei* had lower status (and pay) than *comitatenses*, they were regular troops who patrolled the borders and dealt with minor incursions. *Comitatenses* made up the field armies, which were stationed well behind the borders so they could provide a flexible response to invaders who broke through frontier defences. There were five field armies in the eastern half of the empire and seven in the west (though three of them were small), plus dozens of smaller auxiliary regiments that provided infantry and specialist troops such as archers and cavalry.

In the early empire the backbone of the Roman army had been around 30 infantry legions, each of 5,000 men. In the third century the legionary army, so effective in offence, proved too inflexible to deal with invading barbarians, who often split up into smaller raiding parties and ranged widely over the countryside. In response more legions were created, but each was reduced to about 1,000 men. Legions could serve as *limitanei* or *comitatenses*. The late Roman field armies included many cavalry units, known as *vexillationes*. In some cavalry units, the *cataphracti* and *clibanarii*, both rider and horse were heavily armoured. Most of these troops were stationed in the east, where they were needed to combat the equally well-armoured Persian cavalry.

Though new styles of uniforms, shields and armour gave the late Roman army a very different appearance, its battle tactics remained similar to those of the old legionary force. Despite the increased importance of cavalry, infantry was seen as the main battle-winning arm and still fought in close order behind a wall of shields. The main difference in weaponry was that the infantry's short thrusting sword, the *gladius*, was replaced by the *spatha*, a long slashing sword originally used only by the cavalry.

Reflecting the empire's defensive stance, great efforts were put into fortifications. Fortress walls were built higher and thicker and had the additional protection of projecting bastion towers, which allowed the defenders to pour enfilading fire onto those assaulting the walls. Towers often had platforms on which *ballistae* and other long-range catapult weapons could be mounted. Instead of functioning as patrol bases, fortresses were now refuges, akin to medieval castles, where troops could hold out against invaders and wait for a suitable moment to launch a counterattack.

In earlier times, the highest commands had gone automatically to men of senatorial rank, for whom military service was just a step towards a political career. In the course of the third century senators lost this role, and commands went to career officers who were promoted on merit, not social rank. Many soldier emperors of the third century, including Diocletian and his co-Augustus Maximian, came from humble backgrounds.

Numbering about 400,000 men *c.* 300, the army of the late empire was almost twice as large as it had been a century earlier. However, population decline increased recruitment problems. A form of conscription was introduced by making military service hereditary, but still the army became increasingly dependent on soldiers recruited from Germanic tribes. It became common practice to settle defeated Germani within the empire in return for a regular supply of recruits. In general, Germanic troops were loyal to their commanders, even if sent to fight against their own people. Many were promoted to high rank, becoming romanized in the process. From the late fourth century, the Romans made increasing use of *foederati* (federates), units in which Germani served under their own tribal commanders. These were generally loyal, but their commanders were aware of their own power: in the fifth century the Romans had to make concessions to keep their support.

II
Fall of the Roman Empire

The barbarians end an era

Profound social changes among the Germani had led to the rise of powerful tribal confederations on the northern frontiers that posed a serious threat to the Roman Empire's security. The Germanic peoples originated in the late Bronze Age in southern Scandinavia and the north German plain. The first sign that they were on the move came around 120 BC when two tribes from Jutland, the Cimbri and Teutones (their Latin name), embarked on a seemingly aimless migration through central Europe and Gaul to the borders of Italy, where they were finally annihilated by the Romans in 102–101. This was only the most spectacular manifestation of a generally southward expansion. By *c.* 50 Germanic-speaking peoples occupied a territory from the Rhineland in the west to the Vistula in the east and the Danube in the south.

Fear of renewed invasions led the emperor Augustus to attempt the conquest of Germania. By AD 6 the Romans had pacified the Germanic tribes as far east as the River Elbe. In the year 9 a rebellion broke out under the leadership of Arminius, a chieftain of the Cherusci who had served in the Roman army and was a Roman citizen. Feigning friendship, Arminius led three legions into an ambush in the Teutoburg Forest, where they were massacred. This ended Roman ambitions of conquest. As a consequence, the Romans dealt with the Germani by subsidizing friendly chiefs

The Missorium of Theodosius I, a large silver ceremonial bowl for ritual hand-washing, probably made around 388 in Greece or Constantinople. It depicts the enthroned Emperor Theodosius I, flanked by his son, the future eastern emperor Arcadius and his co-emperor Valentinian II.

The early Germanic peoples

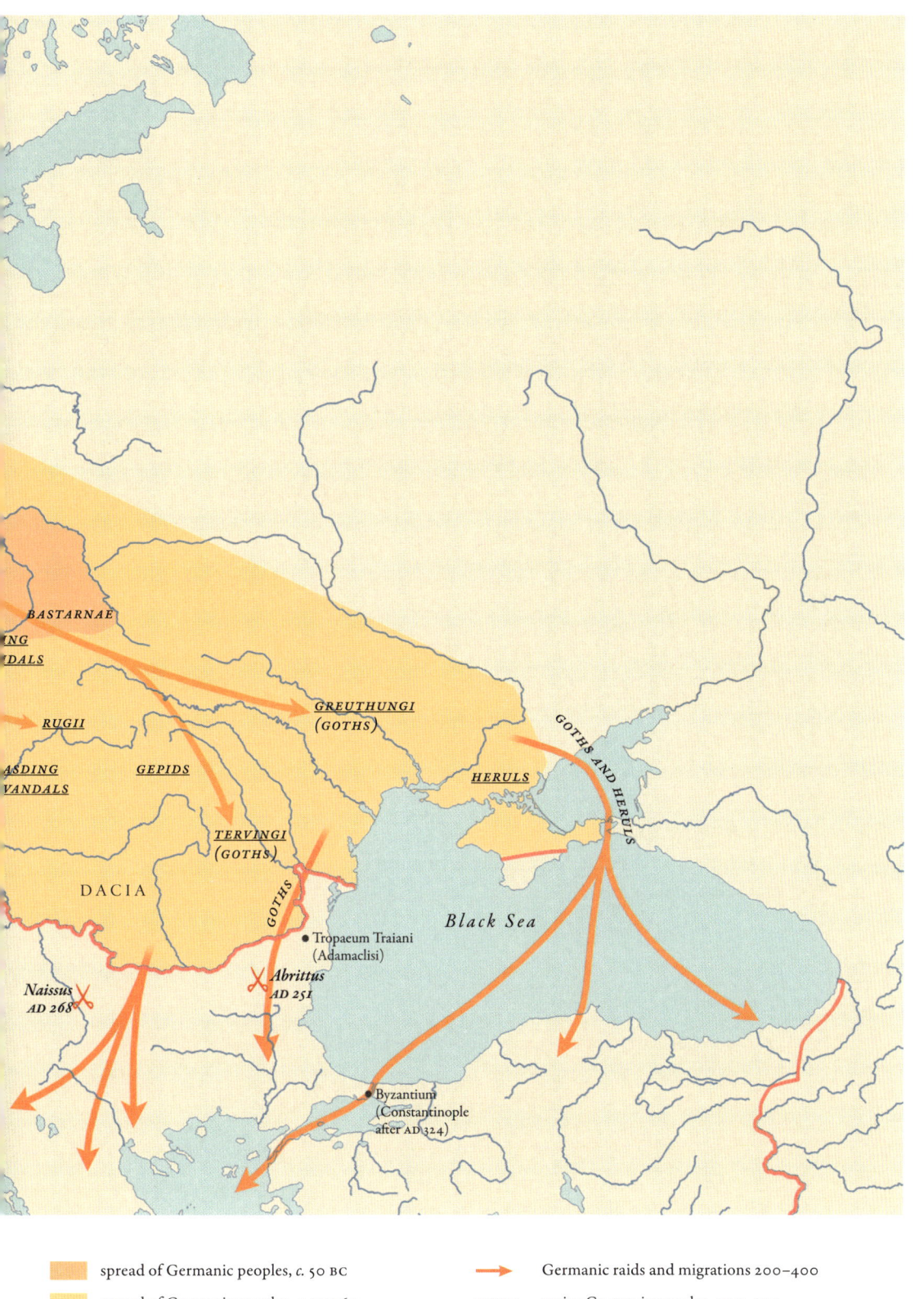

and launching punitive expeditions against troublemakers. There was much cross-border trade and many Germani served as mercenaries in the Roman army.

At this time the Germani were still decentralized tribal peoples, ruled by chiefs and a warrior aristocracy, living in villages and dispersed farms. The most important institution in Germanic society was the *comitatus*, the chieftain's retinue of household warriors who formed the nucleus of a tribal army. Small-scale warfare and raiding were endemic because war provided opportunities to win wealth and status.

Contact with the Roman Empire began to change the structure of Germanic society, initially through its economic impact. Germanic farmers stepped up food production to create surpluses that could be exported across the frontier, where Roman garrisons provided a ready market. Roman luxury products crossed the border in the other direction and the lifestyle and material culture of the frontier tribes became semi-romanized. Those farmers who were most successful in this trade became enriched; differences in wealth and status began to increase. By the second century, a process of political centralization had begun. Tribal kingdoms were emerging and smaller tribes united – voluntarily or coerced by stronger neighbours – to form confederations. On the Rhine, for example, the Chasuarii, Chamavi, Bructeri, Tencteri and other tribes merged to form the Frankish confederation. A major motive behind the formation of confederations was to wage war more effectively. In turn, success in war helped cement an alliance.

As the Romans discovered when the new confederations began making regular invasions in the third century, they made formidable enemies. At this time, invasions were made primarily in search of plunder rather than land, although the Goths forced the Romans to abandon the exposed trans-Danubian province of Dacia, and the Alamanni took the Agri Decumates between the upper reaches of the Rhine and the Danube. As a result of these losses, by 300 the Romans faced powerful Germanic peoples along the whole length of the Rhine and Danube frontiers. Some peoples, such as the Burgundians, migrated closer to the frontier zones, hoping to share in the spoils but disrupting the tribes already living near the borders. A migration by the Gepids split the Goths into the Tervingi and the Greuthungi. While the Tervingi remained settled in Dacia, the Greuthungi built a substantial kingdom extending across the Ukrainian steppes.

A 7th-century Germanic arc-shaped fibula, with geometric and animal interlace, from a Lombard tomb at Nocera Umbra, Italy. Fibulae are large brooches which were worn by both men and women as fastenings for clothing.

The Huns

The sudden arrival of the nomadic Huns in Europe in the 370s destabilized the whole Germanic world and set in train a sequence of events that would ultimately lead to the fall of the Western Roman Empire. The Huns were a Turkic, nomadic, pastoralist tribe of uncertain origin, although they were probably one of the peoples who made up the Xiongnu, a powerful nomad confederation created by Motun (r. 209–174 BC) that dominated the eastern Asian steppes in the last centuries BC. From *c.* AD 48 the Xiongnu confederation began to dissolve, disappearing from history *c.* 400. It was from this breakup that the Huns emerged and began to migrate westwards, scattering or assimilating the Indo-Iranian nomad peoples who stood in their path, such as the Alans and Sarmatians.

Around 370 the Huns ran into the Gothic Greuthungi. For some years their king, Ermanaric, fought a losing battle to hold back the Huns, but gave up the struggle in despair and committed suicide *c.* 375, possibly as part of a ritual sacrifice for the safety of his people. The struggle was continued by Ermanaric's successor, Vithimer, but after he was killed by the Huns, the Greuthungi took the fateful decision to evacuate their lands. The defeat of one of the strongest Germanic peoples spread panic among the rest.

The Huns' success came from their style of fighting. Like all steppe nomads, they spent much of their lives on horseback, in search of fresh pasture for sheep, cattle and horses. They built no dwellings but lived in wagons. This way of life was hard – the steppes are hot in summer and freezing in winter – and bred toughness. Grazing rights were often the cause of fights with other nomadic groups. Huns rarely fought on foot; they prized mobility and were skilled and disciplined light cavalrymen. The favoured weapon of Indo-Iranian nomads, such as the Sarmatians and Alans, was the lance, and both rider and horse wore heavy armour like the *cataphracti* of the Persian and Roman armies. In contrast, the Huns were horse archers and rarely wore armour. They relied on speed, manoeuvrability and the power of their composite bows to keep them from harm.

Made by gluing together layers of wood, horn and sinew, the composite bow's compactness made it ideal for use on horseback and it was widely used by steppe nomads. What gave the Huns the advantage was a unique asymmetrical design that almost

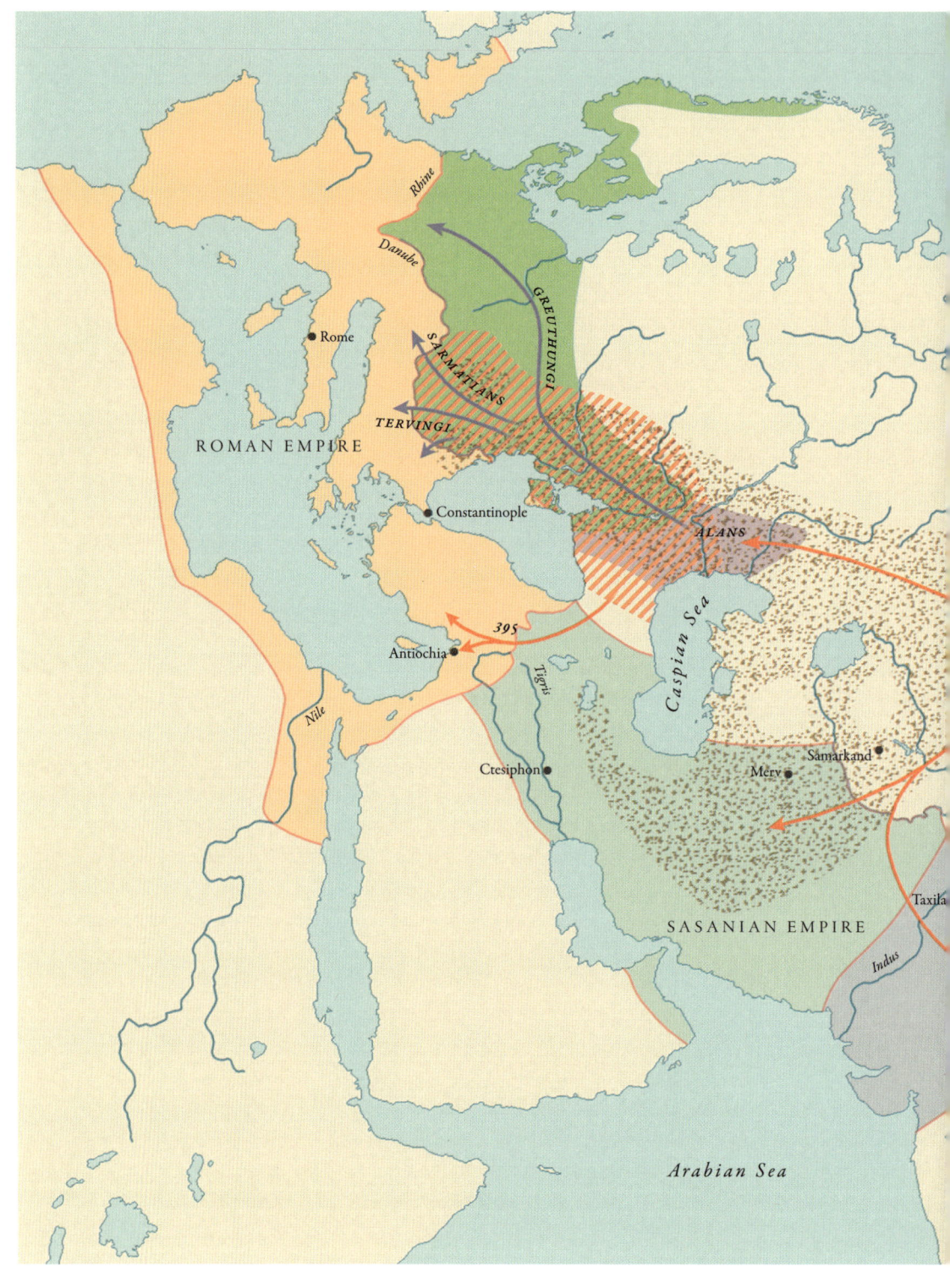

The Huns' arrival in Europe during the fourth century

→ refugees from the Huns, 375–78
→ Hun migrations and raids
■ Germanic peoples, c. 370
■ Alans, c. 370

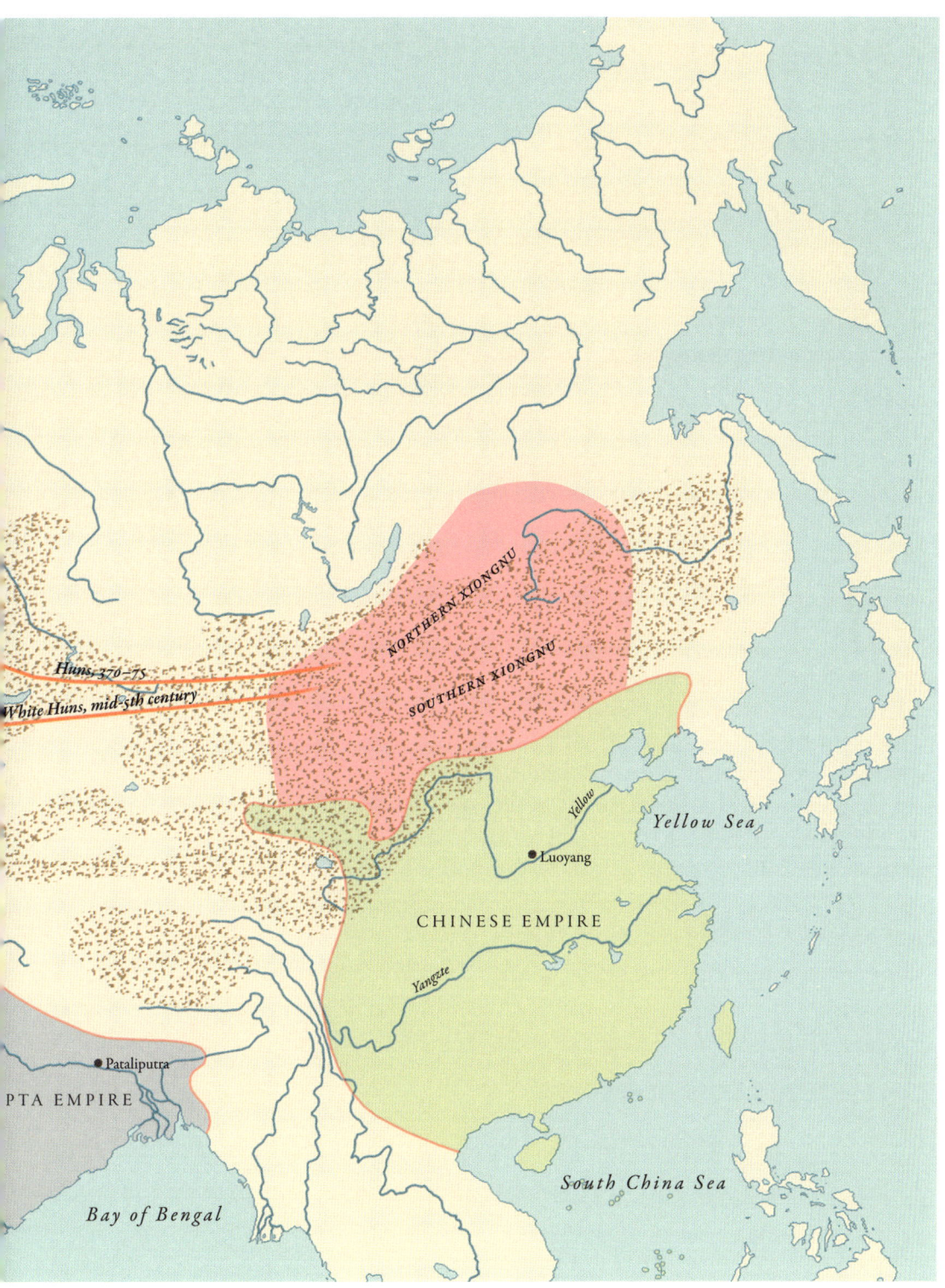

	steppe and semi-desert favourable to mounted nomadism
	Xiongnu, 3rd century BC– 4th century AD
	Hun Empire, c. 410

The ultimate fate of the Roman Empire and its Germanic neighbours was decided by events far beyond their known world. Scattered after the overthrow of the Xiongnu confederation, the Huns' migration created a domino effect, as first they collided with the Alans, who in turn ran into the Germani, who collided with the Romans.

A 5th-century gold Hunnish horse-head fibula. While the basic form of the fibula is inspired by Roman forms, the choice of a horse's head reflects their importance to the nomadic Huns.

doubled the bow's power – it could pierce armour at a range of up to 100 m (328 ft). The importance of the bow was such that it became a Hun symbol of authority: chieftains would be buried with gold-sheathed bows.

The effectiveness of Hun cavalry was enhanced by their terrifying appearance; Roman writers compared them to grotesque beasts. Huns practised deformation of the skull. Infants' skulls were tightly bound above the eyebrows so that as they grew they would be deformed into a long flat shape with no forehead. The Huns also practised scarification, which left them with little facial hair. Their appearance must have been truly unnerving.

At the time of their arrival in Europe, the Huns did not acknowledge a single leader but had several power-sharing kings who operated within a ranking system, one of their number being recognized as senior king. To avoid overgrazing, the Huns needed to disperse over a wide area, which lent itself to a devolved power structure. In the fifth century the Huns came to rely less on pastoralism and more on tribute from subject peoples and mercenary payments from Roman armies. Political centralization became possible and was eventually to unite the Huns under the singular rule of Attila.

The Tervingi and the Battle of Adrianople

News that the Huns were spreading panic among the Germani was at first welcomed by the Romans. However, if they believed themselves immune to the events unfolding on the steppes, they were soon to be disillusioned. Alarmed by the defeat of the Greuthungi, the Tervingi evacuated their lands and sought asylum in the Roman Empire. Some groups of Greuthungi who had escaped the Huns did the same, so in the late summer of 376 some 200,000 Goths set up camp on the north bank of the Danube while their leaders negotiated terms for entry with the Romans.

Dealing with such a huge number of refugees presented the emperor of the east, Valens (r. 364–78), with an enormous problem. Valens had committed the bulk of his troops to a campaign against Persia and was unable to stop the Goths entering by force. He decided on a compromise: allow the entry of the Tervingi and use the available troops to oppose the Greuthungi. Valens did his best to put a positive gloss on the decision. Population decline was having a severe economic impact on the empire. Taxation had to be kept high to pay for the large armies needed to defend the empire's frontiers against unrelenting German and Persian pressure. The upper classes used their influence to avoid paying taxes, so the burden fell most heavily on peasant farmers, who were often left with insufficient means to feed their families. Even in the fertile Nile valley, Egyptian peasants could not afford to pay their taxes and abandoned their fields. In Gaul and other parts of the west, bands of disaffected peasants called *bagaudae* roamed the countryside, plundering the estates of the rich. Population decline also further affected army recruitment.

These problems allowed Valens to present the admission of the Tervingi into the Balkan peninsula as an opportunity. They would be settled on vacant land in Thrace, provide recruits to strengthen the army and increase the tax take. Thousands of defeated Germans had been settled in the empire during the third and early fourth century, so allowing Goths to do the same was, in principle, nothing new. However, Rome had always been in complete control of the earlier settlements. Valens's decision was dangerous because the Tervingi had not been crushed by Roman arms. Their leadership was intact and Valens lacked the troops to control them if things ever went wrong, as they very soon did. Valens left corrupt generals in charge of the Gothic settlement. Promised supplies were not delivered and many Goths were reduced to selling their children to slave traders to get food. The Tervingi rebelled against their treatment in 377 and went on the rampage in Thrace. In the ensuing chaos, bands of Greuthungi crossed the Danube and joined the Tervingi. These two groups

Roman gold medal depicting the eastern emperor Valens. Valens's defeat and death at the Battle of Adrianople in 378 left the Balkans exposed to years of ravaging by the Visigoths.

By invitation – the Gothic invasion, 376–82

Gothic settlement before 376

Roman Empire

battle, with date

Gothic migrations and raids

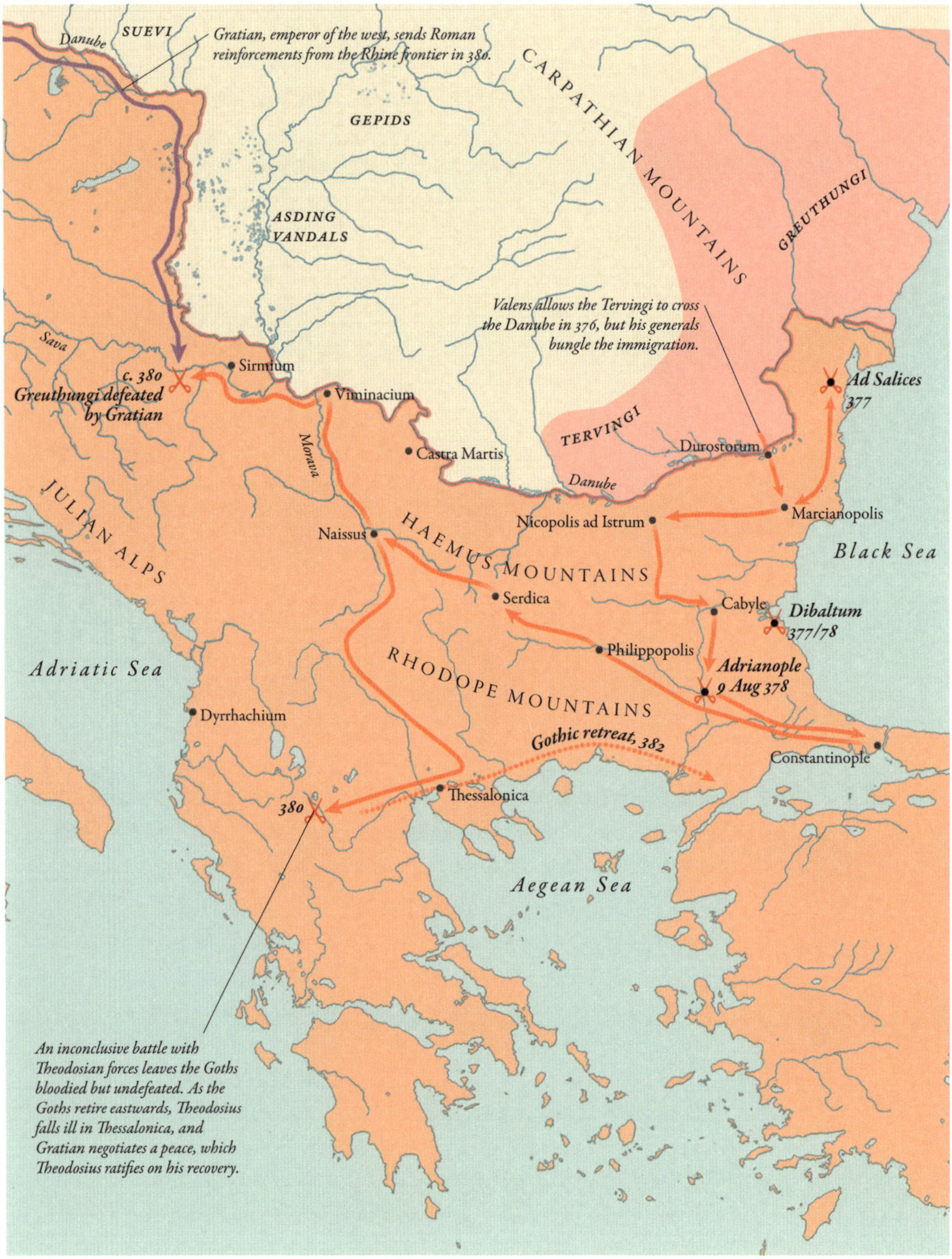

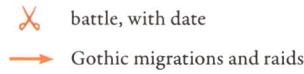

THE TERVINGI AND THE BATTLE OF ADRIANOPLE

Relief carving from the base of the Obelisk of Theodosius at Constantinople shows the emperor standing in state in the *pulvinator* (imperial box), watching a chariot race in the hippodrome.

merged, probably along with other refugees, becoming known as Visigoths.

In 378 Valens patched up a peace with Persia, freeing troops to deal with the Visigoths. On 9 August he launched a badly planned attack on the Visigothic camp near Hadrianopolis (Adrianople, now Edirne) and faced a force very much larger than expected. Crucially, he was unaware that the enemy cavalry was not in the camp. The attack appeared to be going well until the cavalry appeared unexpectedly and attacked the Roman left wing. Taken completely by surprise, the Romans were routed and Valens was killed. It was the worst Roman defeat since Hannibal's victory at Cannae in 216 BC. For four years the Visigoths ravaged the Balkans. They were finally pacified by Theodosius I (r. 379–95), but the cost was high. Unable to inflict a decisive defeat or drive them out of the empire, Theodosius negotiated a treaty and allowed the Visigoths to settle as *foederati* (allies) in 382.

49

11 FALL OF THE ROMAN EMPIRE

The Saxon Shore

As an island, the province of Britannia escaped the worst impact of the Germanic invasions of the third century, and against the trend in most of Rome's western provinces the early fourth century was a time of unparalleled prosperity for the province. The Rhine garrisons' demands for grain and woollen textiles stimulated British agriculture and output from industries such as mining, iron-working and pewter-making. British landowners used the proceeds to build lavish country villas at a time when their counterparts in Gaul were abandoning theirs and retreating to the safety of walled towns. However, the sea was a highway as well as a barrier and Britain's long coastline was vulnerable to pirate raids. To protect the province, the Romans created a coastal defence system known as the Saxon Shore, after the main enemy.

Small-scale pirate raids by tribes living along Germania's North Sea coast had been a sporadic problem since the first century AD but was limited to southeastern Britannia and the province of Belgica on the opposite side of the Channel. The formation of tribal confederations in the third century led to a dramatic increase in the scale and intensity of piracy, just as it had affected Germanic raids across the Roman Empire's land frontiers. The two peoples most often accused of piracy by Roman writers were the Franks and the Saxons, with the former taking the lead in the third century and the Saxons in the fourth. A host of coin hoards, burnt villas and abandoned villages in the coastal areas of Belgica, Gaul, Britannia and even Spain are testimony to their seafaring skills. The Saxons even had a reputation for deliberately sailing in bad weather because it improved their chances of landing undetected. The unpredictability of their attacks greatly increased the Romans' fear of the Saxons, as did their unsavoury habit of sacrificing prisoners to the gods in the hope of getting favourable winds for the voyage home.

The Roman defence of Britannia was based on a chain of coastal forts, each sited on a sheltered harbour so that they could act as bases for operations by both coastguard troops and naval forces. The greatest concentration was around the Thames estuary and the bottleneck of the Dover straits, where naval patrols stood the best chance of intercepting pirates at sea. The forts were built to withstand a siege if necessary, with high walls, strong gatehouses and projecting bastion

Gold disc brooch (centre) and pendants with gold filigree decoration and garnet inlays from early Anglo-Saxon burials in Kent, England.

The Saxon Shore

- → main routes from Britain to Rhine frontier
- ■ Saxon Shore fort
- ▫ possible fort
- ■ 4th-century signal tower
- ■ other military site
- → pirate raids

towers to mount artillery. They were larger than was necessary to accommodate their permanent garrisons, which means they may have also functioned as refuges for local people and may have been used to protect depots where supplies could be gathered for shipping to the Rhine frontier. In the fourth century, defences were supplemented by chains of signal stations.

The Romans did not consider Britannia in isolation and forts on both sides of the Channel were organized into a unified command area known as the *Litus Saxonicum* (Saxon Shore). Though not impenetrable, these defences bought the island province a greater degree of security than most frontier provinces until, in 367, they were overwhelmed by a surprise attack. An alliance of Franks, Saxons, Picts and Irish raiders had bribed Roman agents north of Hadrian's Wall to send back misleading reports, hiding preparations for the attack. The British countryside was overrun by raiders, but they lacked siege warfare skills so Londinium and many other towns were able to hold out against them. The commander of the coastal defences was killed and many soldiers of the Roman garrison simply deserted.

The invaders were driven out by the Gallic field army in 368. Defences were restored and strengthened, but security did not return. The splendid country villas of the Romano-British landowners began to be abandoned, in a pattern that was to be repeated in frontier provinces across the empire, as the fabric of Roman Britannia began to unravel.

Collapse of the Rhine frontier

Before the Romans could solve their problem with the Visigoths in the Balkans, a new disaster unfolded on the Rhine frontier. On the last day of 406, a confederation of around 100,000 Vandals, Suevi and Alans crossed the river near Moguntiacum (Mainz) and invaded Gaul. Rather than seek asylum from the Huns within the empire, the Vandals had chosen to migrate west. After the Goths, the Vandals were the most powerful of the Germanic peoples in eastern Europe, and they also had two main branches, the Asdings, who lived on the Danube, and the Silings. The Silings, from what is now southern Poland, were joined by the Alans, Indo-Iranian nomads who had been displaced from the trans-Caspian steppes by the Huns. The Vandals'

The Rhine collapse, 406/7

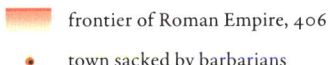
- frontier of Roman Empire, 406
- town sacked by barbarians
- Vandal-Alan confederation invasion

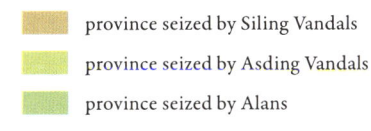
- province seized by Siling Vandals
- province seized by Asding Vandals
- province seized by Alans

planned migration took them into territory already fully occupied by other Germani who were unwilling to make room for newcomers. By the winter of 401–02 the Vandals had reached the upper Danube, but their progress was blocked by the Alamanni. The Vandals tried moving north onto the Rhine, but that brought them into conflict with the Franks. Only the support of the Alan cavalry saved them from annihilation.

In 406 another displaced Germanic tribe, the Suevi, joined the Vandal-Alan confederation. However, the decision to invade the Roman Empire was probably taken out of weakness rather than strength. With the Huns behind them and no available territory east of the Rhine, they had no alternative but to risk an invasion. Fortunately, Roman frontier defences had been drained of manpower in response to a Gothic attack on Italy and on the last day of December the confederates crossed the Rhine unopposed near Mainz. Although no contemporary source mentions the weather conditions, it has been suggested that the Roman fleet that normally patrolled the river was

Ivory diptych portraying the *magister militum* Stilicho, his wife Serena and their son Eucherius. It was probably made to mark his appointment as regent to the young Emperor Honorius in 395.

Gold pectoral cross with garnet cloisonné decoration from a 7th-century Anglo-Saxon burial at Ixworth in Surrey. The cross is one of the earliest examples of Christian influence on Anglo-Saxon art.

immobilized by ice. The invaders sacked Mainz and spread across the countryside. 'All Gaul was filled with the smoke of a vast funeral pyre', wrote the Gaulish poet Orientus.

Considering the situation, it is ironic that a Germanic barbarian should have been the dominant figure in the Roman Empire at this time. Stilicho (d. 408) was a Vandal mercenary who had risen to become master general (*magister militum*, literally 'master of soldiers') of the armies in the west under Theodosius I. Theodosius was the last Roman emperor to rule an undivided realm; after his death in 395 the division into eastern and western empires became permanent. Theodosius was succeeded by his two sons Honorius (Emperor of the West 395–423) and Arcadius (Emperor of the East 395–408). Stilicho was appointed as guardian to eight-year-old Honorius, a weak character who remained in the shadow of his regent.

Stilicho was preoccupied with protecting Italy from the Visigoths and took no action to protect Gaul from the Vandals. The usurper Constantine III (r. 407–10), proclaimed emperor by his army in Britain, gathered his force and crossed the Channel to restore order in Gaul. Under pressure from Constantine, the Vandals, Alans and Suevi crossed the Pyrenees and invaded Hispania in 409. There were few Roman troops in Hispania and Constantine did not follow them: he had fallen out with his generals and was soon to go the way of most usurpers. After years of insecurity and war, the Vandals, Alans and Suevi were desperate to settle down. In 411 they agreed to share out the Hispanic provinces between them and, in all probability, forced the existing Roman provincial administration to gather tax revenues for their upkeep. There was nothing the Romans could do about it. The Visigoths had sacked Rome itself in 410 and were still at large in Italy. Two years later Gaul was invaded by another Germanic race, the Burgundians.

The sack of Rome

The sack of Rome by the Visigoths exposed the empire's decline all too starkly. Not since the Gauls sacked the city 800 years earlier had an enemy taken Rome. Though it was no longer the administrative capital of the empire, it remained a potent symbol of Roman might and its fall caused dismay. In 382 Theodosius's intention had been

The sack of Rome

- Hun movements
- Visigoth movements
- Goth movements
- Vandal, Alan and Suevi movements
- Burgundian movements
- Eugenius and the army of the West (inset)
- Theodosius and the army of the East (inset)
- battle, with date

to withdraw the concession of federate status from the Visigoths as soon as the opportunity arose. However, Theodosius never had that opportunity because he had to spend most of the remainder of his reign suppressing two usurpers who had seized power in the west, Magnus Maximus (r. 383–88) and Eugenius (r. 392–94). Theodosius needed Visigothic support against the usurpers and could not afford to alienate them.

The death of Theodosius in 395 was the signal for the Visigoths to rebel again, under their ambitious new king, Alaric (*c*. 370–410). The Visigoths had suffered heavy casualties fighting for Theodosius, especially at the Battle of the Frigidus in 394, where they had fought in the first rank against Eugenius and his Frankish general, Arbogast. Alaric suspected, probably correctly, that Theodosius was happy to see the Goths weakened in this way and he wanted a new deal that would offer his people greater security. Alaric's demands were that he should be recognized as *magister militum* and that his people should have control of a province and subsidies of grain and gold. A peace was patched up in 397 and the Visigoths were given new lands in Macedonia, but negotiations on Alaric's key demands stalled. Failing to extract concessions from Constantinople, Alaric raided Italy in 402 to put pressure on the western empire but was repulsed by Stilicho. In June 406 Stilicho defeated another Gothic invasion, this time by a group unconnected to Alaric led by a king called Radagaisus.

The collapse of the Rhine frontier six months later changed everything. Stilicho now courted the Visigoths. In return for his support in a dispute with Constantinople over control of Illyricum, the Roman army's main recruiting ground, and a promise of troops to fight in Gaul, Stilicho offered to satisfy all of Alaric's demands. It was a deal that might have worked but it was a step too far for most Romans. As negotiations stalled again, Alaric occupied Noricum, in easy striking distance of Italy. Honorius took the opportunity to free himself of his domineering master general and ordered Stilicho's execution for treason. Unfortunately for the western empire there was no one of similar ability to replace him.

His plans foiled, Alaric invaded Italy in November 408 and laid siege to Rome, his ranks swelled by thousands of runaway slaves and survivors of a pogrom that Honorius had foolishly allowed against Germanic soldiers in the Roman army. Over a year of fruitless negotiations followed, Alaric lifting his blockade when progress

One of a pair of eagle-shaped Visigothic fibulae, decorated using the cloisonné technique. They probably belonged to a wealthy woman who wore them to fasten her dress at the shoulders.

appeared to be made and imposing it again when talks broke down. Fighting was not an option for Honorius: he needed troops to combat the usurper Constantine III in Gaul. Despite his strong position, Alaric was conciliatory, dropping his demands for a generalship and gold and asking only for the province of Noricum and a grain subsidy. His patience ran out in August 410 and after a brief assault Rome opened its gates to him. The sack which followed was surprisingly restrained, with relatively little wanton destruction or killing. Most of the Visigoths were now Christian and they left many church treasures undamaged.

After three days, Alaric withdrew. Safe in Ravenna, Honorius still refused Alaric's demands. Frustrated, Alaric led the Visigoths into southern Italy, meaning to invade Africa, but he died before the year was out. His successor, Athaulf, took the Visigoths to Gaul. Almost unnoticed amid these dramatic events, the Britons kicked out the Roman administration and began to run their own affairs.

The loss of Africa

The Romans still had an unresolved problem with the Vandals and Alans in Hispania, and they now spotted an opportunity to play one alliance of barbarians off against another. In the aftermath of the sack of Rome, Flavius Constantius, a highly able protégé of Stilicho, was appointed *magister militum* of the west. Constantius (d. 421) first dealt with the usurper Constantine III (executed in 411), then turned his attention to the Visigoths, who were now established at Narbonne. Their king, Athaulf, wanted a major role in imperial politics and had married Galla Placidia, the emperor's sister, who had been captured at Rome. Constantius set up a close blockade by land and sea; when food shortages forced the Goths to move to Barcelona, Constantius blockaded them there too.

The Visigoths began to see Athaulf's ambitions as an obstacle to peace with the Romans and in 415 he was murdered. His successor Wallia (r. 415–19) sent Galla Placidia back to her family and agreed to help the Romans recover Hispania. In a brutally effective campaign, the Visigoths destroyed the Siling Vandals and Alans as organized peoples, and returned all of Hispania to Roman control with the exception of Gallaecia, where the Asding Vandals were joined by a ragbag of Alan

The Vandal conquest of Africa

- ---- border of Roman Empire, 411
- • town occupied or attacked by Vandals, with date
- Vandal territory by treaty of 435
- → Visigoths
- → Vandals
- Vandal territory by treaty of 442
- territory seized by Alans and Siling Vandals, 411; returned to Roman control by Visigoths, 415–17; conquered by Suevi, 439–41

Seville town occupied or attacked by Vandals, with date

and Siling refugees. Honorius rewarded the Visigoths with a settlement on rich lands in the Garonne valley of Aquitaine in 418.

Continued attacks by the Romans and Visigoths persuaded the Vandals and Alans to abandon Gallaecia *c.* 422 and move south to Baetica. They were no more secure there and in May 429 the Vandal king, Gaiseric (also spelled Geiseric or Genseric, r. 428–77) organized their transportation across the Straits of Gibraltar to Mauretania Tingitana in north Africa. Together, the Vandals and Alans were about 80,000 strong, of whom about 15,000 were warriors – more than enough to overwhelm the small Roman garrison in Tingitana. Gaiseric's targets were the rich agricultural provinces of Proconsularis, Byzacena and Numidia, and the port city of Carthage. Untouched by war, they were the major source of tax revenue for the western Roman government, as well as the main supplier of grain to Italy. The Vandals travelled east, plundering as they went, meeting no serious opposition until they reached the border of Numidia in late spring 430. Amazingly, given that there had been nearly a year in which the Romans could prepare the defence of this vital region, only token reinforcements had been sent to Boniface, the governor in Africa. He was greatly outnumbered, and his attempt to halt the Vandal advance was swept aside.

In June the Vandals began a year-long siege of Hippo Regius (Annaba, Algeria). Its fall at last provoked a reaction from the Romans. A major force was sent to Africa and Gaiseric was contained in an area centred on Numidia and Mauretania Sitifensis. This became an official Vandal settlement by treaty in 435. With Gaiseric still in easy striking distance of Carthage, the Romans could not afford to relax their guard, but another rebellion by the Visigoths gave them no choice. Taking full advantage of the Romans' problems, Gaiseric broke out of Numidia and seized Carthage in October 439. Recognizing the full seriousness of the situation, Flavius Aëtius, *magister militum* of the west, gathered a massive expeditionary force in Sicily in 442. It never sailed. Aëtius had to withdraw his troops to face a new threat from the Huns.

To maintain grain supplies to Italy, the Romans had no choice but to agree another treaty recognizing Vandal possession of Proconsularis, Byzacena and Numidia. Of all the disasters to befall the empire, this was by far the most serious yet: without the revenues of Africa, the west was no longer fiscally viable and its future was, therefore, bleak. Worse, Gaiseric used Carthage as a base to launch destructive pirate raids on Italy and Sicily. In 455 he sacked Rome itself. It was a much less gentlemanly affair than the Visigothic raid had been, and made the Vandal name synonymous with wanton destruction.

Aëtius and Attila

The years 441 to 453 were dominated by a duel between two men of near legendary stature: Flavius Aëtius, 'the last true Roman of the west', and Attila, the terrifying king of the Huns who styled himself as the Scourge of God. Attila first appears in history in the late 430s, at which time he was joint ruler of the Huns with his brother Bleda. They had inherited power from their uncle Ruga, who it seems had eliminated the other Hunnish kings to make himself sole ruler. Attila's terrifying reputation rests mainly on his effectiveness as a war leader; in his dealings with his subjects he was not tyrannical. Though his political rivals were likely to find themselves impaled on a stake, Attila relied mainly on charisma to maintain power.

Although it was the Huns who were responsible for most of the empire's woes, up to this point relations between the two had generally been good. Many times, Hun mercenaries had played a vital role in strengthening Roman armies in the struggle against Germanic invaders. Attila's adoption of a hostile stance towards the empire may have been partly determined by internal politics – success in war would help consolidate Hunnish unity – but its all too obvious weakness after the fall of Carthage to the Vandals in 439 made it a tempting target.

Attila and Bleda first demanded that the eastern empire double its annual subsidy from 350 to 700 pounds of gold a year. The Romans' rapid acquiescence to their demand was, rightly, seen as another sign of weakness. Using a deliberately contrived border incidence as a *casus belli*, the Huns seized the border towns of Margum and Viminacium and advanced into the Balkans, capturing the strategic town of Naissus (Niš, Serbia) in 442. It was this that forced Aëtius to abandon his expedition against the Vandals. There was a respite in 444–45, in which year Bleda died. This might have been the result of the brothers fighting for sole leadership of the Huns, and it is sometimes said that Attila murdered Bleda, although there is no contemporary evidence to support this view. Whatever the actual

Hunnish gold brooch with a carnelian inlay and geometric decoration with gold wire. The beading around the edge is typical of Hun craftsmanship.

circumstance, Attila returned to the attack, making a failed attempt to capture Constantinople in 447.

Two years later, the eastern Roman government hatched a plot to assassinate Attila using a diplomatic embassy as cover. The plot was betrayed and the ambassadors, most of whom had no idea that their mission was just a diversion, were lucky to escape with their lives. Attila exploited Roman embarrassment over this treachery to extract a huge tribute payment.

Having secured his southern flank, Attila invaded the western empire. Since 433, the Roman *magister militum* and effective ruler of the west had been Flavius Aëtius. Aëtius knew the Huns well; as a young man he had spent three years as a hostage at the Hunnish court and he made considerable use of Hun mercenaries in the 430s in successful campaigns against the Visigoths, Burgundians, Alamanni and Franks, who were threatening Roman control of Gaul.

Fear that Aëtius would loose the Huns on them again if they rebelled kept the Germanic settlers in Gaul quiet through the 440s. Fear of the Huns also pushed the Visigoths, Burgundians and Franks into alliance with Aëtius when Attila invaded Gaul in 451. Attila's army included contingents from the Huns' many Germanic subjects; contemporary reports, almost certainly exaggerated, put it at 500,000 men. Attila had been so confident of victory that in June 451 he contemplated burning himself alive on a funeral pyre after Aëtius fought him to a standstill at the Battle of the Catalaunian Plains, near Troyes. Aëtius made no attempt to follow up his victory and allowed Attila to withdraw from Gaul unmolested: the Huns had been too useful for him to destroy them. This left Attila strong enough to invade Italy in 452. The cities of the Po valley were devastated in turn, but supply difficulties and disease forced Attila to withdraw. A year later it was all over. Attila got drunk at a wedding feast, suffered a haemorrhage and choked to death on his own blood. While Attila's sons squabbled over the throne, his Germanic subjects rebelled and overthrew the Hun Empire at the Battle of Nedao in 454.

Disaster in Africa – the Vandal expedition

Spectacularly destructive though his invasions were, Attila came nowhere near conquering either the Eastern or

Scourge of Europe – campaigns of Attila, 441–52

Western Roman Empires. However, he diverted Roman efforts from reconquering territories that had been occupied by the Vandals, Suevi and Visigoths and whose revenues were essential if the west was to recover. The collapse of the Hun Empire now altered the balance of power. Fear of the Huns had given the Visigoths and other Germani who had sought refuge in the Roman Empire a vested interest in its survival, which acted as a restraint on their actions. From now on they would be harder to control. His skill in dealing with the Huns had enabled Aëtius to maintain his dominant position in the west for twenty years. Now Aëtius no longer seemed so indispensable and in September 454 he was stabbed to death by Emperor Valentinian III (r. 425–55), who hoped by this to become more than emperor in name alone. Valentinian lasted just six months before he was murdered by two of Aëtius's loyal bodyguards: he had no male heirs.

Western emperors began to come and go in rapid succession. Valentinian's immediate successor Petronius Maximus lasted a mere two months before he was killed by a mob when he tried to flee Rome, shortly before it was sacked by Gaiseric's Vandals in 455. His successor, the Gaul Avitus, won power with the backing of Visigothic King Theodoric II (r. 453–66). An emperor appointed by a barbarian ruler was too much for most Romans and after a reign of thirteen months he was overthrown by Ricimer, Aëtius's successor as *magister militum*. As a Goth, Ricimer was unable to become emperor himself, so he placed the general Majorian (r. 456–61) on the throne.

The last western emperor of any true ability, Majorian, understood the importance of recovering North Africa from the Vandals. After stabilizing the situation in Gaul and Hispania, he began to gather a large fleet and army at Cartagena. But Majorian's plans were betrayed to Gaiseric and before the fleet could sail it was destroyed in a pre-emptive Vandal attack. Shortly after this disaster, Majorian was murdered on the orders of Ricimer, who appointed Libius Severus (r. 461–65), a complete nonentity, as emperor. After Libius was poisoned in 465, Ricimer left the throne vacant.

The failure of Majorian's expedition made it clear that the western empire lacked the resources to save itself. Throughout the fifth century it received substantial aid – both money and troops – from the eastern empire but there was a limit to what could be done; the east had its own borders to defend. Stripping the Danube frontier of troops in 442 to support Aëtius's Vandal expedition had, for example, exposed

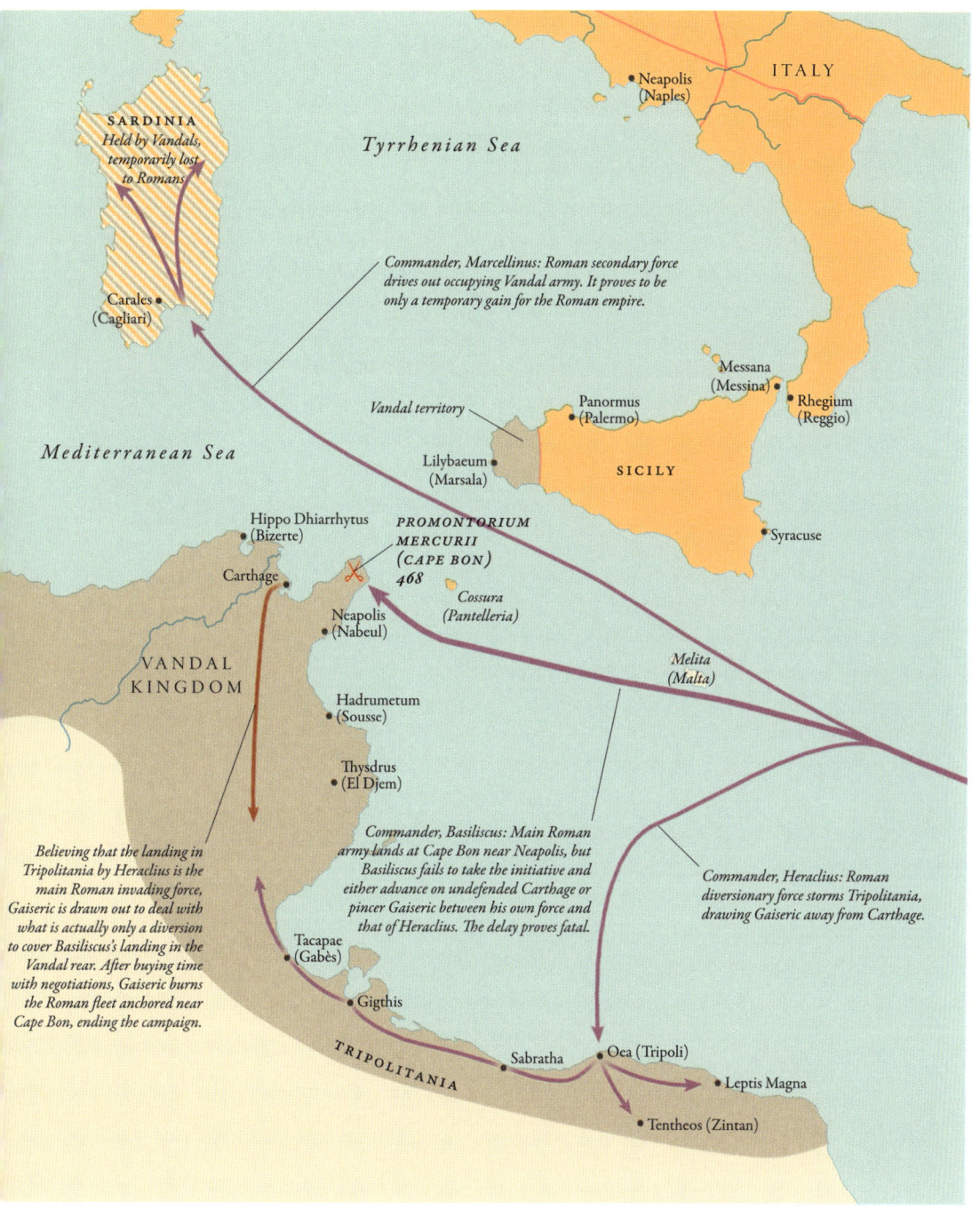

The disastrous invasion of Vandal Africa by Basiliscus, 468

the Balkans to the Huns. A stable peace on the eastern frontier in the late 460s freed Emperor Leo I (r. 457–74) to make a massive last-ditch effort to save the western half of the empire. As a step to restoring stable dynastic rule to the western throne, Leo appointed Anthemius (r. 467–72), an able general with links by marriage to the Theodosian dynasty. Ricimer's support was bought by a marriage to Anthemius's only daughter. The second part of Leo's rescue plan was an expedition to recover North Africa. At the vast cost of 64,000 pounds of gold and 700,000 pounds of silver, in 468 he amassed around 50,000 troops and a fleet of 1,100 ships.

The Roman army landed successfully near Carthage, but things soon began to go wrong. The expedition's commander, Basiliscus, granted Gaiseric's request for a truce, but the wily Vandal king was simply buying time while he prepared a fireship attack that destroyed the Roman fleet at anchor. The Romans never recovered the initiative and withdrew, suffering heavy losses. Leo had emptied his treasury to fund the expedition: there was nothing more the east could do to help the western empire. Its end was not long in coming.

A 5th-century bronze cauldron found near Budapest in Hungary. This unique style of cauldron was probably used in Hunnish burial rituals.

Last emperors of the west

The accession of Anthemius to the western throne in 467, with the full backing of the east (his wife was daughter of Marcian, the previous eastern emperor), created expectation of a revival in Roman power, but the dismal failure of the Vandal expedition exposed the western empire as a hollow shell. Respect for Rome's historic power had persuaded the Visigoths, Burgundians and Franks to acknowledge that the lands they held in Gaul were still formally part of the Roman Empire. Even when they rebelled and tried to seize more land, they always sought formal agreements with the Romans to regularize their occupation within an imperial framework.

All such inhibitions now vanished and by 474, when Julius Nepos became the last officially recognized emperor of the west, all that was left for him to rule was Italy, Dalmatia and some insecure enclaves in Gaul. In 475 the *magister militum* Orestes overthrew Nepos and placed his ten-year old son Romulus Augustulus ('the little emperor') on the throne as a puppet ruler. In Constantinople, Emperor Zeno refused to accept the usurpation and continued to recognize Nepos, who had escaped to Dalmatia, which he continued to rule until his death in 480. Romulus lasted barely a year. Odoacer, a mercenary officer of mixed Hunnic and Germanic descent in Orestes' army, led a mutiny of barbarian soldiers who proclaimed him as king. Orestes was defeated at the Battle of Pavia in August 476 and was executed soon after. Odoacer spared young Romulus and pensioned him off to a country house in Campania. The deposition of Romulus Augustulus is widely seen as marking the fall of the Roman Empire in the west, but it is unlikely that anyone at the time saw things quite so clearly. In most places, the end came more with a whimper than a bang – it may have taken several years before some fully realized that the empire was no more.

Odoacer did not follow up his victory with a declaration of independence, but sent an ambassador to Zeno, offering to recognize the sovereignty of the eastern empire. There was no need, Odoacer argued, for two Roman emperors: Zeno could rule the whole empire from Constantinople, and he would govern Italy as an imperial viceroy. Zeno accepted this face-saving offer, which maintained the legal fiction that Italy was still part of the Roman Empire. Odoacer maintained the Roman administration and, for the vast majority of his subjects, life continued as usual.

A graphic account of what it was like to live through the end of the western empire comes from the *Life of St Severinus* by Eugippius, in which he describes conditions in the Danube border province of Noricum in the 470s. The few remaining garrisons of troops were demoralized and unpaid. One unit sent envoys to Italy to collect their pay: when they failed to return, the unit simply disbanded itself and the soldiers took up farming. The abandonment of frontier defences made life increasingly insecure. In the countryside, villas had been abandoned earlier in the century in favour of walled hilltop refuges. Roman administration struggled on in the towns, organizing citizen militias for their defence, but for their prosperity they had depended on servicing garrisons and river traffic on the Danube. With no garrisons and traffic disrupted by barbarian raids, decline was inevitable. Some towns were destroyed by raiders who carried their populations off as slaves, more were simply abandoned. Those towns that survived sought security by placing themselves under the protection of the king of the Rugii in return for payment of tribute. It was by similar accommodations between Roman provincials and

Germanic kings, as much as by fire and slaughter, that the Roman Empire came to an end in the west.

Why the Western Roman Empire fell

The sack of Rome in 410 ignited a debate about the causes of the decline of Roman power. For pagans the answer was simple: it was because the Romans had abandoned their traditional gods in favour of Christianity. If the Romans only went back to the old ways, pagans believed, the gods would help them restore Roman greatness. The author of the definitive Christian answer to the pagan argument was St Augustine (354–430), bishop of Hippo Regius in North Africa. In his monumental *City of God*, Augustine argued that God had permitted the creation of the Roman Empire for the purpose of spreading Christianity. But the Roman Empire was a sinful state, based on lust for domination, and now that it had served its function God had no further use for it.

Augustine's view was generally accepted by western Europeans until a more rationalistic approach to history emerged during the Enlightenment. In his *Decline and Fall of the Roman Empire*, Edward Gibbon (1737–1797) pinned the blame squarely on Christianity: 'The clergy successfully preached the doctrines of patience and pusillanimity; the active virtues of society were discouraged; and the last remains of the military spirit were buried in the cloister.'

However, Christianity was not evenly spread throughout the empire in the fifth century. The east was strongly Christian and the clergy were politically influential, but much of the west was only superficially Christianized. If Christianity really had sapped the Romans' martial vigour, it should have been the eastern arm that fell first. Yet the thoroughly Christian eastern empire survived the west by a thousand years, falling only when Constantinople was captured by the Ottoman Turks in 1453.

In the late nineteenth century, pseudo-Darwinian theories blamed Rome's decline on racial mixing – intermarriage with 'inferior' subject races supposedly diminished the vigour of the Roman race. In fact, the Romans were not a race in any meaningful genetic sense. The assimilation of conquered peoples was characteristic of Roman

St Augustine of Hippo (left), arguably the most influential theologian of the Middle Ages, and an unidentified saint from a 15th-century antiphony.

imperialism from the earliest times and a major factor in the empire's success and longevity. The Romans were proud to present themselves as a mongrel race in their foundation myths. In the twentieth century Marxist historians advanced class conflict as the cause of the empire's demise. More recently environmental causes, such as deforestation and soil erosion caused by overcultivation, or even poisoning from drinking water supplied from lead pipes, have been proposed.

Most modern historians eschew monocausal explanations. Rome's decline was the result of a complex interaction of external pressure by barbarians and internal political and economic weakness, exacerbated by population decline and the enormous costs of defending the empire. The Roman Empire in the west was less economically developed and less densely populated than the east, thus less able to sustain these costs. With its long northern frontier, the west was also more exposed to barbarian invasion than the east. Once they had broken through the frontiers, invaders could range widely in the west; those who crossed the Danube into the eastern empire could ravage the Balkans, but found their further progress blocked by the walls of Constantinople. The west was not as politically stable as the east. This prevented its rulers from concentrating on fighting the invaders, because they had to hold troops back to protect themselves from usurpers, as Honorius had to do in 410 when the Visigoths sacked Rome.

No single event made the fall inevitable, but three stand out: the destabilization of the Germanic world by the Huns in the 370s; the loss of North Africa to the Vandals in 439; and the failure of Basiliscus's expedition to recapture North Africa in 468. The Romans had great capacity to assimilate immigrants (welcome or otherwise), but the scale of the migrations created by the Huns was overwhelming. The Romans never had the opportunity to deal conclusively with one group of Germanic settlers before they were confronted with another crisis. Because troops were withdrawn to fight a Visigothic rebellion, the Vandals were able to seize the all-important North African provinces, the most serious event in the fall of the western empire. Even so, recovery remained a possibility if only North Africa could be recovered. Had Basiliscus succeeded, the western empire's position would have been transformed and it is possible that the recovery of Hispania and much of Gaul would have quickly followed. Basiliscus's failure extinguished this possibility and doomed the west.

The Western Roman Empire at the accession of Julius Nepos, 474

De Trium Mensis Legalibus Liber I

I. D. electione principium ea-
   rumq; inquisiti... II. ¶.
   D. reparatione peñ̄ e&t adipisce-
   ... III. ¶. D. on moao
   principiu... IIII. ¶. D. legi
   ... V. D. leg...

De Negotiis Tusculearum Liber II

I. ¶. D. ludicis et ludiciis
II. ¶. D. vet pap̃ &t epis dius
III. ¶. D. mandato ñib; et manda-
   ... IIII. ¶. D. ceatb̃ g-
   ... opnis. V. D. cep-
   aut, Mulieris senatusmũ
   ... liber de incog̃ muoli-
   cib; conscribendi

De Origine Coniugali Liber III

I. ¶. D. cuspicacon b̃ nuiaq̃ ñ
II. ¶. D. mmag̃ nupciis. III. ¶.
D. rupau nis nui ut indua ru
IIII. ¶. D. ephularis. V. ¶. T. In

Hh 8.

III
A New Order

The Germanic kingdoms

It is easy to forget that the dissolution of the Roman Empire of the west took a full century. The Germanic peoples' migrations were leisurely, no faster than the speed of the loaded ox wagons that carried their families and possessions. One estimate of the speed of the Vandal migration through North Africa is a mere 5.75 km (3⅔ miles) a day. Barbarian settlements were a less dramatic affair than might be imagined. The settlements of the Visigoths, Ostrogoths and also of Odoacer's followers were based on laws introduced by Emperor Theodosius II (r. 408–50) to regulate the billeting of barbarian *foederati* on landowners. Estates were divided into thirds for sharing; the landowner had first choice of the thirds, the *foederati* had second choice and the landowner kept the final third. The Burgundians went further and took half-shares; it was only the Vandals who employed complete expropriation of estates.

Recognizing the new political reality, Roman landowners accepted the newcomers with reasonably good grace. The Gallo-Roman writer Sidonius Apollinaris, who had Burgundians billeted on his Auvergne estate, complained of the stench of the rancid butter which they used as a sort of hair gel, but he also left us an admiring description of a Frankish prince.

The survival of Roman administrative institutions was encouraged by the practice of allocating the tax revenues of a province to the

> The *Lex Visigothorum*, the Law of the Visigoths, was promulgated by King Recceswinth in 654. It abolished legal distinctions between Romans and Visigoths, allowing for greater assimilation of the two populations.

The Germanic kingdoms, c. 511–525

upkeep of *foederati* settled within it. The *foederati* had every interest in preserving a system that worked to their benefit. Other factors, however, worked against the long-term survival of the Roman system. The division of the Western Roman Empire into independent kingdoms disrupted what had been a huge free trade area, causing a general economic decline, especially in regions lacking easy access to the Mediterranean. At a local level, economic disruption was caused by the division of estates, as well as by looting and a general sense of

A manuscript of 1253 depicts the Council of Toledo, when the Visigoths abandoned Arianism and became Roman Catholic.

insecurity in wartime. The infrastructure of the Roman state had been expensive to maintain and, as its economic base collapsed, life reverted to a simpler level. Much of that infrastructure, such as aqueducts supplying water to depopulated towns, was by now irrelevant anyway.

The Germani were small minorities in their new kingdoms, outnumbered by the natives by as much as twenty to one. The problem with the native population was not that they were hostile; years of high taxes had undermined loyalty to the empire and there was little popular resistance to the invaders. Peasant farmers simply had new landlords, and without the regulations of the Roman state they may even have been better off. The main problem for the Germani was that they would be assimilated and lose their national identities, so they employed various means to prevent this.

The main marker of ethnicity for the Germani was law, which they used to maintain a distinction between themselves and their Roman subjects, who continued living under Roman law while Germani lived under their own customary laws. A German could not be judged by a Roman, but where a German was in dispute with a Roman it was Germanic law that prevailed. Intermarriage between Romans and barbarians was usually forbidden, in theory if not always in practice.

A more serious obstacle to assimilation was religion. Most of the Germanic peoples were still pagan when they entered the empire, but the Goths had been converted to Christianity by the Arian bishop Ulfila ($c.$ 311–383), who was consecrated bishop of the Christians living in Gothia in 341. The Goths clung to Arianism after it was condemned as a heresy in 381 and, through their influence, it was adopted by many other Germanic peoples, including the Burgundians, Suevi, Vandals and Lombards. Arianism became a badge of identity and created an unbridgeable religious gulf between them and their Catholic Roman subjects. It was also a political statement. The emperors claimed sovereignty over the Church so becoming Catholic was a sign of submission to Rome.

The Visigothic kingdom

For over forty years after their settlement in Aquitaine, the Visigoths remained mainly loyal to the terms of their federate agreement. The Visigoths' pro-Roman stance ended after

Kingdom of the Visigoths, 418–631

- kingdom of Toulouse, 418
- Visigothic kingdom, 476
- temporary Visigothic conquest, 477–500
- territory lost to Franks, 507
- territory lost to Eastern Roman Empire, 554; reconquered by Visigoths, 571–631
- Vandal kingdom
- Suevic kingdom
- main area of Visigothic settlement
- main area of Suevic settlement
- battle, with date

King Theodoric II was murdered in 466 by his ambitious brother Euric (r. 466–84). Though the Visigoths' attempt to seize the Rhône valley in the 430s diverted Roman troops and thus contributed to the loss of Africa to the Vandals, the Visigoths provided the bulk of the Roman army that defeated Attila at the Catalaunian Plains in 451, suppressed peasant rebellions and fought the Suevi in Hispania. After the defeat of Basiliscus's expedition against the Vandals in 468, Euric recognized that the western empire was in terminal decline. Breaking out from Aquitaine, he quickly conquered all of Hispania except for Gallaecia, where the Suevi held out, and by 477 he also occupied Auvergne and Provence. In 475 the weak Emperor Julius Nepos had formally recognized Euric's sovereignty over his conquests.

Though Euric employed both Roman and Gothic advisers at his court in Tolosa (Toulouse), he maintained a form of apartheid. The Visigoths lived under their own laws, codified by Euric, while the native population continued to live under Roman law. The two peoples were forbidden to intermarry. Euric maintained the Goths' traditional Arianism as an important part of their identity and a barrier to their assimilation with the native Catholics. This division between the Visigoths and their Roman subjects may have been a factor in their defeat by Catholic Franks at Vouillé in 507, which lost them most of their lands in Gaul. The Visigoths retreated over the Pyrenees and established a new capital at Toledo. After years of hostility, the Visigoths conquered the Suevi in 585. A civil war had allowed the Eastern Roman Empire to occupy Baetica in 554, but after it was retaken by the Visigoths in 631, their control of the peninsula was resisted only by the Basques in the far north.

Their defeat at the hands of the Franks divided the Visigoths into pro-Arian and pro-Catholic factions. A civil war in 582–85 was won by the Arian Leovigild, but he died within a year and his son Reccared I (r. 586–601) converted to Catholicism. Internal conflict continued and the Catholic triumph was not secure until the reign of Sisebut (612–21). Conversion to Catholicism won Visigothic kings the enthusiastic backing of the Spanish Church, which moved its headquarters from Seville to the royal capital. During Sisebut's reign one churchman who had a particularly strong influence was Isidore of Seville, best known for his efforts to preserve the knowledge of the Classical world in his encyclopaedic *Etymologiae*. The acceptance of Catholicism removed the legal distinction between Goth and Roman;

both became subject to the same laws and were formally allowed to intermarry. However, a study of aDNA from human remains from a sixth-century cemetery, identified as Visigothic on the basis of grave goods, suggests that intermarriage had already been going on for a long time. Of the nine individuals sampled all had a mixed genetic heritage from both central European and local populations.

Despite ruling Spain for 250 years, the Visigoths were too few in number to have much influence on its languages or cultural development: there were probably no more than 200,000 of them out of an estimated sixth-century population of over six million. This is borne out by recent genetic studies indicating that less than 5 per cent of Spanish men carry Y-chromosomal DNA that could be compatible with Visigothic or other central European ancestry. The main cultural influence on Spain through the Visigothic period was the Byzantine Empire, which is evident even in the style of the crowns worn by Visigothic kings. Another sign was the introduction of ferociously anti-Semitic laws. Persecution of ethnic minorities was virtually unknown in the other Germanic kingdoms.

One of the realm's weaknesses was its elective kingship, which encouraged divisive factionalism and usurpation. After the death in 531 of Amalric, the last of Alaric's descendants, the Visigothic monarchy became increasingly unstable and civil wars more common – the main reason for its rapid collapse after the Muslim invasion in 711.

The Ostrogothic kingdom

The Ostrogoths – the name probably means 'eastern Goths' – were mostly the descendants of those Greuthungi Goths conquered by the Huns in the 370s. After the fall of the Hun Empire, Goths led by the brothers Valamir and Thiudimir of the Amal dynasty seized control of the former Roman province of Pannonia. However, the Romans still claimed sovereignty over Pannonia and in 459 forced the Ostrogoths to accept federate status. The Ostrogoths, who felt threatened by the Gepids (Germans who had defeated the Huns in 454), rebelled and transferred their settlement to northern Greece in 473, and then to Thrace by 484.

By this time, the Ostrogoths were under the sole rule of Thiudimir's son Theodoric (r. 471–526). Under the terms of the federate agreement,

THE OSTROGOTHIC KINGDOM

Under the generally benign rule of Theodoric, the Romans in Italy found a degree of peace and prosperity unknown for almost a century. Images of Theodoric and his court at Ravenna were all erased on the orders of Justinian.

Theodoric had been sent as a hostage to Constantinople when he was aged seven, absorbing Greco-Roman cultural values more thoroughly than any previous Germanic ruler by the time of his release aged 18. After his return to the Ostrogoths, Theodoric continued to be honoured by the emperors, and in 484 he was even elected a consul of Constantinople. But if the Romans were hoping to dazzle him into becoming an obedient puppet, they were sorely disappointed. Among his own people Theodoric continued to play the role of Germanic war leader and in 486 he rebelled again, ravaging the countryside to within 9 km (14 miles) of Constantinople.

Theodoric's policy of intermittent hostility towards Constantinople was getting the Ostrogoths nowhere and in 488 he accepted Zeno's commission to overthrow Odoacer (435–493) and rule Italy until the emperor was able to claim sovereignty in person. Zeno was probably indifferent whether Theodoric won or lost – either way it would eliminate a potential threat to the eastern empire. Theodoric invaded Italy and trounced Odoacer in three straight battles in 489–90. He blockaded Odoacer's refuge of Ravenna by land and sea, but the city held out for three-and-a-half years. Its surrender was obtained only after negotiations in which Theodoric and Odoacer agreed to share Italy. This was merely a ploy on Theodoric's part, and he murdered Odoacer a few days later at a feast held to celebrate the end of the war.

Like Odoacer, Theodoric formally ruled Italy as part of the Roman state. Though proclaimed king by his soldiers, he never described himself as King of Italy, which would have implied territorial sovereignty: technically Theodoric was only king of the country's Ostrogoths. The emperor's right to appoint senators and the consuls of Rome was still respected, as was his right to make laws. However, there was no doubt that Theodoric was the power in the land, as his Roman subjects recognized when they called him by the traditional imperial titles *dominus* and *Augustus*. For his part, Theodoric respected the Roman Senate (though he ruled from Ravenna), held games in the Circus Maximus, distributed free grain to the Roman poor and restored aqueducts and other public buildings in many Italian cities. He relied on Roman bureaucrats to run his government, but Goths alone could serve in the army.

Most estimates put the total number of Ostrogoths at just 40,000. One of Theodoric's aims was to prevent his people being assimilated by the Romans. The Goths' Arianism was a major barrier, and Goths

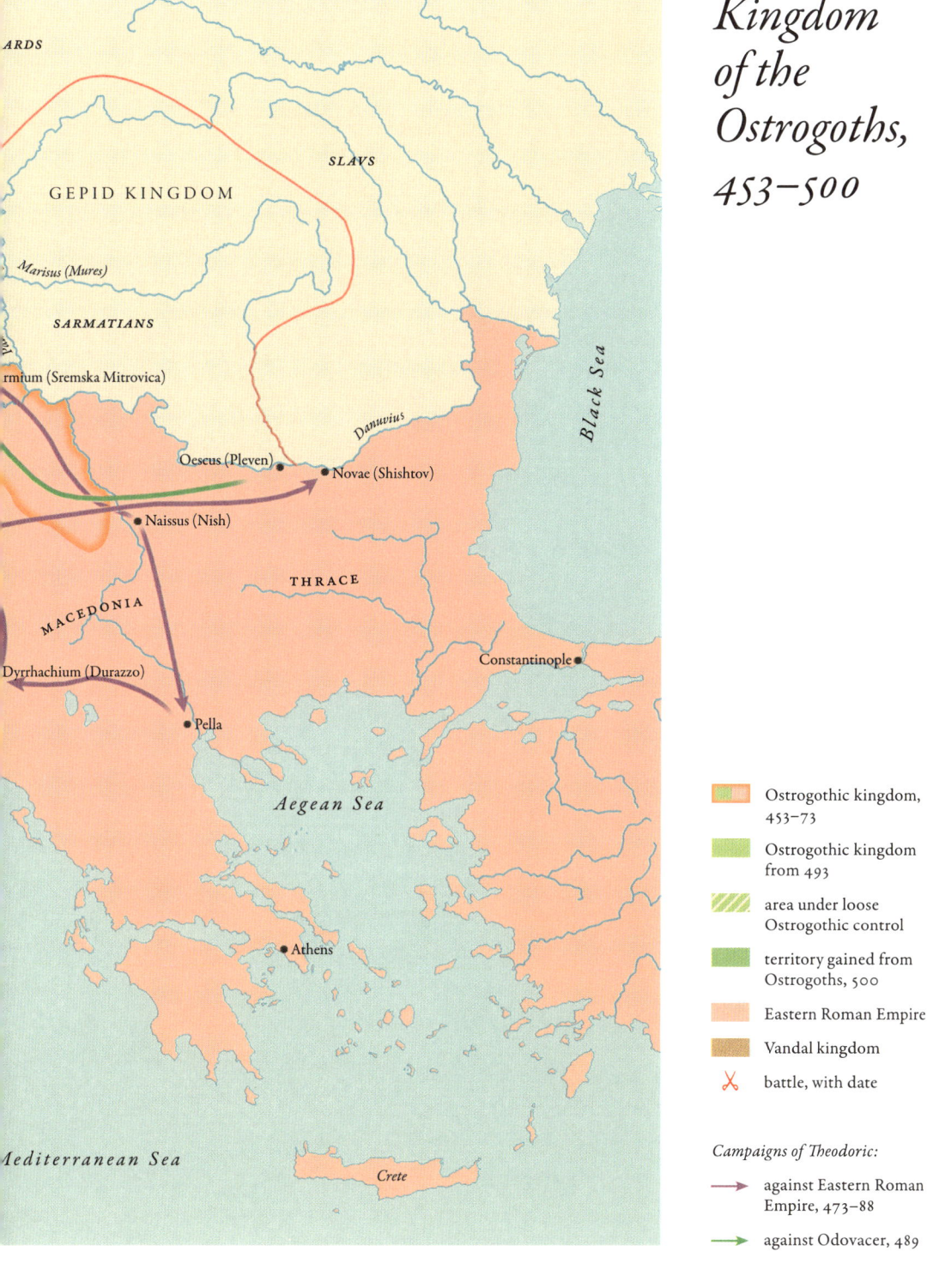

Kingdom of the Ostrogoths, 453–500

and Roman citizens could not legally marry. Though Ostrogoths were subjected to Roman law, they were not tried by Roman judges. To help maintain their cohesion as a people, Gothic settlement was concentrated in the Po valley, with smaller settlements at strategic locations in other areas. The Ostrogoths lived on the revenues of the estates they had been allocated and on annual donatives from Theodoric, who recognized the hostility many Ostrogoths felt towards the Romans. He urged them to show restraint, pointing out that 'it is in your interests that the Romans should be left undisturbed, for while they enrich our treasury they multiply your donatives [donations]'.

Towards the end of his reign Theodoric increasingly doubted the loyalty of his Roman subjects and as a result his rule became more oppressive. One of his most prominent victims was the senator and philosopher Boethius, who was executed in 524 on suspicion of treason.

Late Roman and Ostrogothic Ravenna

For much of the late Roman and early medieval periods, the most important city in western Europe was Ravenna. As the seat of Roman emperors, Germanic kings and Byzantine exarchs, Ravenna prospered as Rome decayed, wealthy patrons embellishing it with the finest late antique churches, palaces and art outside Constantinople. Ravenna had become the capital of the Western Roman Empire in 402 when Honorius transferred his court there from Milan, which had been the capital for most of the fourth century. A prosperous provincial market town, port and naval base, Ravenna had much to recommend it. It was still conveniently close to the threatened northern frontier and it had much better land and sea communications with the eastern empire than either Milan or Rome.

The salt marshes which surrounded Ravenna would make life uncomfortable for any army attempting to lay siege and, of course, supplies and reinforcements could be brought in by sea. To its natural defences Honorius added a new circuit of strong walls with bastion towers; he and his successors also commissioned many public buildings and churches to give Ravenna a suitably imperial grandeur.

Ravenna proved the strength of its position in 410 when reinforcements sent by sea from Constantinople forced Alaric to lift his siege of the city. In 490–93 Odoacer held out against Theodoric for over three years despite receiving no outside help. Theodoric made Ravenna his capital and its surrounding countryside became one of the main Ostrogothic areas in Italy. There was little interaction between the Ostrogothic and Roman populations of Ravenna; they existed as parallel societies. The Ostrogoths lived outside the walled city and had their own Arian churches. Orthodox Catholics kept their churches and enjoyed freedom of worship under Theodoric's rule, but he was irked that the same tolerance was not extended to Arians in Catholic-controlled areas.

Theodoric added many outstanding churches to Ravenna, both orthodox and Arian. The masterpiece was the octagonal basilica of San Vitale with its lofty central dome, which still stands today. Begun *c.* 526 and financed by Julianus Argentarius, a wealthy Roman banker who provided 26,000 gold coins to pay for its construction, the church was not completed until 547, by which time Ravenna was back under (eastern) Roman control. The interior of the church is lavishly decorated with mosaics of the highest quality, which include portraits of the conquering Emperor Justinian and his wife Theodora. Other noteworthy churches include San Apollinare in Classe (outside the city), the Arian baptistery and the Arian cathedral of San Apollinare Nuovo, built next to the palace for use by the royal family. Shortly before his death Theodoric commissioned a mausoleum for himself. Its most remarkable feature is its roof, cut from a single slab of limestone weighing approximately 300 tons.

After its capture by the eastern Roman (or, as it would soon be known, Byzantine) Empire in 540, all Arian churches were confiscated and handed over to the Catholic Church. Sculptors and mosaicists were brought from Constantinople to further embellish Ravenna's churches and palaces – and also to remove evidence of the Ostrogothic occupation, as in San Apollinare Nuovo, where mosaic portraits of the Ostrogothic royal family were replaced with mosaics of curtains. As the seat of the exarchs, the imperial viceroys who governed Italy, Ravenna was the centre of Byzantine power in Italy until its capture by the Lombards in 751. They held the city for only three years before losing it to the Frankish king, Pippin III, who handed it over to the papacy in 757. By this time, the silting up of its harbour had sent Ravenna into decline.

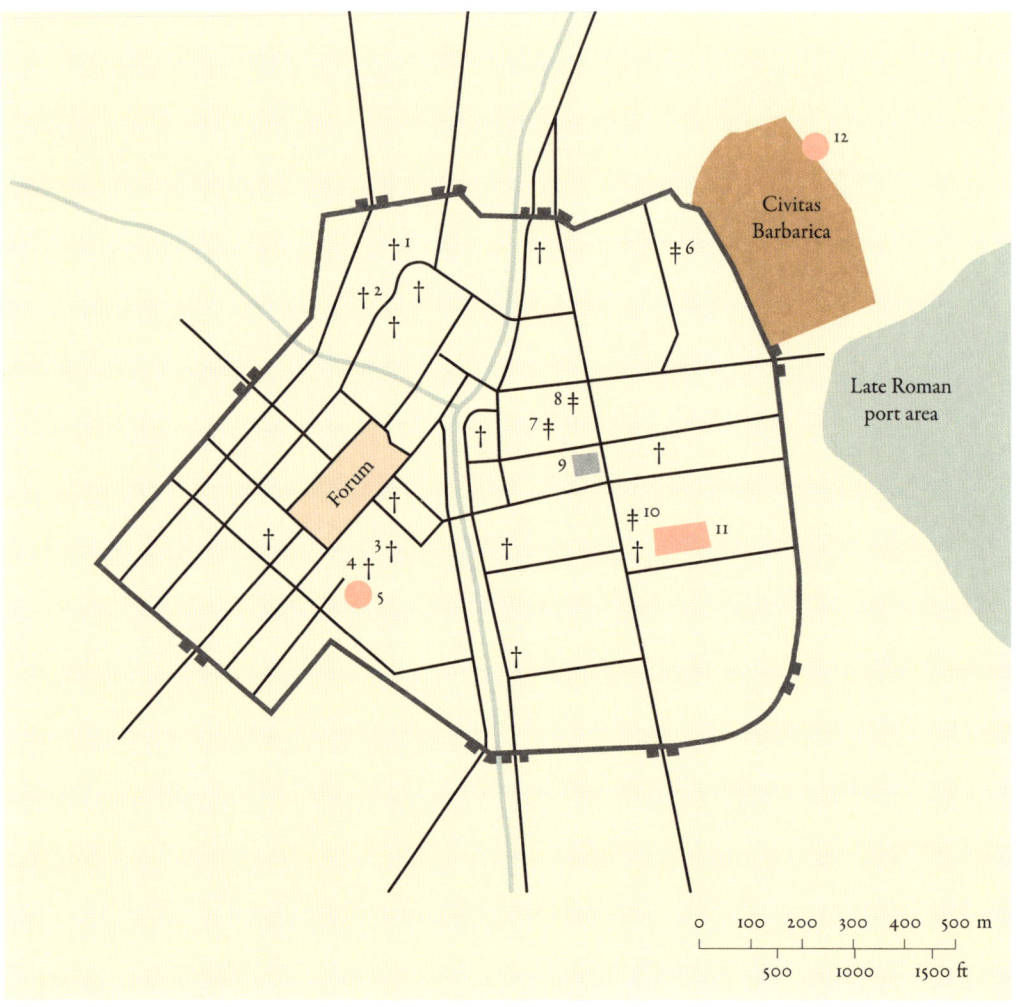

Ostrogothic Ravenna, c. 600

- main area of Gothic settlement and cemeteries
- ‡ Ostrogothic church
- † other church

1. Mausoleum of Galla Placidia
2. San Vitale
3. Orthodox baptistry
4. Orthodox cathedral
5. archbishop's palace
6. Ecclesia Gothorum
7. Arian baptistry
8. San Spirito
9. royal mint
10. San Apollinare Nuovo (Arian cathedral)
11. royal palace
12. Mausoleum of Theodoric

The Vandal kingdom

The kingdom of the Vandals was the first Germanic territory to become fully independent of the Roman Empire. After his capture of Carthage in 439, Gaiseric had a very strong negotiating position. Italy relied on North Africa for its grain supplies and in threatening an embargo Gaiseric blackmailed the Romans into recognizing his kingdom's independence, formalized by a peace treaty in 442. Gaiseric also negotiated a politically advantageous marriage for his son Huneric to Eudocia, Emperor Valentinian III's daughter.

These major concessions only bought the Romans a temporary respite from Vandal aggression, and within a few years Mauretania and Tripolitania were added to their kingdom. Gaiseric turned Carthage into a pirate base and raided as far afield as Greece. These raids were very opportunistic, with little forward planning. Once when his helmsman asked him against whom they were sailing, he reportedly replied, 'Let us go against the people with whom God is angry'.

Rome itself was sacked in 455. Sardinia, Corsica and the Balearic Islands fell to Vandal rule around this time, but victories on land and sea by the master general Ricimer in 456 prevented Gaiseric getting more than a foothold in Sicily. Gaiseric's greatest triumph – his victory over Basiliscus's expedition to reconquer Africa in 468 – made such an impression on the Romans that it was over sixty years before they plucked up the courage to attack the Vandals again. This was just as well for the Vandals, for their kingdom was very much Gaiseric's creation. None of his successors came close to matching his outstanding abilities and it was only the fearsome reputation he had won for the Vandals that masked the kingdom's serious weaknesses.

Unlike most Germanic peoples, the Vandals were actively hostile to the Romans. This was nowhere more evident than in religion. During the time they were settled in Spain, the Vandals became almost fanatical converts to Arian Christianity. Even allowing for a degree of exaggeration by indignant Catholic writers, the Vandals seem to have persecuted Catholic clergy with enthusiasm and cruelty. The persecution reached its peak under Gaiseric's son Huneric (r. 477–84), who ordered all Catholic churches to be confiscated for use by Arians or demolished. The Vandals were also more hostile to the Roman landowning classes than other Germanic peoples.

The Vandal kingdom

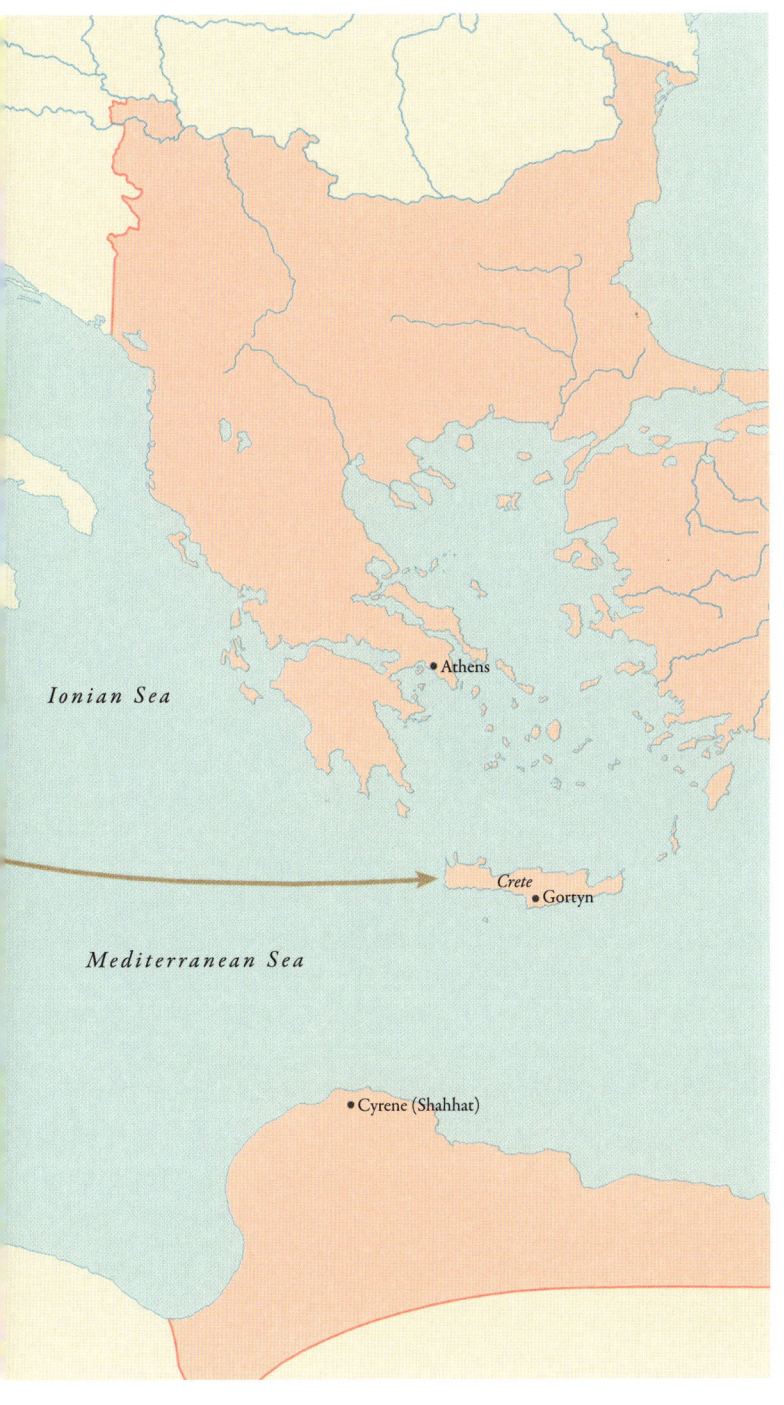

- Vandal kingdom, 435
- Vandal kingdom, 442
- maximum extent of Vandal kingdom at the death of Gaiseric, c. 477
- Eastern Roman Empire
- Vandal pirate raids
- main centres of Vandal settlement
- battle, with date

The dome of the Arian baptistry, late 5th century, in Ravenna is decorated with a mosaic depicting the baptism of Christ by John the Baptist. The seated figure on the left is a personification of the River Jordan.

While landowners were able to reach agreements to share their land with the new rulers in most of the Germanic kingdoms, the Vandals simply expelled most Roman landowners and took over their land wholesale.

However, the Vandals were not hostile to all things Roman. Aristocratic Vandals who took over the estates of dispossessed Romans lived in country villas and commissioned elaborate mosaic floors, just like their former owners. Even Vandal commoners must soon have adopted an essentially romanized lifestyle and material culture, because they are archaeologically indistinguishable. Only a few obviously Germanic graves and artefacts have been found in North Africa, while the modern populations of the region have no discernible genetic inheritance from the Vandal presence.

For military reasons, Vandal settlement was concentrated in only a few areas: around Carthage, Constantine in Numidia, and Cherchell and Tipasa in Mauretania. Before the Vandal conquest, North Africa had been the most prosperous region of the western empire, exporting large quantities of grain and olive oil to Italy.

This did not continue long under the Vandals. Their piracy disrupted Mediterranean trade, leading to the decline of agriculture in North Africa. Only Carthage seems to have remained prosperous. Economic decline was reinforced by Berber raids, which the Vandals proved incapable of suppressing.

The Vandals were not a numerous people and their hostility to Romans would have helped them resist assimilation by the native population, but it ensured that they could form no meaningful connections with it either. It also ensured the continuing hostility of the eastern emperors, who saw themselves as protectors of religious orthodoxy. In the sixth century, this would prove the Vandals' undoing.

Early Frankish kingdoms

The Franks are first named in Roman sources in about 245 when they tried to attack Mainz. By the 260s they were also making a name for themselves as pirates. Frankish raids on Gaul continued through the third and early fourth centuries. Many small groups of Franks, captured by the Romans during these raids, were allowed to settle in the empire as *laeti* – peasant-farmers with an obligation to provide recruits for the army. From the mid-fourth century the Franks gradually expanded into Roman territory west of the lower Rhine. Compared to the great migrations of other Germanic peoples it was unspectacular, but it created a solid power base for the Frankish conquest of Gaul, which occurred under the Merovingian dynasty after the final collapse of Roman power in the 470s.

The Franks were not newcomers but a confederation of tribes that had been living along the east bank of the Rhine between the River Main and the North Sea since at least the first century BC. The name 'Frank' is presumably one which they gave to themselves, as the word means 'bold' in their language. The Franks began their territorial expansion in 358 when the Caesar, Julian – who became sole emperor three years later – settled a group of Frankish invaders within the empire's borders as *foederati* in Toxandria, the region between the mouths of the Scheldt and Maas rivers. Julian intended this to be a temporary expedient until such time as he could expel them, but he was killed campaigning in Persia a few years later and, as they

The early Frankish kingdom

- original Frankish homeland
- Frankish federate settlement, 358
- Frankish territory, c. 482
- SALII Frankish tribe, c. AD 200
- frontier of Roman Empire, c. 400
- British migration, c. 460
- campaign of Childeric, 460–82
- royal Frankish centre
- key centre held by independent Roman ruler, 460–80
- distribution of Germanic warrior graves in late Roman Gaul
- battle, with date

generally proved themselves to be reliable allies, the Franks stayed put. Many Franks became career soldiers in the Roman army and at least two attained the rank of *magister militum*. The collapse of the Rhine frontier after 406 gave the Franks the opportunity for further expansion, and by around 440 their lands reached as far west as the River Somme. The Roman general Aëtius stopped further Frankish expansion, and they fought alongside him against the Huns at the Battle of the Catalaunian Plains in 451.

The Franks had no centralized institutions at this time; they were ruled by a number of petty kings who set up their headquarters in captured Roman cities. Outwardly, what set Frankish monarchs apart from their subjects was their long hair, which embodied the mystique of kingship. To cut a king's hair was to depose him, for he could not rule if his hair was short. Though they were politically disunited, the Franks had begun to lose their original tribal identities and coalesce into two main groups, the Ripuarians, who lived in the original homeland on the Rhine, and the Salians, on the new lands west of the Rhine. The distribution of pagan warrior burials indicates that Frankish settlement was densest between the Rhine and the Seine.

The eponymous founder of the Merovingian dynasty was Merovech (d. *c.* 460). His name means 'sea-fighter' and later legends claimed that he was the offspring of a sea monster – perhaps in reality a successful pirate. Nothing is known about him other than that he was the father of Childeric, king of the Salian Franks settled around Tournai. Still a pagan when he died in 482, Childeric's richly furnished burial, discovered at Tournai in 1653, indicates he was a ruler of considerable wealth and magnificence. However, when he became king *c.* 460 Childeric was only one of several protagonists trying to fill the power vacuum created by the collapse of Roman power in Gaul which followed the death of Aëtius in 454.

There were the Ripuarian Franks, with their own kingdom centred on Cologne, while Britons who had settled in Armorica were attempting to push east under King Riothamus, and Saxon settlers were trying to control the Loire valley – a region into which, and beyond, the Visigoths also hoped to expand. The Gallo-Roman *civitates* (self-governing communities) between the Loire and Somme may have been functioning independently, though two Roman generals, Aegidius and Count Paul, were still active in the area in the early 460s. Arbogast, another Roman general of Frankish descent, ruled the city of Augusta Treverorum (Trier) until *c.* 477. For a time Childeric seems to have been expelled from his kingdom by Aegidius but, however he did it, by the time of his death in 482, Childeric had emerged as the major military power in northern Gaul and had laid the foundations for rapid Frankish expansion under his ruthless son Clovis.

Minor Germanic kingdoms

If the Goths, Vandals and Franks were the main players of the barbarian invasions, they were accompanied by a large supporting cast, including Gepids, Sarmatians, Rugians, Scirians, Heruls, Bavarians, Burgundians, Suevi and Alamanni. Most of these peoples were absorbed into the major Germanic confederations but three founded short-lived kingdoms.

Originally an east Germanic people, in the third century the Burgundians muscled their way onto the Rhine frontier opposite Mainz in order to raid Roman territory. They took advantage of the collapse of the Rhine frontier to invade Gaul in 412 and seize lands around Strasbourg, Worms and Speyer. The Romans finally contained the Burgundians after Aëtius unleashed the Huns on them in 436. Their catastrophic defeat forms the basis of the medieval German legend of the *Nibelungen*. Aëtius settled the surviving Burgundians as *foederati* in the Saône valley and around Lakes Geneva and Neuchâtel. They remained loyal until Roman power began to collapse in the 460s, when they occupied much of central Gaul, establishing their capital at Lyons.

The Burgundian kings cultivated a close relationship with the Gallo-Roman aristocracy and their kingdom was prosperous and well ordered. Still pagan when they entered Gaul, they converted to Catholicism early in the fifth century, though some later switched to Arianism. Burgundian settlers became more integrated with the native population than was the case with other Germanic peoples and they often shared settlements and cemeteries. Despite this, the Burgundian kingdom was not destined for a long history. Taking advantage of a succession dispute, the Franks conquered it in 532–34.

Alamanni and Suevi

Alamannic bronze-gilt fibula dating to the 6th century with geometric and animal-inspired decoration.

The Alamanni were a confederation of tribes that formed in the Black Forest area of southern Germany in the early third century. Their mixed origins are reflected in their name, which means 'all men'. From 233 onwards they began regular attacks on the Romans and in 260 forced them to withdraw from the Agri Decumates, an exposed salient between the Rhine and Danube rivers. Despite their success in war, the Alamanni remained a loose confederation with several kings, each ruling from a hilltop stronghold. After the Rhine frontier was breached by the Vandal-Alan-Suevic confederation in 406, the Alamanni began to occupy Alsace and the northern foothills of the Alps. As the fifth century progressed, their failure to develop centralized leadership began to tell and the Alamanni found themselves hemmed in by more powerful neighbours. Their attempts to expand northwards into the Rhineland were repulsed by the Frankish king Clovis in 497 and by 536 the Alamanni had fallen under Frankish domination.

The Alamanni were slow to accept Christianity, their conversion not complete until the seventh century. They continued to be ruled by their own *duces* and when Frankish power entered a period of decline in the seventh century, they regained independence. Their reconquest by the Carolingian mayor Pippin III in 744–45 was accompanied by mass executions and the Alamanni thereafter lost their identity. Their name survives in the modern French word for the Germans, Allemands.

The Suevi (or Suebi) were a major but ill-defined group of Germanic peoples whose recorded history goes back to the first century BC. The Suevi were distinguished from other Germans by the hairstyle of males, which involved tying their long hair into a knot on the side of their heads. By the third century AD some tribes which grouped with the Suevi, such as the Lombards and Marcomanni, had emerged as distinct ethnic groups, while others had been absorbed into new tribal confederations, such as the Alamanni. However, a core group of Suevi, retained their identity in the mid-Danube region and it was they who, under pressure from Huns, joined the Vandals and Alans to invade Gaul in 406.

When the alliance occupied Spain in 411 they were settled in Gallaecia with the Asding Vandals. After the Vandals and Alans migrated to Africa, the Suevi occupied the whole province. Gallaecia was poor and mountainous, and the Suevi lived mainly by plundering neighbouring provinces. Under King Rechila, the Suevi occupied Baetica and Lusitania in 447 but were driven out again in 456 by the Romans and their Visigoth allies. In 465 the Suevi converted to Arian Christianity. They retained their independence in Gallaecia until 585, when they were finally conquered by the Visigoths.

The Germanic warrior

In Germanic society, the surest route to wealth, status and power was success in battle. Its most important institution was the *comitatus* or war band, the personal retinue of elite warriors that every king or chief tried to gather around him and which formed the core of the tribal army. The need to keep the war band together often dictated the politics of early German chiefdoms and kingdoms. Warriors needed war as an arena to display their prowess and win status and wealth. Kings and chiefs needed success in war to provide the means to reward their warriors and keep them loyal. In such a society long periods of peace were impossible to sustain. Success bred success, as more warriors would be attracted to the war band of a triumphant leader. The confederations and political centralization of the third and fourth centuries were in part driven by particularly successful war bands.

Warriors were expected to be loyal to their leaders, unto death if necessary. There was no formal discipline; fear of dishonour was generally sufficient to prevent a warrior abandoning his comrades in battle. Loyalty to the war leader was higher than loyalty to one's people (modern ideas of nationalism are not appropriate to the early Middle Ages). Germanic mercenaries maintained this attitude when they enrolled in the Roman army – they were no more likely to mutiny than Roman soldiers and were loyal to their Roman commanders even when asked to fight against their own people. In early Germanic society all able-bodied free men were expected to bear arms. The favoured offensive weapon was a long two-edged sword, the finest of which were made by the Roman pattern-welding or damascening technique. Swords were very expensive and most warriors fought with only a spear and a large single-bladed knife for close combat. Also employed were the bow and arrow and the throwing axe, especially popular among the Franks.

An S-shaped, garnet inlaid Lombardic fibula, terminating in stylized eagles' heads, made around 600. This was a popular style among the Lombards.

For protection, a well-equipped Germanic warrior would have a coat of chainmail or scale armour (a leather coat to which overlapping metal plates were riveted), a conical iron helmet with cheek plates and a mail neckguard, and a large circular wooden shield covered in leather and sometimes rimmed with metal. Such protection was not cheap. Frankish laws assessed the value of a chainmail coat at two horses or six oxen and a helmet at one horse, so it was only affordable to high-ranking warriors. Most Germanic warriors went into battle protected only by a wooden shield and perhaps a toughened leather cap – a serious handicap when faced with regular Roman troops, who all wore mail or scale armour. As their migrations progressed, Germanic warriors acquired more and more Roman equipment, especially swords and armour.

Most Germans fought on foot. Only the Goths, under the influence of steppe nomads, had developed effective cavalry, and its role was decisive in their victory over the Romans at Adrianople in 378. Stirrups were not used in Europe until the sixth or seventh century, but saddles were designed to allow warriors to fight effectively on horseback without the risk of dismount by the shock of impact with an opponent. Among the other Germans, cavalry was important for skirmishing, raiding and reconnaissance, but in a defensive engagement even those warriors who had horses usually dismounted and fought on foot. By giving up the easy means of escape, war leaders showed their willingness to share the same fate as their less well-equipped followers.

The Germans did not employ sophisticated battle tactics and lacked siege warfare skills. Visigoth leader Fritigern said that he 'had no quarrel with stone walls'. Attacks were launched in deep formations, with the high-ranking, best-equipped warriors in the first rank and the humblest at the rear. The favoured defence formation was the shield wall, where the warriors formed tightly together behind their overlapping shields. The formation was probably inspired by Roman legionary tactics. Germanic warriors were not drilled like Roman soldiers: if a formation was broken there was little chance of it reforming and a rout would ensue.

IV
Birth of Byzantium

The bulwark of Christianity

After the Roman Empire of the west fell in the fifth century, the eastern empire rallied and survived for another thousand years. At first, the eastern emperors continued to use Latin as the language of law and administration but, as few of their subjects spoke it as their everyday tongue, Greek eventually supplanted it. At the same time the culture of the eastern empire became increasingly Hellenized. Its inhabitants continued to think of themselves as Romans, but modern historians distinguish it from the Roman Empire of Classical times by calling this medieval Greek-speaking realm the Byzantine Empire, from Byzantium, the old Greek name for Constantinople. Historians do not agree when it is appropriate to start calling it the Byzantine Empire. Some do so from the foundation of its capital, Constantinople, in 324, others from the final and permanent division of the empire into eastern and western halves after the death of Theodosius in 395. The most common time is 476, when the last western emperor, Romulus Augustulus, was deposed. However, the Hellenizing of the eastern empire was not a single event but a gradual process only completed in the reign of Heraclius (610–41). By recognizing the transformation that had taken place and making Greek the empire's official language, Heraclius has perhaps the best claim to be the first Byzantine emperor.

A 10th-century Byzantine reliquary containing fragments of what was believed to be the True Cross, the cross on which Jesus was crucified. Now in Limburg cathedral, Germany, the reliquary was probably brought to the west after the sack of Constantinople in 1204 during the Fourth Crusade.

While it was not welcomed by the eastern emperor Zeno (r. 474–91), the fall of the west at least simplified things and allowed him to concentrate on the survival of his own realm. The east was inherently stronger, but was riven by religious disputes and had its own problems with over-mighty Germanic generals. Zeno made little headway in reconciling the feuding Orthodox and Monophysite religious factions, whose bitter dispute centred on the nature of Christ. The empire would later pay a heavy price for this religious disunity. Zeno had greater success with his German problem. By sending Theodoric and his Ostrogoths to Italy to fight Odoacer, he rid the east of its most dangerous Germanic federates.

The standing of the east continued to improve under Zeno's cautious successor Anastasius (r. 491–518). Despite fighting wars with Persia and the Bulgars, Anastasius cut taxes and still left his successor Justin (r. 518–27) with a full treasury. Justin was an unlikely emperor, an uneducated Thracian peasant who had joined the army and risen through the ranks to become commander of the imperial guard. For most of his reign Justin ruled with the guidance of his nephew Justinian, who caused a scandal by marrying an actress, Theodora. In 527 Justinian was crowned co-emperor and when Justin died later that year became sole Augustus.

Arguably the last great Roman emperor, Justinian (r. 527–65) was ambitious to restore the full glory of the empire. He believed it was a Roman emperor's duty to uphold the law, maintain religious orthodoxy and, above all, maintain the unity and territorial integrity of the empire. Justinian thought it a disgrace that the western provinces were still occupied by barbarians, and his reign was dominated by determined but ultimately only partially successful campaigns to recover them. At thirty-eight years, Justinian's reign was the longest enjoyed by any Roman emperor since Augustus in the first century. This was a considerable achievement in itself, for the heavy taxes he imposed to fund his ambitious plans ensured that he was never a popular ruler.

Conquest of the Vandals

The Vandals had struck the most serious blows against the Western Roman Empire, so Justinian's first target was their

CONQUEST OF THE VANDALS

North African kingdom. He could not immediately implement his plans, because he had inherited a war with Persia from his uncle Justin's reign. As so often in the past, the Persians initially had much the better of the fighting, but a remarkable victory by the youthful general Flavius Belisarius (505–565) at Dara (now in eastern Turkey) in 530 was enough to stalemate the war and allow Justinian to negotiate an 'endless peace' in 532. The peace lasted only eight years and was sealed with a hefty price tag of nearly 5,000 kg (11,000 pounds) of gold, but it was enough to free Justinian's forces for campaigns in the west.

The Persians were not Justinian's only problem. In the same year he made peace, there was a popular uprising by the circus factions in Constantinople. These originated in republican times as chariot racing teams and were known as the Blues, Greens, Whites and Reds, from their team's colours. Chariot racing had a mass following in Constantinople and the rivalry between the main factions, the Blues and Greens, was intense, often extremely violent and extended into the political and religious arenas. Blues tended to support religious orthodoxy and the emperor; Greens were Monophysites and opposed him. By clamping down on the political activities of both factions, Justinian achieved the near impossible and united them against him. Mobs crying '*Nika! Nika!*' (Victory! Victory!) took over the

This 6th-century mosaic from the basilica of San Vitale in Ravenna presents a powerful image of the late Roman state, with Emperor Justinian flanked by courtiers, soldiers and clergy. The figure by Justinian's right-hand side is thought to be the general Belisarius.

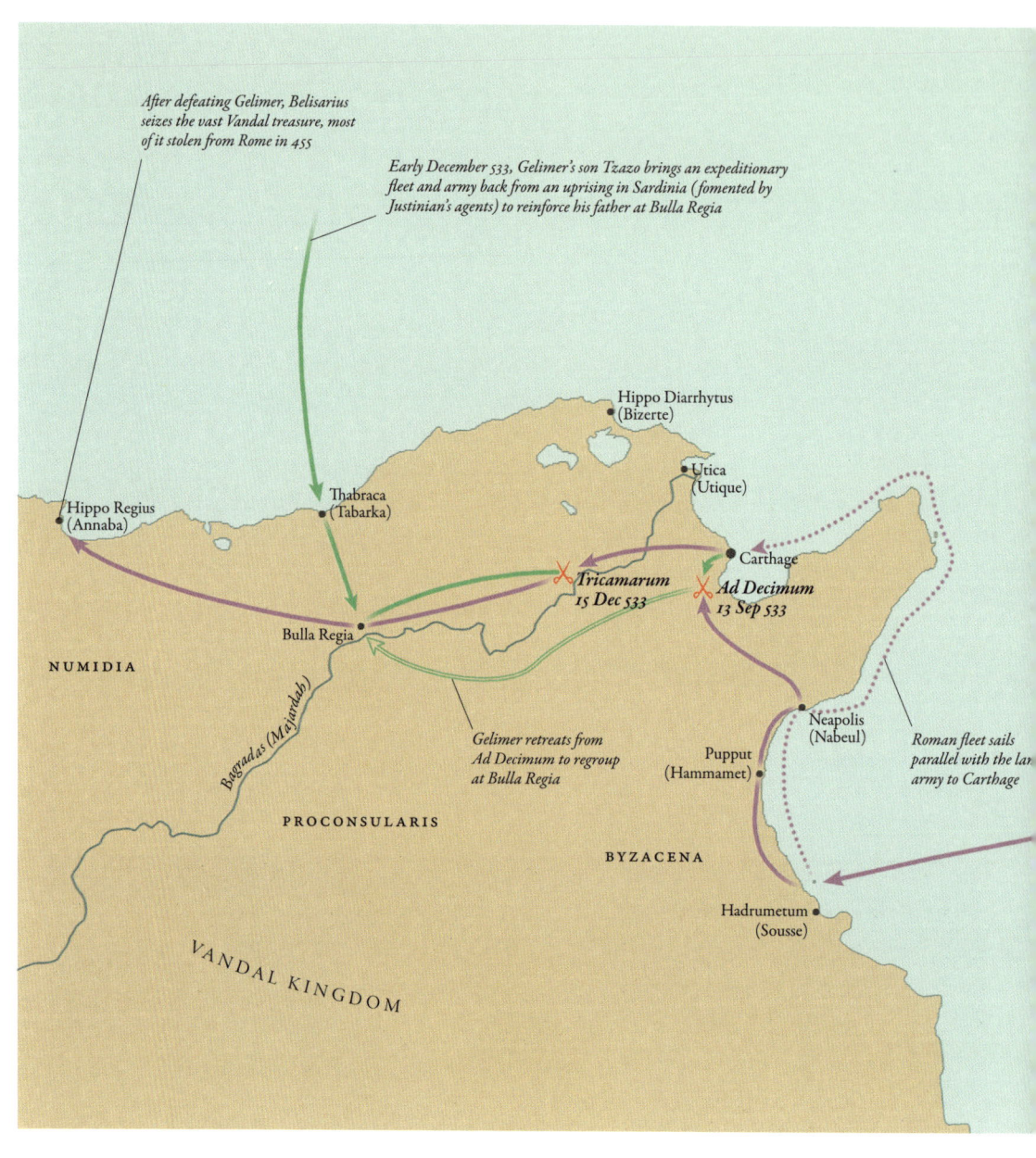

Belisarius's conquest of Vandal Africa

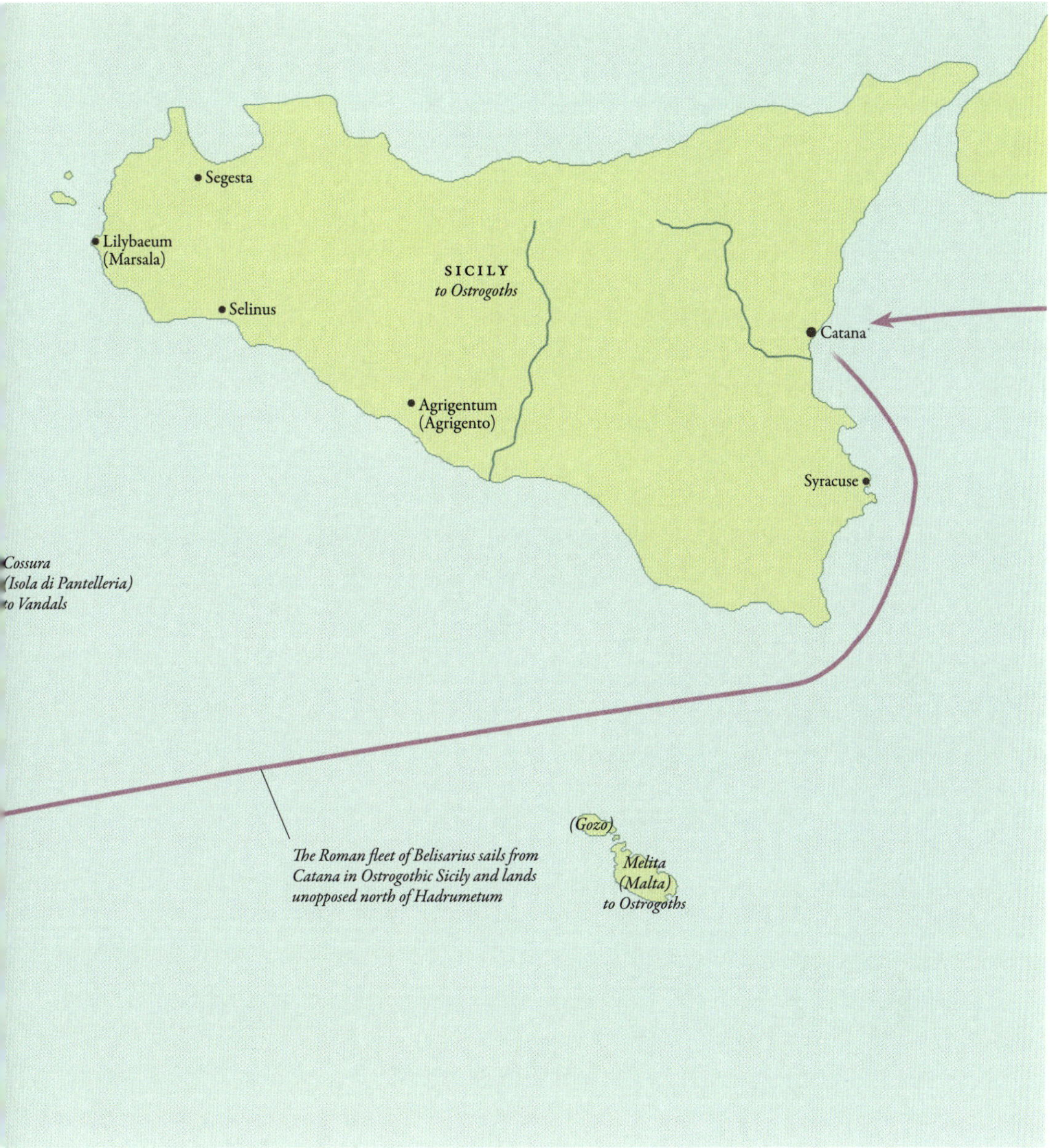

Segesta
Lilybaeum (Marsala)
Selinus

SICILY
to Ostrogoths

Catana
Agrigentum (Agrigento)
Syracuse

Cossura (Isola di Pantelleria)
to Vandals

The Roman fleet of Belisarius sails from Catana in Ostrogothic Sicily and lands unopposed north of Hadrumetum

(Gozo)
Melita (Malta)
to Ostrogoths

→ Belisarius's movement
→ Vandal movements
✗ battle, with date

Ostrogothic kingdom
Vandal kingdom

city, torching public buildings and attacking soldiers. Justinian was on the brink of fleeing, but Theodora shamed him into staying, saying she would rather die as an empress than live as a refugee. Belisarius again demonstrated his outstanding skills and gathered a small force that trapped the rioters in the hippodrome and massacred them. The riots left tens of thousands dead and much of Constantinople in ruins, but it broke internal opposition to Justinian for good.

Belisarius's conquest of Vandal Africa

Justinian was now free to deal with the Vandals. Memories of Basiliscus's disastrous campaign of 468 were still raw and had given the Vandals an aura of invincibility. Most of the emperor's advisers argued against the campaign, but Justinian believed that in Belisarius he had a general capable of meeting the challenge. The emperor's justification for the war was religious: he wanted to rescue African Catholics from the oppression of their Arian rulers. It helped that the Vandal king Hilderic (r. 523–30), who had been brought up as an orthodox Catholic by his Roman mother, Eudocia the daughter of Valentinian III, had recently been deposed by his Arian nephew Gelimer (r. 530–34). The force Justinian entrusted to Belisarius was only a third the size of that given to Basiliscus: 500 transports, 92 war galleys, 10,000 infantry, 5,000 heavy cavalry and 1,000 Hun horse archers.

Diplomatic preparation for the campaign was impeccable. Permission was obtained from the pro-Roman Ostrogothic queen Amalasuntha to use Sicily as a forward staging post, while 5,000 Vandal troops and the bulk of the navy were diverted to Sardinia after Roman agents fomented a rebellion there. Belisarius's force set sail in June 533, landed in North Africa in early September near Hadrumetum (Sousse), and began to advance on Carthage. At *Ad Decimum* (the tenth milestone from Carthage) Gelimer ambushed the Roman army but failed to press home an early advantage; two days later Carthage fell without a fight. Gelimer fled to Bulla Regia, rallied his troops, and by December 533 he was ready to try to retake Carthage. This time it was Belisarius who ambushed Gelimer, when his army pitched camp at Tricamarum, about 32 km (20 miles) from Carthage.

In this 15th-century French manuscript, Emperor Justinian is shown receiving Belisarius on his return to Constantinople after his conquest of the Vandal kingdom in North Africa.

Despite a huge advantage in numbers, the Vandal army scattered and Belisarius advanced to Hippo Regius to take possession of the Vandal treasury. Gelimer surrendered a few months later and was allowed to retire to an estate in Anatolia. Though greatly aided by the Vandal king's lacklustre leadership, Belisarius's victory was a stunning achievement. Justinian would soon entrust him with an even more ambitious mission.

The Ostrogothic campaign

Events in the Ostrogothic kingdom presented Justinian with his pretext for intervention. Theodoric (r. 471–526) had been succeeded by his young grandson Athalaric (r. 526–34) under the regency of his pro-Roman daughter Amalasuntha. When Athalaric died, still in his teens, the throne passed to Amalasuntha's cousin Theodahad (r. 534–36), who wasted no time in imprisoning her. Justinian offered her his protection, and when Amalasuntha was strangled in her bath in April 535 he declared his intention to avenge her murder. Diplomatically isolated, the Ostrogoths could expect no help from the Visigoths or Franks.

Justinian's campaign to reconquer Ostrogothic Italy started as promisingly as the African Vandal campaign, but soon degenerated into a lengthy war of attrition that left Italy devastated and impoverished. For the conquest, Belisarius was given a force of only 7,500 men – only 50 per cent greater than a single legion of Julius Caesar's time. Belisarius faced little opposition in achieving his first objective – the forcible occupation of Sicily in December 535 – and he crossed to the mainland in 536, capturing Naples after a short but bitter siege.

The Ostrogoths were dismayed by Theodahad's failure to save Naples, so he was deposed and killed. In his place they chose Witigis (or Vitiges, r. 536–40), who proved to be an equally inept general. By choosing to concentrate on the threat of a Frankish invasion in the north, Witigis left Rome exposed and it was occupied by Belisarius in December; its Ostrogothic garrison had withdrawn peacefully after negotiations with Pope Silverius. In March 537 Witigis arrived outside Rome with a large Ostrogothic army. Belisarius had spent the winter restoring Rome's defences. Though Witigis besieged it for a year and nine days, the city held out. Disease and hunger took a heavy toll on both sides. The arrival of reinforcements in spring 538 allowed Belisarius to break the siege and regain the initiative. In a war of sieges, Belisarius took stronghold after stronghold over the next eighteen months, finally trapping Witigis in Ravenna at the end of 539. Only two other major Ostrogoth cities held out: Pavia and Verona.

In May 540 Belisarius obtained Ravenna by deception. The Ostrogoths offered to surrender if the Byzantine genral agreed to become their king. Ignoring instructions from Justinian, Belisarius agreed but was loyal to the empire and reneged on the deal as soon as he held Ravenna. Witigis was sent into honourable retirement on an estate in Anatolia. Justinian was not the most trusting of monarchs and Belisarius's actions at Ravenna bred suspicion. The general was recalled to Constantinople to take command in a new war with Persia, but instead of appointing a new commander Justinian divided authority in Italy between eleven generals. At this point, the empire

Overleaf: Completed in 537, the greatest of the churches Justinian built in Constantinople was the cathedral of Hagia Sophia (Holy Wisdom). The minarets were added when it was converted to a mosque after the Ottoman Turks captured Constantinople in 1453.

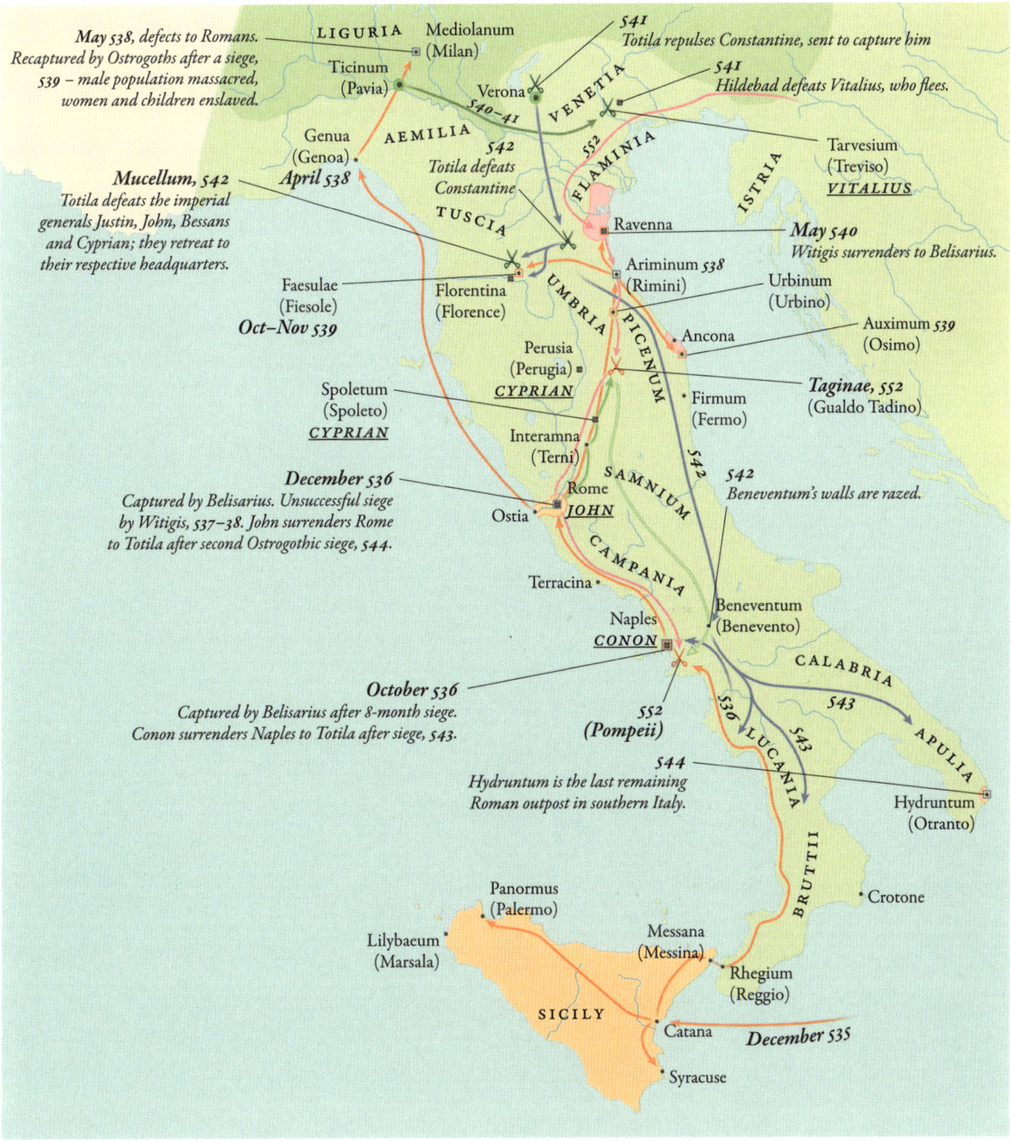

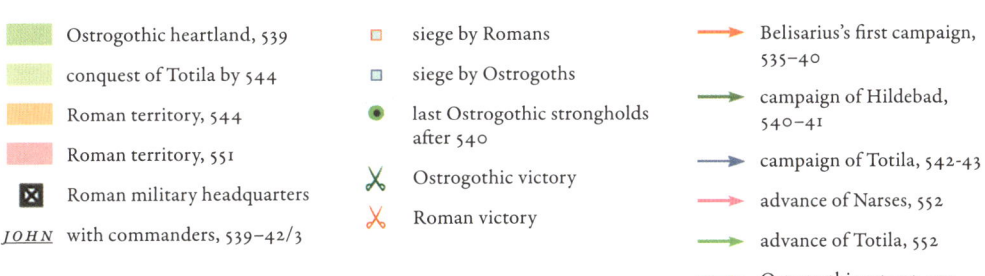

Belisarius's first campaign and the Ostrogothic revival, 535–44

Ostrogothic heartland, 539

conquest of Totila by 544

Roman territory, 544

Roman territory, 551

Roman military headquarters

JOHN with commanders, 539–42/3

siege by Romans

siege by Ostrogoths

last Ostrogothic strongholds after 540

Ostrogothic victory

Roman victory

Belisarius's first campaign, 535–40

campaign of Hildebad, 540–41

campaign of Totila, 542-43

advance of Narses, 552

advance of Totila, 552

Ostrogothic retreat, 552

was paralyzed by a plague pandemic. In 541 rebellion broke out at Verona, where the Ostrogoths proclaimed Totila king (r. 541–52). A skilled tactician and wily politician, Totila was supported by many Italians who were disillusioned by the imperial restoration.

Against an uncoordinated imperial response, Totila swept through Italy, and by 544 the Romans held only a few fortified towns. Even Rome had been lost. Justinian sent Belisarius back to Italy, but with insufficient troops to win a decisive victory. A long stalemate followed and it was not until 551 that Justinian sent another major army into Italy, this time under the eunuch general Narses (*c.* 478–573). The arrival of fresh troops proved decisive. Narses defeated the war-weary Ostrogoths at Taginae (Gualdo Tadino, Umbria) in 552, killing Totila. The Ostrogoths rallied under a new king, Teia, but Narses defeated him too in October on the slopes of Mount Vesuvius. By 554 Gothic resistance had been crushed, but if Italy was now securely under imperial control, its economy was so ruined that it was more of a liability than an asset.

Gold *solidus* of Justinian I. Such coins were used mostly for foreign trade.

Justinian's legacy

By the end of his reign, Justinian had achieved a large part of his ambition to restore the Roman Empire. In addition to reconquering North Africa and Italy, his forces had recovered all the islands of the western Mediterranean and a sizeable part of southern Spain. For the first time in over a century, the Roman Empire extended from the Euphrates to the Atlantic Ocean, but the cost had been high. The financial consequences of Justinian's attempt to recover the west were enormous. He did nothing to reduce the Roman army's reliance on expensive barbarian mercenaries, and while in theory campaign costs should have been recouped in taxes from reconquered provinces, Justinian's armies were usually too small to win quick victories and get revenue flowing.

In Italy the war against the Ostrogoths dragged on for twenty years, leaving the province economically ruined. Even Belisarius's quick victory in North Africa was wasted, because the garrison left behind was too small to protect it from economically damaging Berber raids. The eastern empire was exposed to Persian and Slav invasions, because Justinian had stripped the Danube and Persian frontiers of troops to fight in the west. The empire was financially exhausted by the time of Justinian's death in 565 and his successors were unable to hold what had been won. The destructiveness of the wars sapped the provincials' enthusiasm for imperial restoration and in Italy Justinian's officers came to be seen not as Roman liberators but as Greek invaders. The Western Roman Empire had been too long gone for its spirit to be revived.

Justinian's activities were not confined to the military sphere; his concept of the responsibilities of imperial office was a wide one. Over the centuries, Roman law had accumulated such an enormous body of legislation and case law that it was difficult to make consistent judgments. Justinian saw law as central to the Roman spirit: reviving it was as important as reconquering the west. On Justinian's orders the complete codification of Roman law was undertaken by a commission headed by the lawyer Tribonian. The result, the *Corpus Juris Civilis* (Body of Civil Law), reduced the number of volumes a lawyer needed from 106 to a much more manageable six. It was the finest achievement of the Roman legal tradition but, ironically, the code had little influence in its own time because it was written in Latin, a language few people in the east now spoke.

Justinian believed that it was the emperor's duty to maintain religious orthodoxy in order to secure God's favour towards the empire. The main challenge to orthodoxy in the sixth century came from Monophysitism. While Catholic orthodoxy held that Christ had indivisible human and divine natures, Monophysites believed that Christ had only a single divine nature. Monophysites were numerous in the eastern empire and were the majority in Egypt, Palestine and Syria. In the old western empire, the majority were orthodox Catholics ruled by Arian Germans. To pose as the liberator of western Catholics, Justinian needed to champion orthodoxy – but this meant alienating many of his existing subjects.

Despite occasional persecution of Monophysites and the bullying of uncooperative popes, Justinian's policy was mainly one of persuasion. He tried to bring the parties together by offering theological compromises but these, naturally, pleased no one. There was no reconciling the irreconcilable. Justinian's successors were more heavy-handed and by the beginning of the seventh century Monophysite areas were seething with discontent. More successful was Justinian's persecution of the empire's remaining pagans. By the end

One of a pair of gold Avar earrings, made around 550–560. A nomad people, originally from the East Asian steppes, the Avars arrived in Europe in the 6th century.

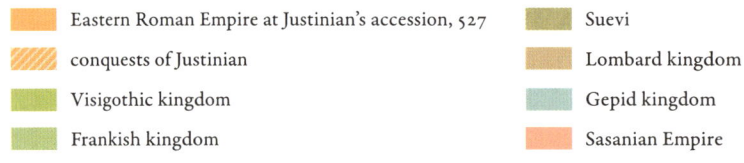

European reconquests during Justinian's reign

- Eastern Roman Empire at Justinian's accession, 527
- conquests of Justinian
- Visigothic kingdom
- Frankish kingdom
- Suevi
- Lombard kingdom
- Gepid kingdom
- Sasanian Empire

of his reign all public worship of Greco-Roman and ancient Egyptian gods had been suppressed, the last temples razed.

Justinian also sought to revive the glory of the empire with the creation of impressive public buildings, fortifications and churches. The finest of these was the cathedral of Hagia Sophia (Holy Wisdom) in Constantinople, which until the sixteenth century remained the greatest domed building in the world. On a less massive scale, but more haunting, are the glittering mosaic portraits of Justinian and Theodora and their courtiers which face one another across the chancel of the church of San Vitale at Ravenna. Seen as they were intended, reflecting the light of hundreds of flickering candles, the awesome figures of the emperor and his wife would have seemed to be alive, while all around them shadows gathered.

The Lombard invasion of Italy

After concluding the Ostrogothic war in 554, Justinian realized that the empire needed peace to consolidate its gains and for its economy to recover. He was willing to avoid war at almost any cost and adopted a policy of paying tribute to buy off potential invaders, but threats continued. Among those threatening the empire were the Avars, Mongolian nomads who arrived in eastern Europe *c.* 560. Though on a smaller scale than that of the Huns, the Avar migration had a similar destabilizing effect, as the Slavs and Lombards invaded the empire in an effort to escape them.

The Lombards – from Langobardi or 'long beards' – were a Germanic people whose earliest known homeland was near Germany's Baltic Sea coast: recent aDNA studies point ultimately to a Scandinavian origin. In the turbulent years of the fourth and fifth centuries they migrated south, settling on the Danube in modern Austria *c.* 486. The Lombards adopted a form of social organization based on late Roman military ranks, with a hierarchy of dukes, counts and others commanding warrior bands based on kinship groups, all under a relatively weak monarchy. It was around this time that the Lombards converted to the Arian form of Christianity.

In the early sixth century the Lombards fought the Gepids for control of Pannonia. Justinian encouraged the Lombards in these wars and employed their king, Audoin, against the Ostrogoths.

The Lombard invasion of Italy

- border of Eastern Roman Empire, 568
- initial Lombard invasion, 568–69
- *568* date of Lombard acquisition
- lands of Lombard kingdom in Italy, *c.* 600
- division of Lombard kingdom
- territory lost from the empire, 600–700
- territory still under imperial control, *c.* 700
- main area of Lombard settlement based on cemetery evidence
- patriarchate
- archdiocese
- major road
- advance of Slavs

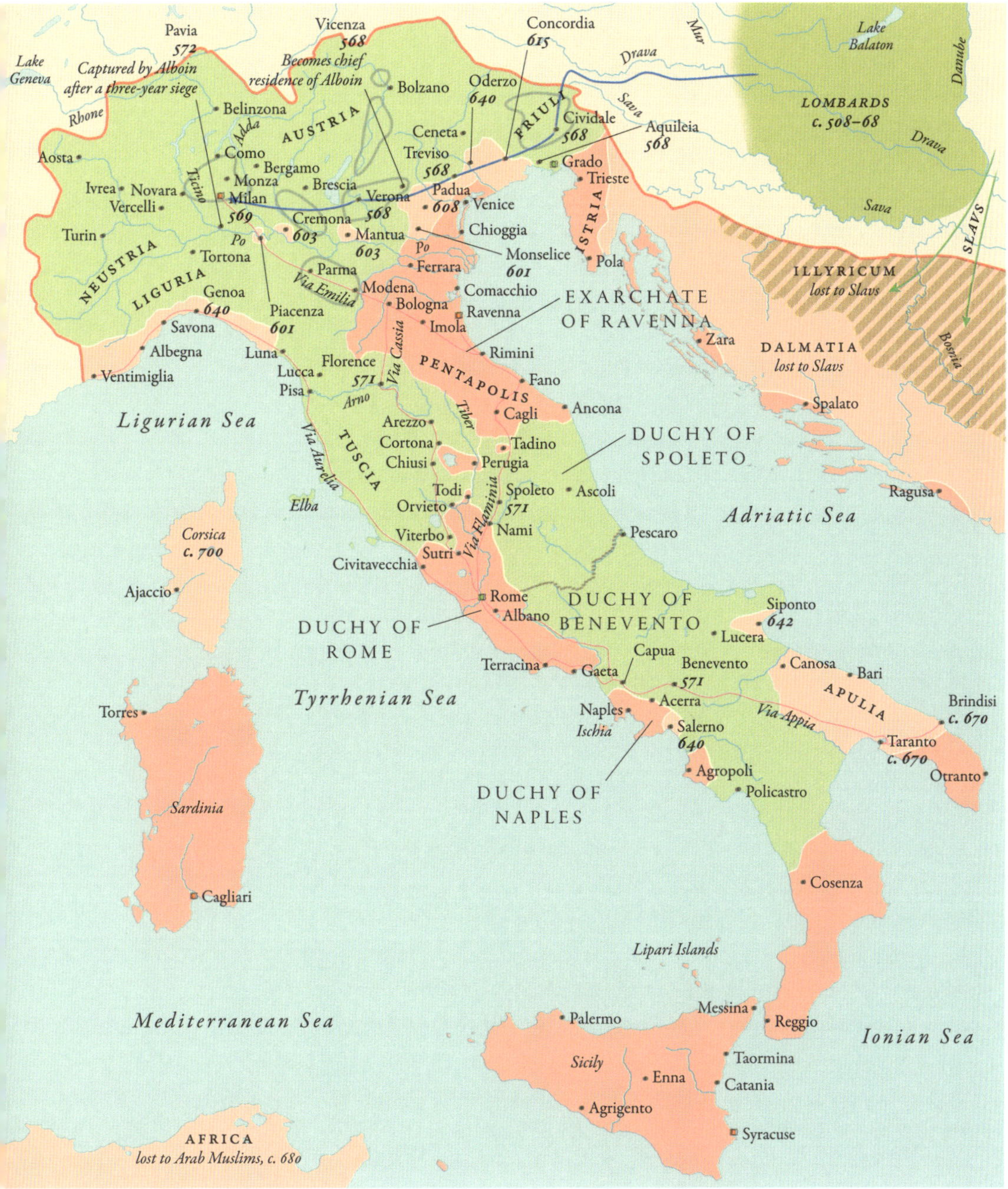

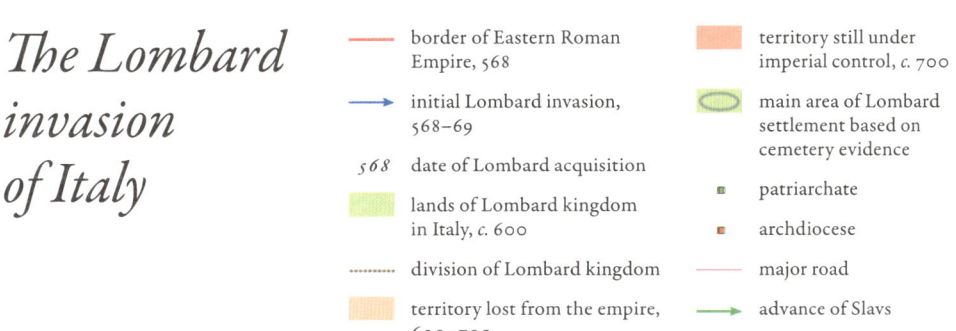

The wars against the Gepids were brought to a decisive conclusion by Audoin's son Alboin (r. *c.* 565–72) with the help of the Avars. Alboin personally slew the Gepid king Cunimund and forcibly married his daughter Rosamund. Any sense of triumph Alboin might have enjoyed was surely short-lived, for the Avars turned out to be a far graver threat than the Gepids had ever been. In 568 Alboin tamely agreed that the Lombards would hand over their lands to the Avars and migrate to Italy.

Italy had still not fully recovered from the Ostrogothic war prosecuted by, first, Belisarius and then Narses, and was weakly defended. Justinian's successor, his nephew Justin II (r. 565–78), rashly provoked conflict with the Persians and Avars. In only three years the Lombards overran almost all of the Po valley and Tuscany, as well as Spoleto and Benevento in southern Italy, while avoiding the Exarchate of Ravenna as being too well defended. The imperial position in Italy looked past saving but then, in 572, Alboin was murdered at Rosamund's instigation. His insistence during a feast that she drink from a cup made from her father's skull apparently proved one humiliation too many. Alboin's successor, Cleph, was murdered after reigning for only eighteen months and, this time, no agreement could be reached on a successor. The Lombard kingdom shattered into thirty-six independent duchies.

The monarchy was restored by Cleph's son Authari in 584, but he was only able to impose his authority in the north; Spoleto and Benevento remained independent duchies. The interregnum gave the eastern empire an opportunity to create an effective military government for Italy under the exarch (military governor) of Ravenna. The popes stiffened resistance in Rome, and the emperors encouraged Frankish invasions of northern Italy to distract the Lombards. The empire retained control of the seas and, because the remaining imperial strongholds were mostly on the coast, they could be supplied easily if they were besieged. For these reasons, neither Authari nor his successors were able to repeat the sweeping advances of Alboin's reign, but neither were the exarchs given sufficient forces to reconquer any significant territory from the Lombards.

The main areas of Lombard settlement were all in the north, in the area now named after them: Lombardy. The heavily fortified city of Pavia was adopted as the royal capital. The Lombards were only ever a small minority in Italy and like the other Germanic peoples clung to Arianism as a badge of identity and a barrier to assimilation by the native Catholics. Only in the reign of King Liutprand (712–44) did they feel confident enough to convert to Catholicism.

Slavs, Avars and Persians

The Balkans paid the heaviest price for Justinian's reconquests in the west. Lack of garrisons to man its many fortresses left the Balkans exposed to increasingly severe raids by the Slavs, who on one occasion plundered as far south as Corinth. Meeting little resistance, Slavic settlement began in the late sixth century, and Avars became the new raiders. The Slavs' origins are poorly understood. The many cultural disruptions caused by migrating Germanic and Asiatic nomads in the history of eastern Europe mean that archaeology provides no clear answers. At the time of their first recorded attacks on the Eastern Roman Empire in the 520s, the Slavs were still a preliterate tribal people who left no records of their early history, and Greek and Roman historians are notorious for their lack of interest in barbarian peoples. Linguistic and place name studies, however, show that by *c.* 500 they already occupied a large part of eastern Europe.

The arrival of the Avars on the Danube in the 560s at first provided the empire with an ally against the Slavs. The Avars were fearsome

A 6th-century gold belt fitting featuring a griffin, a popular motif in Avar metalwork.

warriors, fighting in typical nomad fashion as highly mobile horse archers, and Justinian paid them a handsome subsidy to attack the Slavs. The Avars rapidly became a serious threat in their own right. In 568 Justin II decided to end subsidies to the Avars and added insult to injury by seizing Belgrade, which the Avars also claimed as their own. The Avars vented their fury by repeatedly ravaging the Balkans, but it was not until 580 that their khan, Baian, recaptured Belgrade. The key border fortress of Sirmium (Sremska Mitrovica, Serbia) fell to the Avars in the same year.

In 591 and 597 Avar raiding parties even reached the Aegean Sea. The Slavs joined in the raiding, attacking Thessalonica in 584 and 586 and settling unhindered in a region that was rapidly becoming depopulated. Tireless campaigning by Emperor Maurice (r. 582–602) forced the Avars back north of the Danube in 601. Maurice's load was lightened by a peaceful eastern frontier: in 596 he had intervened in a Sasanian civil war at the request of the deposed Khusrau II (or Khosrow, r. 590–628) and restored him to the Persian throne. Maurice was rewarded with a magnanimous peace treaty.

Maurice was a fine soldier – his reflections on the art of war, the *Strategikon*, is a military classic. But his imposition of strict discipline was resented by an army already demoralized by pay cuts and seemingly endless wars. In an effort to keep the pressure on the Avars, Maurice ordered his army to winter on the far side of the Danube in 601–02. It was too much to ask and the soldiers mutinied, appointing an undistinguished junior officer called Phocas as their spokesman. As the army marched on Constantinople, the circus factions joined the rebellion and Maurice was overthrown. Almost by default, Phocas was acclaimed emperor in 602. His first act was the brutal execution of Maurice and his family, but this was only the beginning. Phocas had none of the qualities needed to be an effective leader and his rule quickly descended into a reign of terror. Phocas was popular only in Rome where, in 607, Pope Boniface III erected a pillar in honour of the emperor's recognition of the papacy as the head of the Church. Phocas further demonstrated his enthusiasm for orthodoxy by launching a vicious persecution of Monophysites.

The empire began to collapse into civil war. To eliminate potential rivals, Phocas purged the army of its best generals. Deprived of effective leadership, the army was unable to prevent the Avars and Slavs overrunning the Balkans. Then, taking advantage of the growing anarchy in the empire, Khusrau II announced his intention of avenging his former benefactor and occupied Mesopotamia. To free troops for the east, Phocas tried to buy off the Avars: they took the money but carried on regardless. By 608 a Persian army had reached the Bosporus before withdrawing, while an Avar army had briefly laid siege to Constantinople itself.

The Persian wars

Salvation came from an unlikely direction. Disgusted with Phocas's incompetent tyranny, in 610 the exarch of Carthage equipped a fleet and sent his son Heraclius (r. 610–41) to Constantinople to overthrow him. Eliminating Phocas was no quick fix for the empire's problems, however – Heraclius faced a gargantuan task. The empire was bankrupt, its economy and provincial administration were shattered, and with no money to pay mercenaries the army hardly functioned. By 616 Armenia, Syria, Palestine, Egypt and most of Anatolia had been occupied by the Persians. Most of the Balkans was in the hands of the Slavs and Avars.

Fresco depicting a battle between the Byzantine emperor Heraclius and the Persians under Khusrau II, one of a series of ten telling the story of the True Cross, in the Basilica of St Francis in Arezzo. It was painted by Piero della Francesca in *c.* 1452–66.

The Eastern Roman Empire under Phocas, 608

For the next ten years Constantinople was almost continuously blockaded by Persian and Avar forces. Heraclius sued for peace, even offering to become a vassal of Khusrau II, but his offers were rejected. Encouraged by the lack of resistance encountered, Khusrau was set on nothing less than the complete destruction of the Roman Empire. Heraclius realized that it was pointless trying to revive what little survived of the civil and military institutions that had served the empire since Diocletian's time. Only complete reform could save it. The provinces still under Heraclius's control were reorganized into military districts called 'themes' under a *strategos* (general). Soldiers were settled in the themes on inalienable grants of land in return for hereditary military service, freeing the empire of its reliance on expensive mercenaries and giving its soldiers a stake in its survival.

Most of the unwieldy bureaucracy that typified the late Roman state was disbanded as it was no longer needed. Recognizing the Hellenization of the empire, Heraclius made Greek the official language of government. His reforms were a clear break from the Roman past, and for this reason he can be regarded as the true founder of the medieval Byzantine Empire.

The Church also played an important role. When they had captured Jerusalem in 614, the Persians burned the Church of the Holy Sepulchre and carried off what was believed to be the True Cross. Sergius, the patriarch of Constantinople, created a morale-boosting atmosphere of religious fervour by presenting the struggle against the fire-worshipping (Zoroastrian) Persians as a war in defence of Christ himself, a kind of forerunner of the Crusades. Sergius also placed the vast wealth of the Church at the emperor's disposal. Heraclius was ready to commit his new army in 622. Bypassing the ravaged lands of Anatolia, Heraclius sailed to the Bay of Issus near Antioch and struck north into Cappadocia to cut the lines of the Persian army besieging Constantinople. Fired by a victory over the leading Persian general Shahr-Baraz, the Byzantine army wintered in Trebizond on the Black Sea and the next year struck deep into the Persian Empire, winning a succession of victories, culminating in the decisive Battle of Nineveh in Mesopotamia in December 627. Discredited by his failures, Khusrau was overthrown and executed by his son, Kavad II, who immediately came to terms. All occupied Byzantine territory was to be returned and Kavad agreed to pay a huge indemnity. At Easter 630 Heraclius personally returned the True Cross to Jerusalem, concluding what had become a holy war.

The Byzantines were still recovering from the war with Persia when they faced a new and unexpected threat from the newly united and Islamized Arabs. Neither Heraclius, now ailing and worn out, nor the empire were in any condition to resist. By the time Heraclius died in 641, much of the territory won back so painfully from the Persians had been lost again. Yet Heraclius's work had not been in vain. His new military system was durable and recovered from its early catastrophes. The sense of Christian mission endured and the Byzantines would never lose the conviction that they were the true defenders of Christendom.

Constantinople

The longevity of the Byzantine Empire was due in no small part to its impregnable capital, Constantinople. Founded by Constantine the Great in 324 as a new eastern capital for the Roman Empire, it was built on the site of a small Greek port called Byzantium. Ideally placed for its purpose, Constantinople stood on an easily defended peninsula with sheltered harbours at a strategic crossroads of major land and sea routes. Officially inaugurated by Constantine the Great in 330, it was loosely modelled on Rome: it had seven hills and was divided into fourteen districts, and had its own Senate and consulship. The whole city was protected from attack by land and sea by an 8-km (5-mile) circuit of walls.

A gold *aureus* of Constantine the Great, minted in 324, the year he founded Constantinople as a new, eastern, capital for the Roman Empire.

Above all, however, Constantine planned Constantinople to be a Christian city, free of Rome's pagan associations – though that did not prevent him from plundering the east for pagan statuary, and even an ancient Egyptian obelisk, to adorn the city. Constantinople was centred on three great churches, dedicated to Holy Wisdom (St Sophia), Holy Power (St Dynamis) and Divine Peace (St Irene). Both St Sophia and St Irene were rebuilt on an even grander scale by Justinian after the Nika riots in 532 and still stand today. A church dedicated to the Holy Apostles was built as Constantine's mausoleum, and it was there in 337 that he was buried in a tomb surrounded by memorials to the twelve apostles.

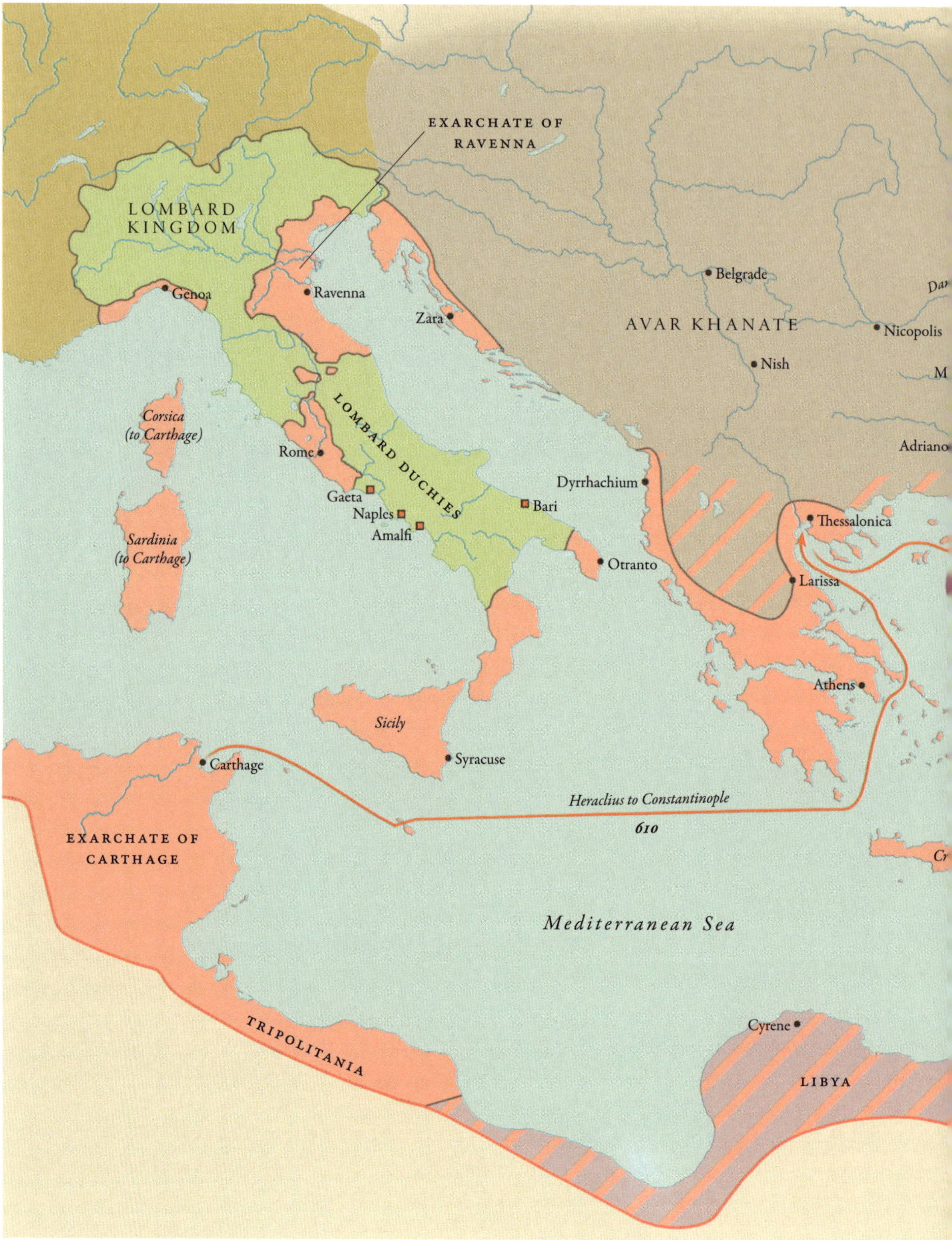

Byzantine recovery under Heraclius

- Byzantine territory, 622
- Lombards
- Franks
- Avars
- Sasanian Empire

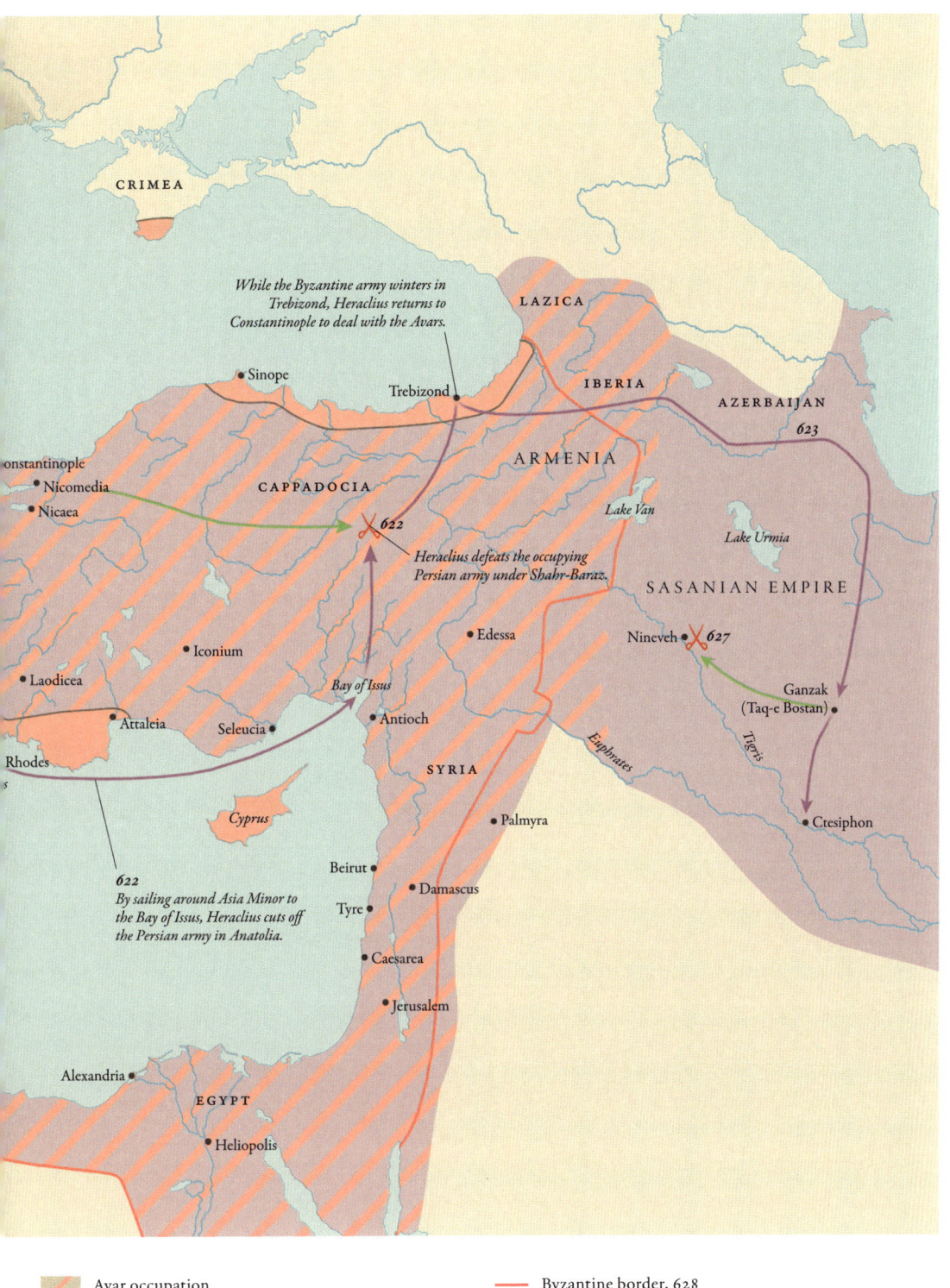

Financial benefits for house builders and the offer of free bread for the poor were used to encourage settlers. The city grew with amazing speed and by the end of the fourth century it had already spread outside its original walls. By this time Constantinople had 11 imperial palaces, at least 14 churches, 5 markets, 8 public baths and 150 private bath houses, 20 public and 120 private bakeries, and a hippodrome for chariot races (but no amphitheatre – gladiatorial combat had never been popular in the Greek east and was outlawed by Theodosius I). There were 322 streets and 4,388 houses, not including the many slum dwellings of the poor.

Because of its strategic location, Constantinople was already a major international trade centre. Expansion continued less rapidly until the seventh century, by which time it had a population of over half a million, making it by far the largest city in Europe. Globally, only Chang'an (the Tang dynasty capital in China) was larger. To accommodate the growing population, new walls were built in 413, 1.6 km (1 mile) further out than Constantine's original walls. Built by the *praefectus praetorio* Anthemius, and named after Theodosius II, who was only twelve at the time, these walls were one of the best investments in military architecture ever made. The walls gave impressive defence. First there was a 20 m (65 ft) wide flooded moat and stone breastwork, then an outer wall 12 m (40 ft) high and 2 m (6 ft) thick, and finally the main defence line, the massive inner wall, 20 m (65 ft) high and 5 m (16 ft) thick. The towers on both walls overlapped, so that defenders on the inner wall could give covering fire for those manning the outer wall and breastwork. The walls were badly damaged in an earthquake in 447 and had to be repaired in haste, because Attila was advancing on the city. All citizens, regardless of rank, were ordered to help with the repairs, which were completed just in time to repel the Huns.

The Theodosian walls continued to resist all assaults for another thousand years until they were finally breached, after a six-week bombardment, by Ottoman cannon in 1453. By this time Constantinople was a shadow of its former greatness; whole districts within the walls had been abandoned to nature and the population had fallen to only 100,000.

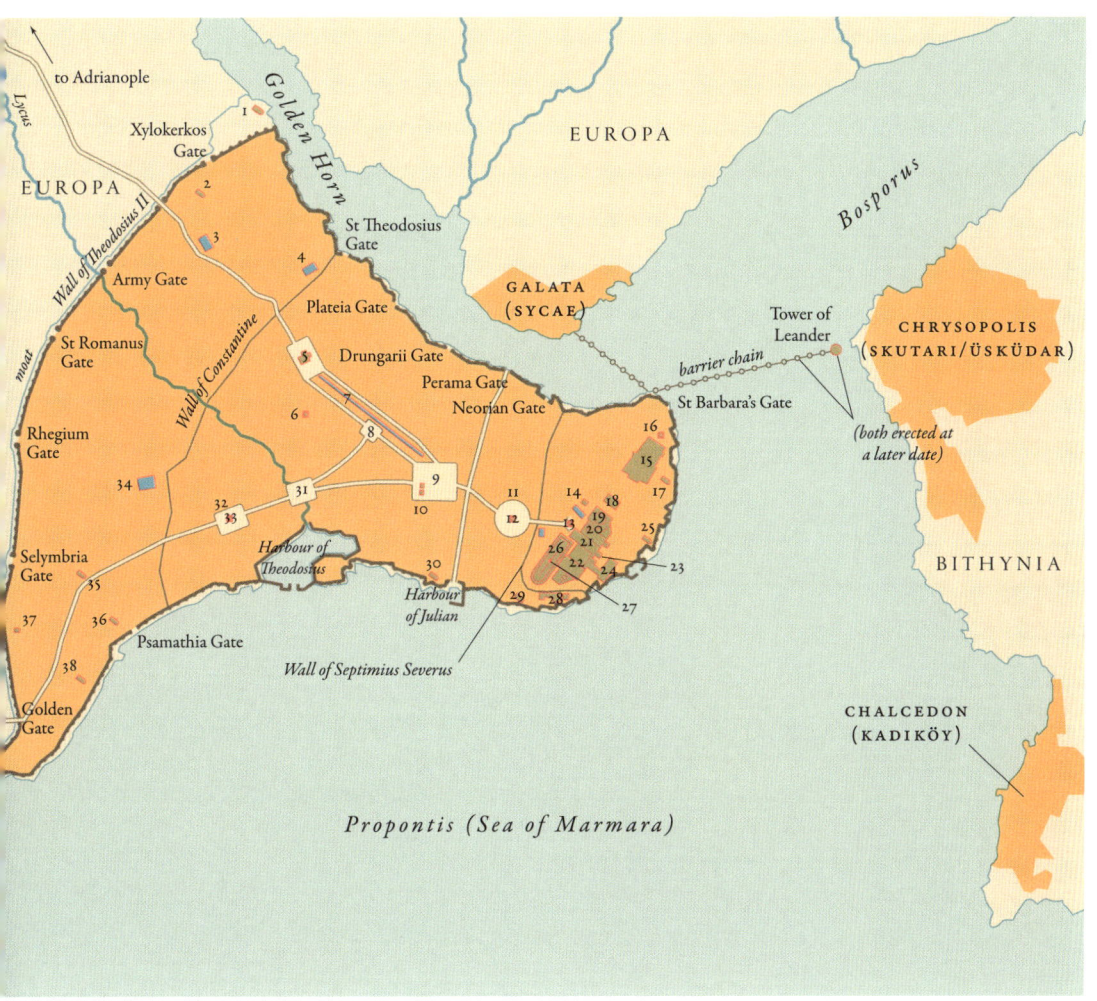

Constantinople in the time of Justinian

1 St Mary in Blachernae
2 St Salvador
3 Cistern of Aelius
4 Cistern of Aspar
5 Church of the Holy Apostles
6 Column of Marcian
7 Aqueduct of Valens
8 Amastrianum
9 Forum Tauri
10 Arch of Theodosius
11 Forum of Constantine
12 Column of Constantine
13 Millon
14 St Mary Chalkoprateia
15 Acropolis
16 Column of Claudius Gothicus
17 Monastery of Magnana
18 St Irene
19 St Sophia
20 Augusteion
21 Baths of Xeuxippus
22 Imperial Palace
23 Senate House
24 Bucoleon Palace
25 St Mary Hodegetria
26 Hippodrome
27 Obelisk of Theodosius
28 Palace of Justinian
29 St Sergius and St Bacchus
30 St Thomas
31 Forum Bovis
32 Forum of Arcadius
33 Column of Arcadius
34 Cistern of Mocius
35 St Andrew in Krisel
36 Martyrum of St Carpus and St Papylus
37 Monastery of St Menas
38 St John Studios

V
Britannia

Forgotten island

The years between 400 and 600 are a true dark age in British history. Britain produced almost no contemporary chroniclers in this period, while continental writers seem almost to have forgotten about the island, which for them became a land of ghosts and mists. Increasing troubles on the continent led the imperial government to neglect Britain in the late fourth century. The last major intervention was by Stilicho in 396–98, but three years later he was withdrawing troops to defend Italy against the Goths. Isolation meant that the British aristocracy and commanders of the field armies missed out on imperial patronage. This bred rebelliousness and Britain earned a reputation for producing usurpers.

In 406–07 the Roman army in Britain elevated three usurpers in quick succession: Marcus, Gratian and Constantine III (r. 407–10). When Constantine withdrew the field army for his doomed adventure on the continent, the Britons seem to have decided that the empire was no longer working for them, and in 409 they kicked out the Roman administration and set up their own government. Britain thus became the only province to leave the Roman Empire voluntarily.

It is likely that the Britons tried to maintain a Roman-style administration, as this was the only model they would have known. Any attempt to maintain political unity quickly broke down, however, as long-suppressed tribal rivalries re-emerged. Leadership probably

A 7th-century helmet found in a richly furnished Anglo-Saxon ship burial at Sutton Hoo in Suffolk, England, associated with Rædwald, the king of East Anglia. The helmet was made of iron with decorative panels made of tinned bronze.

devolved on the local Romano-British aristocracy who established themselves as hereditary rulers, so by the sixth century Britain was divided into several small kingdoms. Some of these, like Dumnonia in the southwest and Gwynedd in north Wales, were based on old Celtic tribal identities that had survived the Roman occupation. Other kingdoms were based on Roman towns: Aquae Sulis (Bath), Corinium (Cirencester) and Glevum (Gloucester) had their own kings in the sixth century. To what extent these towns remained functioning urban communities is uncertain. A few towns, such as Luguvalium (Carlisle), Verulamium (St Albans) and Viroconium (Wroxeter), continued to flourish until the mid-fifth century, but most had been abandoned by this time due to economic dislocation. In Eburacum (York), the headquarters of the legionary fortress was in use, probably as the palace of a local king, long after the rest of the city was in ruins. The limited occupation at other towns may have been of a similar nature. Some Iron Age hillforts, such as South Cadbury, were reoccupied, but in most areas the population dispersed across the countryside.

The Britons found themselves under attack by Picts from the un-romanized far north of Britain, the Irish (confusingly known as *Scotti* or Scots) and, from across the North Sea, by the Saxons and other Germanic tribes now known collectively as Anglo-Saxons. The distribution of inscriptions in the early Irish *ogam* alphabet indicates considerable Irish settlement in south Wales and Dumnonia, but their main success was against the Picts: the only British territory the Irish won permanent control of was the Isle of Man.

Archaeological evidence shows that Germanic settlement began in the south and east of Britain within a few years of the end of Roman rule. In his *On the Ruin of Britain*, the monk Gildas (d. 570), the only contemporary British chronicler of the period, claimed that a tyrannical king, probably called Vortigern, invited Saxon mercenaries to settle in Britain in return for military service against the Picts and Scots. If that is true, he was probably following the Roman policy of settling barbarians as federates. However, the Saxons rebelled and began to take over the country. British resistance was rallied by an obscure war leader called Ambrosius Aurelianus who defeated the Saxons at the Battle of Mount Badon (location unknown) *c.* 500 and halted their expansion. Gildas paints a very negative picture of the Britons in the immediate post-Roman period: their rulers were mostly

A ship's figurehead, one of five dredged from the River Schelde in the 1930s. Made of oak and carved with lozenge-shaped lattice-work, the figurehead has been radiocarbon dated to AD 220–665.

The end of Roman Britain

- northern frontier of Roman Britain, 410
- Britons, *c.* 410
- Picts, *c.* 410
- Irish, *c.* 410
- DÉISI kingdoms and peoples, *c.* 500
- Aergol king known from literary source, *c.* 500

Raids and migrations, 4th–5th centuries:

- Pictish
- Irish raider-settlers
- Anglo-Saxon raider-settlers
- British settlers, 5th century

Late Roman towns or forts:

- coastal fort
- certainly occupied, 5th century
- probably occupied, 5th century

Other sites:

- stronghold, 5th–6th centuries
- early Christian site
- distribution of Anglo-Saxon cemeteries, 5th century
- Irish *ogam* inscription

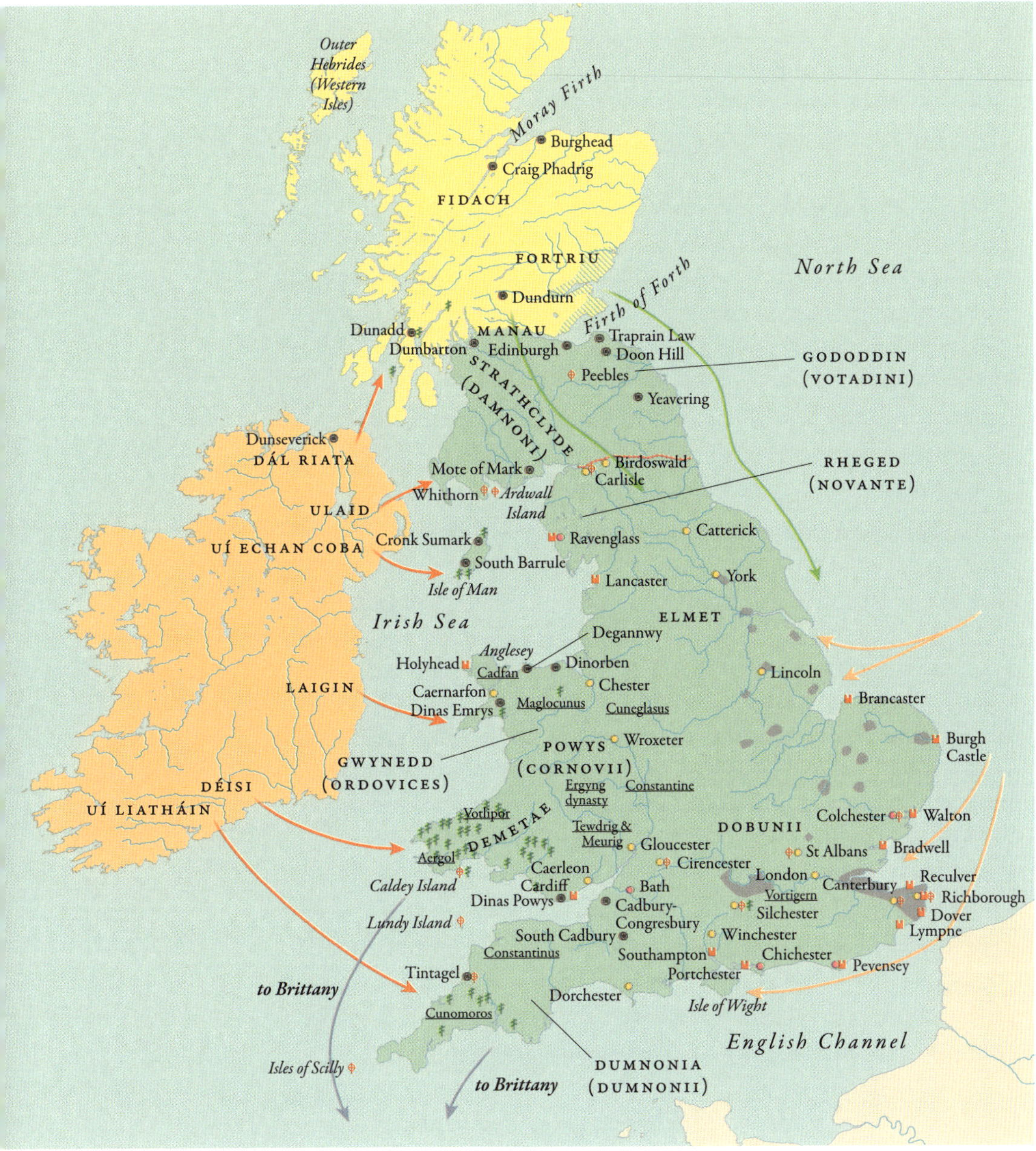

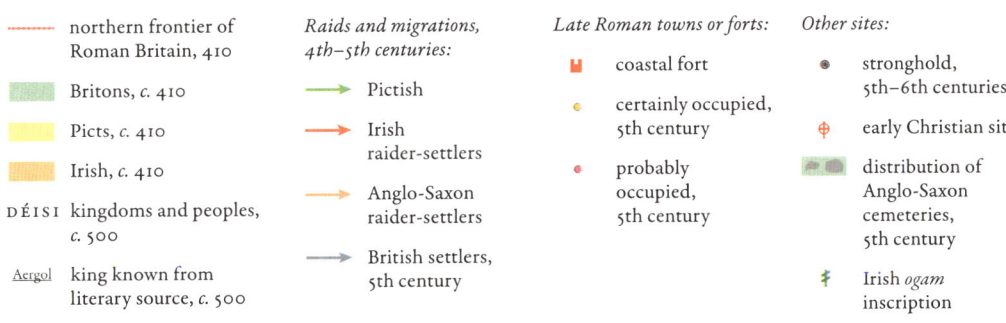

immoral tyrants and, to escape genocidal massacres by the Saxons, Picts and Scots, the survivors sought refuge in the mountains of the west or fled abroad to Brittany. Archaeological and genetic evidence, however, indicates that Gildas's account was greatly exaggerated, probably for rhetorical effect.

Christianity had become well established among the Britons by the end of the fourth century. In the next century British missionaries began to convert the Picts and Irish, though the southeast reverted to paganism after it was conquered by the Anglo-Saxons. Political and physical isolation from Rome allowed the British Church to develop its own customs and practices, characterized as 'Celtic Christianity'. The same isolation revived Iron Age Celtic art forms, which had never died out in Ireland and the Pictish north.

The Anglo-Saxon settlements

The Anglo-Saxon conquest and settlement of much of Britain was the first step in the creation of the modern English nation. The earliest detailed account of the Anglo-Saxon settlements was recorded by the monk Bede (672/3–735) in his *Ecclesiastical History of the English People*. Bede based his history mainly on that of the monk Gildas, some fragmentary chronicles and now lost oral historical traditions. According to Bede, a small band of Saxons led by Hengist and Horsa were settled in Kent by Vortigern in 449 in return for their service fighting the Picts and Scots. The Saxons rebelled, murdering the Britons' leaders at a feast with weapons smuggled in their boots. They brought in reinforcements from across the sea and began to conquer Britain.

Bede tells us that three peoples, all of them still pagan, took part in the conquest: the Saxons from the North Sea coast of Germany; Angles from the neck of the Jutland peninsula; and the Jutes, from northern Jutland. The Angles are said to have settled in East Anglia and Northumbria; the Saxons in Sussex ('South Saxons'), Essex ('East Saxons') and Wessex ('West Saxons'); and the Jutes in Kent and the Isle of Wight. Genetic evidence is not precise enough to confirm Bede's account in detail, but research into aDNA from human remains in early medieval cemeteries across eastern England is consistent with a substantial migration of people of Continental

Anglo-Saxon settlements, c. 550–700

- main area of Anglo-Saxon settlement, c. 550
- Anglo-Saxon expansion to c. 600
- Anglo-Saxon expansion to c. 650
- British territory, c. 650
- direction of Anglo-Saxon expansion
- 616 date of Anglo-Saxon conquest
- Anglo-Saxon royal burial
- British royal centre
- early Anglo-Saxon royal centre
- linear earthwork
- POWYS British kingdom, 6th–9th centuries
- KENT Anglo-Saxon kingdom, 7th–9th centuries

North European (CNE) descent into Britain from across the North Sea in the aftermath of the end of Roman rule there. It is not clear which group predominated, for while the English take their name from the Angles, the British Celts take their names for the English from the Saxons (*Saesneg* in Welsh, *Sassenach* in Gaelic). The Jutes were clearly the junior partner and some historians believe, for no very good reason, that their participation in the settlements is purely legendary.

The location of the earliest identified Anglo-Saxon settlements supports the idea that they were invited to Britain. There is a concentration of settlements in Kent and many others are inland. However, Bede's date for the first settlement is far too late, as archaeological evidence, notably cemeteries of pagan burials containing typically Germanic grave goods, proves that it started within ten years of the end of Roman rule. Hengist and Horsa are almost certainly legendary figures but, in the light of contemporary events on the continent, a rebellion by Saxon federates is not incredible. By whatever means, the Anglo-Saxons had taken over most of southeast Britain by 500, and in the next century several

Scenes from a 12th-century copy of Bede's *Life of St Cuthbert*. Cuthbert played a key role in the evangelization of the Anglo-Saxon kingdom of Northumbria.

small kingdoms emerged. Their progress was checked by the British victory at Mount Badon, but in 577 the West Saxons resumed the advance, reaching the Bristol Channel after defeating a coalition of British kings at Dyrham. A last-ditch effort by the Gododdin to hold the line in the north was crushed at Catterick *c.* 600 and the fragmentation of British territories was completed in 616 when the Northumbrian king Aethelfrith defeated the Britons at Chester.

Of all the inhabitants of the former Roman Empire, the Britons put up the stiffest resistance to Germanic invaders. As a result, the Anglo-Saxon settlement was not peaceful and resulted in far greater cultural, economic and political disruption than the Germanic settlements on the continent. The *Anglo-Saxon Chronicle*, compiled from earlier chronicles in the late ninth century, records many violent incidents, such as the storming of the old Roman fort at Pevensey in Sussex in 491, when the victorious Saxons massacred the Britons who had taken refuge there. However, there is considerable documentary evidence for the survival of the native population – in early Anglo-Saxon law codes and religious biographies, for example – and this is now backed up by genetic evidence. Even as late as 700, the East Anglian fenlands were populated by Celtic-speakers.

The CNE genetic imprint decreases towards the west of Britain. This suggests that the later stages of Anglo-Saxon expansion were more in the nature of a political takeover than a migration, the conquered Britons remaining on the land and being gradually assimilated to Anglo-Saxon identity. This is borne out by place name studies, which show a higher survival of Celtic place names in western England than in the east, where they are rare. The victorious Anglo-Saxons adopted barely half-a-dozen Celtic words into Old English, suggesting that the conquered Britons had a low social status. Some British aristocrats integrated with the Anglo-Saxon aristocracy: Cerdic (d. *c.* 534), the founder of Wessex and the kingdom that would one day unify England, had a Celtic name (Caradoc).

King Arthur, man or myth?

The most famous and mysterious figure of early medieval Britain is King Arthur, usually thought of as a great Celtic leader who triumphed over the invading Anglo-Saxons at the Battle of Mount Badon *c.* 500, which bought the Britons a generation of peace. However, it is unlikely that Arthur was a king, if he existed at all. The nearest thing to a contemporary source for this period is Gildas's *On the Ruin of Britain*. Writing within forty years of the Battle of Mount Badon, Gildas attributes the Anglo-Saxon defeat to the leadership of Ambrosius Aurelianus, a romanized Briton whose ancestors 'had worn the purple', and makes no mention of Arthur. Gildas does not describe Ambrosius as a king and his role appears to be akin to that of a *magister militum* of the late Roman army.

The earliest document to mention Arthur as the victor at Badon, the *History of the Britons* by Nennius, another British monk, dates to no earlier than the ninth century. It includes much that is obviously legendary and should be regarded not so much as evidence that Arthur was a historical figure but that he had come to be regarded as one by the time it was written. Because of the lack of contemporary evidence, many historians believe that Arthur was simply a folkloric figure, like Robin Hood, who was historicized when real events became associated with his name. If Arthur did exist, the most likely possibility is that he and Ambrosius were one and the same person. Arthur, which means 'bearman', perhaps was originally a nickname given to the tough warrior.

Dozens of British locations have become associated with Arthur. Some are relatively recent in origin. The tradition that Arthur and his knights lie sleeping in the prehistoric copper mines at Alderley Edge in Cheshire dates only from the eighteenth century, for example, but many can be traced to the Middle Ages. One such is Arthur's O'en (oven), a ruined Roman building near the Antonine Wall, first recorded in 1293. What is particularly striking about the distribution of these sites is that almost all of them lie within the areas where the Britons remained independent longest: southwest Scotland, Cumbria, Wales and Cornwall. This neither proves nor disproves that Arthur was a real person, but it emphasizes the British origin of the stories.

Emigrant Britons took Arthurian traditions with them to Brittany, where there are several Arthur-related sites. Arthurian tales then spread to France, where they inspired the literature of chivalry and courtly love in which Arthur was transformed from a rough warlord into an idealized medieval king, presiding over an equally idealized court of gallant knights errant and fair damsels. The group of sites most frequently associated with Arthur are prehistoric monuments,

such as megalithic tombs (Coetan Arthur), tumuli (Bwrdd Arthur), hillforts (Moel Arthur) and henges (King Arthur's Round Table), built centuries before the Battle of Mount Badon.

Other sites have become associated with the Arthurian stories on etymological grounds. In the Middle Ages, Colchester was thought to have been Camelot because its Roman name was Camulodunum. The fort at Birdoswald on Hadrian's Wall, known to the Romans as Camboglana, has been identified with Camlann, the site of Arthur's legendary last battle. Carmarthen in southwest Wales was said to derive from Kaermerdin, 'Merlin's fortress'; it actually derives from Moridunum, the Roman name for the town.

Not all Arthurian associations are fanciful, however. Archaeological excavations have shown that South Cadbury, Tintagel, Dinas Emrys, Mote of Mark (i.e., King Mark of Cornwall, the rival of Arthur's father Uther Pendragon) and Dumbarton Rock were Dark Age power centres. Recently excavations at Birdoswald have shown that it too was the stronghold of a British chieftain in the immediate post-Roman period.

Early Christian Ireland

Peaceful trade contacts between Ireland and Roman Britain began as early as the first century AD. As Roman power declined in the late fourth century, the Irish began raiding Britain for loot and slaves. One Irish king, Niall of the Nine Hostages, is said to have led seven expeditions to Britain. The Irish did not become significantly romanized as a result of raiding, but the raids led to the development of the *ogam* alphabet and the first contacts with Christians.

The first Christians to live in Ireland were probably British slaves. St Patrick was one such; captured around the end of the fourth century he escaped after six years, only to return as a missionary bishop *c.* 435. Patrick's mission to Ireland is the most famous, but it was not the first. The evangelization of Ireland was begun by missionaries from Gaul in the late fourth or early fifth century, and by 431 there were enough converts for Pope Celestine to appoint Palladius of Auxerre as bishop of the Irish. This early missionary work was concentrated in southeastern Ireland; Patrick's mission was to begin the conversion of the pagan northern half of Ireland.

After Patrick's arrival, Gaulish missionaries were gradually superseded by ones from Britain, who introduced the practices of the Celtic Church. As a result, the Irish Church did not develop a formal diocesan structure; its main centres were monasteries rather than cathedrals and its dominant figures were abbots rather than bishops. Irish monasteries became outstanding cultural centres. Under the patronage of the monasteries, craftsmen produced superb works of art in metal and stone, such as the chalices of Ardagh and Derrynaflan, and sculptured high crosses, many of which still stand. The monks copied Classical manuscripts and produced intricately illuminated gospel books as acts of devotion.

Early Christian Ireland was a complex mosaic of hundreds of local kingdoms, over kingdoms and high kingdoms. An ordinary king (*rí tuathe*) was the ruler of a *tuath*, which was defined as a people or community, rather than a territorial unit. The territory of a *tuath* could be very small, often less than 260 square km (100 square miles), but each would have its capital, usually a small ring fort or a *crannog* (a lake settlement on an artificial island); a church or monastery; and an inauguration site, typically a prehistoric barrow on a prominent hilltop believed to be the grave of an illustrious royal ancestor. In theory, the people of a *tuath* belonged to an extended kinship, with the king as the head of the senior lineage. He was responsible for the fertility of his people's land and cattle, no doubt a legacy of pagan times. Kings also had duties of lawmaking, judgement and leadership in war.

In return, all free families of the *tuath* owed the king tribute and military service. Kings would themselves owe tribute (mainly paid in cattle), hospitality and military service to an over king (*ruiri*), who in turn might owe it to a *rí ruirech* or provincial over king. Over kings did not exercise direct rule outside their *tuath*; their power rested entirely upon their ability to call on the services of client kings. There were seven provincial over kingdoms, the most powerful of which were those ruled by the northern and southern Uí Néill dynasties. As rulers of the prehistoric ritual centre of Tara, the southern Uí Néill kings enjoyed superior status and were sometimes given the title 'kings of Ireland' (*rí Érenn*). The High Kingship of Ireland did not develop as a formal institution until the late tenth century, however.

Irish kings kept warrior retinues, not unlike the Germanic *comitatus*, and warfare between kingdoms was endemic. Early Irish

Early Christian Ireland

ULAID	provincial over-kingdom	
LÓIGIS	major sub-kingdom and dynasty	
CORCA	minor kingdom and peoples (*tuatha*)	

- densest concentration of early Christian *ogam* inscriptions, 4th–7th centuries
- major missionary church
- church of the Patrician (Armagh) *paruchia*
- church of the Columbian (Iona) *paruchia*
- royal centre
- Culdee foundation
- other monastery
- high cross
- production centre of illuminated manuscripts

warfare centred around cattle raids of the type described in the epic poem *Táin Bó Cúailnge* (Cattle Raid of Cooley), believed to be set in the fourth century, which describes how the legendary Ulster hero Cú Chulainn defeated a raid by Queen Medb of Connacht to seize a prize bull.

The Celtic Church

After the pagan Anglo-Saxons conquered southeast Britain, British Christians became isolated from the Roman Church and began to develop an ascetic monastic Church known as 'Celtic Christianity'. The Britons spread their Celtic Church to Ireland, Brittany and Galicia, and in turn the Irish spread it to Pictland and the Anglo-Saxon kingdom of Northumbria. The Irish were also active in the Frankish kingdoms as monastic founders and reformers, and as teachers and scholars.

The main doctrinal difference between the Celtic and Roman Churches – an arcane variation in the methods used for calculating the date of Easter – occurred accidentally. Reforms in the dating method enacted by the Roman Church in the fifth century did not reach Britain. Its conservative method of calculating Easter, however, became a symbol of the Celtic Church's independence. Other differences concerned organization. The Catholic Church had a hierarchical structure of dioceses and archdioceses based on the administrative divisions of the late Roman Empire. Though bishops were respected and influential, the Celtic Church did not develop a formal diocesan structure, and pastoral care for the laity was often provided by ascetic Culdee monastic communities.

Monasteries that were believed to share a common founder were grouped in loose associations called *paruchiae* (parishes). Celtic monks were readily distinguishable by their unique tonsures: they shaved the front of their heads instead of the top as was the Roman practice. Celtic monasticism had a strong ascetic and eremitical tradition, inherited from the Desert Fathers. An important expression of this tradition was the desire for isolation from the world. Monks seeking solitude for contemplation settled in small communities or hermitages on remote islands around the British coasts. Others deliberately set sail into unknown waters, putting their fate into the hands of God. The Irish called this practice *peregrinatio* – 'travelling for God'. Many *peregrini* must have disappeared without a trace, but some made safe landfalls and returned to tell the tale. By *c.* 800 Irish monks had become the first human inhabitants of the Faroe Islands and Iceland.

Not all *peregrini* turned their backs on the world. St Columba, who founded a monastery on the Hebridean island of Iona in 563, became closely involved in the conversion of the Picts to Christianity. St Aidan, another monk from Iona, played a major role in the conversion of Anglo-Saxon Northumbria. Irish missionaries such as Fursa and Columbanus took Celtic monasticism to the continent. Although Irish influence extended as far as Italy, it was concentrated in the economic and political heartland of the powerful Frankish kingdom, between the Seine and the Rhine. The tradition of *peregrinatio* died out after the eighth century, with the increasing influence of Benedictine monasticism and its emphasis on stability.

The activities of British missionaries in Europe have attracted less attention. They were mainly active in areas of British settlement overseas, primarily in Brittany but also in a little-known colony in Galicia known as Britonia, which survived from the mid-sixth until the early ninth century. Galician monasticism developed a distinctively Celtic character, with monks living in small communities or hermitages along the rugged coast or on small offshore islands. Unlike the Irish, the Britons played no role in converting their Anglo-Saxon neighbours. Bede believed that this was a deliberately malicious policy on their part, intended to keep the Anglo-Saxons out of heaven.

The practices of the Celtic Church became increasingly controversial in the seventh century. Missionaries like Columbanus were bringing Celtic practices to the continent and at the same time Roman missionaries in southern Britain converted the Anglo-Saxons. In Northumbria, both Celtic and Roman missionaries were at work. Conflict was inevitable. In 664 King Oswiu of Northumbria called an assembly at Whitby to settle the issue of the calculation of Easter, deciding in favour of the Roman method. In 716 it was formally adopted in Ireland, but the Britons held out until the ninth century. This capitulation marked the beginning of the end of the independent Celtic Church, as it gradually accepted Roman practices and papal leadership.

Decorated with biblical scenes, the 9th- to 10th-century Muirdach's High Cross at Monasterboice in county Louth is considered one of the finest examples of early medieval stone carving. High crosses were used as preaching stations but they were also status symbols.

The Anglo-Saxon kingdoms

Anglo-Saxon England before the Viking Age is often described as the Heptarchy, from its division into seven main kingdoms: Kent, Wessex, Northumbria, Mercia, East Anglia, Essex and Sussex, which fought among themselves for supremacy. The earliest of the Anglo-Saxon kingdoms to achieve prominence was Kent, whose kings traced their ancestry back to the legendary founders of Anglo-Saxon England, Hengist and Horsa. Though small, Kent prospered from its position astride the main trade routes between Britain and the continent and developed close links with the Frankish kingdom.

Although he was still a pagan, King Ethelbert (d. 616) married Bertha, a Frankish princess and a Christian. Ethelbert allowed Bertha to practise her religion and in 597 he welcomed the missionary Augustine, who had been sent by Pope Gregory I to evangelize the Anglo-Saxons. Soon after he became the first Anglo-Saxon king to convert to Christianity. With his support, the Roman missionaries began to evangelize the neighbouring kingdoms of Essex and East Anglia. Marriage politics also played a part in spreading Christianity. When King Edwin of Northumbria married Ethelbert's daughter Ethelburh in 625, one of the conditions was that Paulinus, a Roman missionary, be allowed to preach. Most Anglo-Saxon kingdoms had short periods of apostasy, but they were quickly re-evangelized by a second wave of missionaries, many of whom were Irish. The last Anglo-Saxon kingdom to become Christian was Sussex in the 680s.

Ethelbert was a powerful king, whose pre-eminence was recognized by the other Anglo-Saxon kingdoms: later Anglo-Saxon writers considered him the first *bretwalda* or high king of Britain. Later in the seventh century, Northumbria became the pre-eminent Anglo-Saxon kingdom. Northumbria was formed from two smaller kingdoms, Bernicia and Deira, united by King Aethelfrith (r. c. 592–616) of Bernicia. It reached its greatest territorial extent under King Edwin (r. 616–33), when it controlled most of northern England and southern Scotland, the small Anglo-Saxon kingdom of Lindsey, and the islands of Man and Anglesey.

In the late seventh and eighth centuries Northumbria experienced a golden age of monastic culture, producing outstanding works like the Lindisfarne Gospels, the historical writings of Bede and many fine sculptured crosses. Northumbria went into decline after King Ecgfrith

A Victorian statue of King Ethelbert of Kent, the first Anglo-Saxon ruler to convert to Christianity, on the west porch of Canterbury cathedral.

was defeated and killed at Nechtansmere during an invasion of Pictland in 685. The main beneficiary of this was Northumbria's great rival, the Midland kingdom of Mercia. Seven members of the Northumbrian house, Edwin among them, were killed in battle with the Mercians between 616 and 679. Mercia originated in the valley of the River Trent, but under Kings Penda (r. c. 632–55) and Wulfhere (r. 658–74) it expanded to incorporate neighbouring peoples and minor kingdoms, such as the Middle Angles and the Hwicce, so that it dominated England between the Humber in the north and the Thames in the south.

Under Ethelbald (r. 716–57) and Offa (r. 757–96), Mercia became the leading Anglo-Saxon kingdom. Offa was recognized by both the papacy and the powerful Frankish king Charlemagne as the most important king in Britain and all Anglo-Saxon kingdoms except Northumbria were forced to acknowledge Mercian overlordship. Offa modelled his kingship on that of Charlemagne and adopted the Frankish-style silver penny as the basis of his coinage. The dyke which Offa built to protect his frontier with the Welsh is lasting testament to his power and command of resources. However, the Mercian hegemony was less secure than it looked. Rebellions were common and suppressed with great brutality. When Offa's son Ecgfrith died within a few months of succeeding his father in 796, it was widely seen as a judgment of God for Offa's sins.

Under Coenwulf (r. 796–821), Mercian power began to decline. After a rebellion in Kent, Coenwulf attempted to relocate the archbishopric of Canterbury to London, where it would be securely under his control. Faced with a hostile Church, he backed down. Coenwulf also faced invasions from Northumbria and was unable to force the new king of Wessex, Ecgberht (r. 802–39),to acknowledge his overlordship. In 825 Ecgberht crushed a Mercian invasion at the Battle of Ellendun. Mercia's vassals rebelled and its hegemony collapsed, leaving Wessex as the most powerful Anglo-Saxon kingdom.

Overleaf: Difficult to reach even today, the 8th-century monastery on the precipitous island of Skellig Michael, off the coast of county Kerry, is the most spectacular expression of the Celtic Church's belief that God could be found in solitude.

The Picts and Scots

The Picts are perhaps the most mysterious people of early medieval Britain, known only from their enigmatic carved stones and the hostile chronicles of their enemies. The Picts – the name means 'painted people',

as it is believed they decorated themselves with tattoos – were descendants of Caledonian tribes who had never been conquered by Rome. They were divided into several small kingdoms ruled from forts on craggy hilltops or coastal headlands. The earliest historical Pictish king was Bridei of Fidach (r. *c.* 550–84), who exercised a high kingship over all of Pictland, which encompassed most of Britain north of the Forth-Clyde isthmus. After his death, power and the high kingship shifted to the kingdom of Fortriu (roughly modern Perthshire).

Few records of the Pictish language have survived: our knowledge is restricted mainly to personal and place names. Most Pictish words show that the language was related to Brithonic, the language of the ancient Britons ancestral to modern Welsh. Recent genetic research on human remains from Pictish burials confirms that they were closely related to the ancient Britons.

The most famous Pictish artefacts are magnificently sculpted symbol stones. The earliest known symbols appear on fourth-century jewelry, but the first symbol stones were probably not erected until the fifth or sixth centuries. Between forty and fifty different symbols are known. Their meaning is not understood, but they continued to be used after the conversion to Christianity, suggesting that they did not have religious significance. Symbols were usually used in groups of two to four; a combination may have identified an individual, family or tribe. Stones found in association with burials were probably memorials.

The Irish pirates who began raiding Britain in the fourth century described themselves as *Scotti*, meaning simply 'raiders'. Soon all the Irish, whether pirates or not, were described as Scots. In the late fifth century the Dál Riata dynasty of Ulster established control of Argyll, ruling from the hilltop citadel of Dunadd. Over the next five centuries, their descendants extended their rule over most of northern Britain to create the kingdom of Scotland. According to tradition, the Scots' settlement of Argyll was led by King Fergus MacErc (d. 501), who conquered Kintyre while his brothers Loarn and Oengus conquered Lorn and Islay. The story may have been invented to explain the division of the Scots of Argyll into three tribes: Cenel Loairn, Cenel nGabrain (named for Fergus' grandson Gabran) and Cenel nOengus. Fergus and his successors ruled both Irish Dál Riata and Argyll until 637, when the halves of the kingdom became independent of each other.

The Scots introduced the Gaelic language to Britain, and also the Irish *ogam* writing system, which was adopted by the Picts.

Carved Pictish stone from Hilton of Cadboll, Easter Ross, Scotland, showing a hunting scene. The Picts developed an eclectic art style which incorporated Anglo-Saxon, Irish and continental motifs together with symbols unique to themselves (at the top). The meaning of the symbols and the stones themselves is poorly understood.

The Picts and the Scots

Chief kindreds of Dál Riata:

- Cenel Loairn
- Cenel nGabrain
- Cenel nOengus
- Irish Dál Riata

- Pictish territory
- ● Pictish symbol stone (single)
- ◉ Pictish symbol stones (multiple)
- ⚒ Pictish *ogam* inscription
- ⚒ Irish *ogam* inscription
- ⊕ freestanding Irish cross
- ◉ royal or aristocratic centre
- ● monastery
- ✕ battle, with date

1. Fortriu: main centre of Pictish power, 7th–8th centuries
2. Dunadd: capital of Scottish Dál Riata
3. Craig Phadrig: seat of Pictish kings, 6th century
4. Iona: founded by St Columba in 536 as a base for the conversion of the Picts

153

Irish monks followed the colonists and founded monasteries. St Columba's monastery on Iona became the major centre for the conversion of the northern Picts in the late sixth century. Conversion of the southern Picts had been begun by the Briton St Ninian in the fifth century. Christianity was a stimulant to Pictish art, leading to spectacular sculptured cross slabs combining native, Northumbrian and Irish decorative styles.

In 843 the Scots king Kenneth MacAlpin (r. *c.* 840–58) conquered Pictish Fortriu, creating a new kingdom known by *c.* 900 as Alba, from the Irish word for Britain, or Scotia. This was the culmination of a century of increasing Scots influence over the Picts. From the early eighth century, many Pictish kings had Scottish origins and it was the death of one of them, Eoganan, in battle against Vikings in 839 that gave Kenneth his opportunity. The Picts did not long retain their identity under Scottish rule. The traditional Pictish symbols died out before the end of the ninth century and the last contemporary reference to the Picts dates to 904. The Pictish language became extinct soon after, replaced by Gaelic. No Pictish literature has survived; it is thought to have been deliberately suppressed by the Scots.

Origins of Wales

The modern Welsh people are descendants of romanized Britons who resisted the invading Anglo-Saxons during the Dark Ages. They were the only inhabitants of the Roman Empire of the west not conquered by migrating Germanic peoples. The modern country of the Welsh came into existence in the course of the seventh century. Anglo-Saxon victories at Dyrham in 577 and Chester in 616 drove wedges between the Britons, creating enclaves in Wales, Cumbria and southern Scotland, and Dumnonia in southwest England. The northern and southwestern British enclaves were gradually reduced by the Anglo-Saxons and the equally expansionist Scots.

The Britons in Wales were perhaps fortunate in possessing a natural frontier where the rugged Cambrian mountains rise from the plains of the English Midlands. The Anglo-Saxon kingdom of Mercia had expanded to the foothills of these mountains sometime before 700 but was halted by Welsh resistance. This still roughly marks the modern England–Wales border.

The kingdoms of Wales

Places associated with early Welsh kingdoms by literary or archaeological evidence:

- 🟩 Powys
- 🟥 Dyfed
- ⬜ Builth
- 🟦 Gwynedd
- 🟧 Brycheiniog
- 🟪 other Welsh kingdom

DYFED key major Welsh kingdom
GWENT key minor Welsh kingdom

kingdom of Rhodri Mawr, 844–78
linear earthwork
British territory, c. 700
✂ battle, with date

The Britons had begun calling themselves Cymry, the people of Cymru, the British word for the country that then included not only modern Wales but also the surviving British kingdoms of Rheged and Strathclyde (now in northwest England and southwest Scotland). After Rheged and Strathclyde fell to Anglo-Saxons and Scots, Cymru and Cymry applied only to modern Wales and its people, but traces of the original wider identity survive in the names of the English county of Cumbria (the Lake District) and the Cumbrae islands in the Firth of Clyde. The words 'Wales' and 'Welsh' derive from the Anglo-Saxons' name for the Britons, *waelisc* – foreigners.

Wales was divided into several kingdoms, of which the most important were Dyfed, Powys and Gwynedd, all derived from Iron Age tribal identities. Dyfed was based on the territory of the Demetae, but its ruling dynasty was probably of Irish origin. Powys was the kingdom of the Cornovii and originally included most of northeast Wales and, until it was overrun by Mercia in the seventh century, the modern English county of Shropshire, whose administrative centre in Roman times was Viroconium Cornoviorum (Wroxeter).

Gwynedd, founded by Cunedda *c.* 440, was based on the territory of the Ordovices in northwest Wales. Gwynedd emerged as the strongest Welsh kingdom in the ninth century, but an attempt by its king, Rhodri Mawr (d. 878), to impose political unity on the Welsh achieved only temporary success. Because of the Welsh custom of partible inheritance, Rhodri's kingdom was divided between his sons after his death. A reluctance to abandon this custom ensured that later attempts to unite the Welsh failed.

Though neither as large nor as wealthy as the Anglo-Saxon realms, the Welsh kingdoms were far from impotent. Mercia, which established hegemony over its Anglo-Saxon neighbours in the eighth century, went to enormous trouble to fortify its Welsh border with a series of defensive earth ramparts running between the Irish Sea and the Bristol Channel. The most impressive and best preserved of these is Offa's Dyke, constructed under orders of King Offa. The dyke was a 5.5-m (18-ft) high rampart running 103 km (64 miles) from Llanfynydd near Wrexham to Kington in Herefordshire. The dyke is often thought of as an impressive attempt by the Mercians to define the frontier, but it lacked the gates necessary if it were to be crossed for peaceful trade. The Mercians were clearly afraid of the Welsh. The construction of the dyke is best understood in the context of the

Many prehistoric monuments, like this octagonal Iron Age stela at Lampaul-Ploudalmézeau (Finistère), were Christianized following the conversion of Brittany.

Pillar of Eliseg near Llangollen in North Wales, a weathered stone monument with an inscription celebrating the success of Eliseg, King of Powys in the mid-eighth century, in winning back Welsh territory from the English after a nine-year war. The Welsh later won back even more territory from Mercia and the course of the dyke now lies mostly in Wales. Successes like this kept alive Welsh hopes that they would one day drive the Anglo-Saxons out of Britain altogether.

Britannia Minor

The only remaining Celtic-speaking area on the continent today is the rugged peninsula of Brittany. After the Roman conquest, Celtic languages became extinct in most of continental Europe and would have done so in Brittany too had its Celtic character not been revitalized by waves of Celtic-speaking settlers from western Britain. Brittany, then known as Armorica, suffered severely from Frankish and Saxon piracy during the third century. The economy collapsed, country villas were burned, settlements were abandoned and the population declined. Then, in the fourth century, newcomers began moving into the region and reoccupied sites abandoned in the previous century. Fragments of southern British pottery identify the newcomers as Britons. These settlers were reinforced by further waves of immigration, which continued into the sixth century.

The main evidence for areas of British settlement comes from the obvious similarity of Welsh, Cornish and Breton place names. *Plou-* (from Latin *plebs*, Welsh *plwyf*, people) is common in Brittany and associated with *gui-* and *guic-* names (from Latin *vicus*, settlement). Other common elements of British origin include *lan* (Welsh *llan*, church), *tré-* (Welsh *tref*, the subdivision of a parish), *coët* (Welsh *coed*, wood) and *ker* (Welsh *caer*, hamlet). The main distribution of British place names is in the north and west. In the southeast the place name elements *-ac*, *-é*, and *-y*, derived from the Gallo-Roman suffix *-acum* (place), are common, indicating that British settlement was less dense here.

These conclusions are supported by traditions preserved in the *vitae* (religious biographies) of early saints of Brittany, most of whom like Mawes (Maudez), Samson and Winwaloe (Guénolé) were born in Cornwall or south Wales. The earliest monasteries founded by these

British settlement of Brittany, fifth to sixth centuries

- eastern limit of the Breton language, c. 800
- main concentration of *plou-*, *guic-*, *tré-* and *lan* place names
- main concentration of place-name suffix *-ac* and related names
- monastic foundation and associated saint, 5th–6th centuries
- late Roman fort
- early British settlement

saints all lie along the north coast of the peninsula. British churchmen brought with them the practices of the insular Celtic Church.

No contemporary writer noticed the arrival of the earliest British immigrants, but legendary traditions recorded by Geoffrey of Monmouth in the twelfth century tell of a British noble, Conan Meriadec, who went to Gaul with the Roman usurper Magnus Maximus (r. 383–88) and was granted Armorica as a reward for his loyalty. Conan slaughtered the local Armoricans and repopulated the province with Britons, turning it into a 'little Britain' (Britannia Minor, whence Brittany). The sixth-century British writer Gildas believed that the Britons were refugees from the Anglo-Saxon invasions of their country. Though there was certainly no massacre of the Armoricans, it is likely that Geoffrey of Monmouth's fanciful tale is closer in spirit to the truth than that of Gildas. The British emigrants came mostly from areas that had repelled the Anglo-Saxons so were probably not refugees but people who saw the collapse of Roman power as an opportunity to seize new lands.

The political organization of early Brittany is unclear. The Britons seem to have settled under several chiefs. One early leader, Riothamus, who fought the Visigoths on behalf of the Romans, is described as a king by a contemporary writer. The Romans retained nominal authority in Brittany until the 460s, but by the end of the century the Franks laid claim to the region.

By the mid-sixth century three regional powers had emerged: Cornouaille (Cornovia) in the west, about which almost nothing is known; Domnonée (Dumnonia) on the north coast, which was ruled by a dynasty with links to British Dumnonia; and Browaroch in the south, founded by a chieftain called Waroc sometime after 560. The Bretons came under pressure from the Franks in the seventh century and in 635 King Judicael of Domnonée was forced to become a vassal of the Merovingian king Dagobert I. However, by 691 Brittany had regained full independence as a result of the decline in the Merovingian dynasty.

VI
Islamic Expansion

The force of a new faith

The breakup of the Mediterranean-centred world of Classical antiquity begun by the Germanic invasions was completed by spectacular Arab conquests in the seventh century. From a highway that united all around its shores into a single cultural area, the Mediterranean became a frontier between mutually hostile civilizations. The origins of the Arab conquests can be traced directly to their conversion to Islam. The faith, meaning 'submission (to the will of God)', was founded by the Prophet Muhammad (*c.* 570–632), a member of the Quraysh tribe of Mecca, an important trading and religious centre on Arabia's main north–south caravan route.

Pre-Islamic Arabia was a land of religious diversity. Most Arabs, including the Quraysh, were polytheists, but several Arab tribes had converted to Judaism and there were many Nestorians, Monophysite Christians and Zoroastrians. According to Islamic tradition, Muhammad was in his fortieth year when he experienced the first of a series of revelations that formed the basis of the Qur'an (or Koran), which Muslims believe to be the word of God. Rather than founding a new religion, Muhammad claimed that he was restoring the original religion of Abraham that Jews and Christians had misinterpreted.

Muhammad's first converts were members of his immediate family and it was three years before he preached in public. His emphasis on

Visigothic votive crown of King Recceswinth, *c.* 649–62. The crown was buried near the Visigothic capital of Toledo to prevent it falling into Arab hands.

VI ISLAMIC EXPANSION

social justice attracted converts among the poor and slaves, but most of the Quraysh were hostile. Muhammad was mocked wherever he went. He and his followers were boycotted and he survived at least one assassination attempt. Though he was unappreciated at Mecca, Muhammad's reputation as a religious visionary spread widely and in 622 he and his followers left Mecca for Medina (then known as Yathrib), where he had been invited to act as a judge between conflicting tribes. Known as the *hijra* (migration), this event marks the beginning of the Muslim calendar. By negotiation with the tribes of Medina, Muhammad established the first Muslim community or *umma*, a theocracy in which religious and political authority was exercised by Muhammad acting in the name of God. However, there was strong opposition to Muhammad from the Jews of Medina. Muhammad had expected the Jews to welcome his religious teaching, but having failed to win them over he expelled them and distributed their property among his supporters. According to Arabic historical traditions, one Jewish tribe who resisted expulsion by force, the Banu Qurayza, was massacred, while other critics of Muhammad at Medina were assassinated.

Muhammad made Medina a base from which to propagate Islam by diplomacy and force, teaching his followers that it was their religious duty to make war on unbelievers. Raiders were sent out to attack Meccan caravans travelling to and from Syria, provoking war with the Quraysh. An unlikely victory by the small Muslim army at Badr in 624 gave apparent substance to Muhammad's claims to be God's messenger. Mainly by diplomacy, Muhammad steadily won over more and more tribes to Islam until, in 630, he captured Mecca without a fight. Stripped of its idols, the Ka'aba, Mecca's pagan shrine, became the holiest place of Islam because of its legendary associations with Adam and Abraham. After his victory, Muhammad continued to live at Medina, where he died two years later. Muhammad had no sons and had not categorically nominated a successor, so his father-in-law Abu Bakr (*c.* 574–634), one of the earliest converts to Islam, was chosen as the first *khalifat rasul Allah* (successor of the Prophet of God) or caliph in 632. Many tribes had accepted Islam because of Muhammad's personal charisma; now that he was dead, they considered the relationship ended and rebelled. In crushing 'the Apostasy', Abu Bakr completed the political and religious unification of the Arabs.

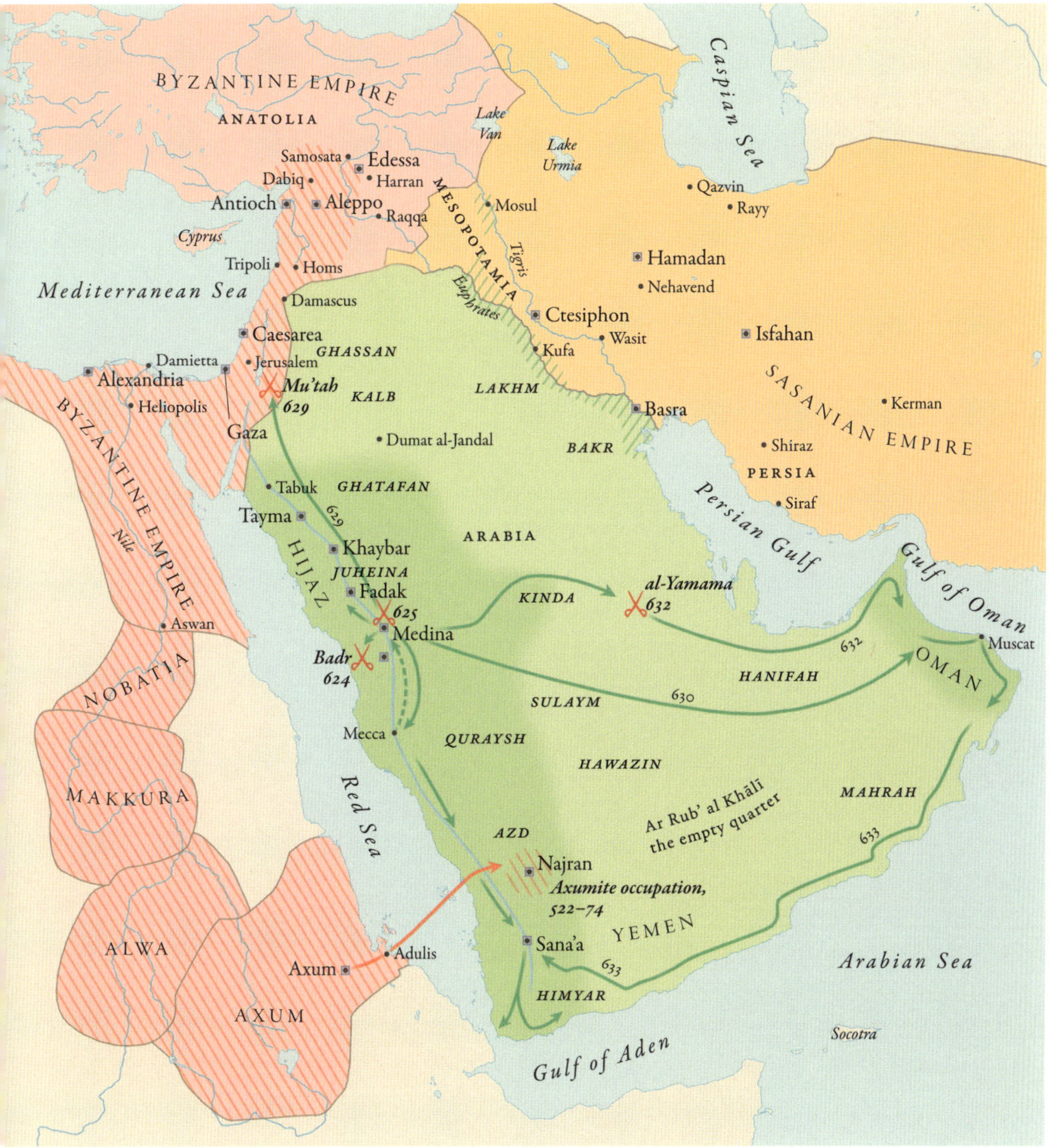

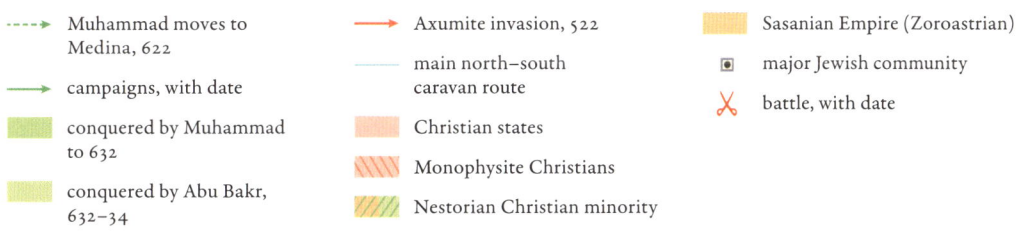

Muhammad and the establishment of the caliphate, 522–634

- Muhammad moves to Medina, 622
- campaigns, with date
- conquered by Muhammad to 632
- conquered by Abu Bakr, 632–34
- Axumite invasion, 522
- main north–south caravan route
- Christian states
- Monophysite Christians
- Nestorian Christian minority
- Sasanian Empire (Zoroastrian)
- major Jewish community
- battle, with date

قرنداشنك حالى نه حالن دورنجه سوزر ابرنجه كتورلر
كوزله كوره دورالا بكزى متغير اولدى كوزى ياشپله

طولدى رسول حضرت ابوخذيفه نك يوزنه بقدى بكرينه
دكر كوز كوردى ايتدى يا اباخذيفه ايتكى قرنداشكى

The Arab conquests

Within eighty years of their conversion to Islam, the Arabs created an empire that stretched from the Atlantic Ocean to the River Indus – the largest yet seen in the history of the world. The first expeditions against the Byzantine and Sasanian Empires were launched by Abu Bakr (r. 632–34), as a way to consolidate Arab unity, and under his successors Umar (r. 634–44) and Uthman (r. 644–56) the Arab armies won a succession of spectacular victories. The entire Sasanian Empire of Persia was conquered by 652 and the Byzantines lost their rich provinces of Egypt, Libya, Tripolitania, Palestine and Syria.

After Uthman's death, a civil war broke out between supporters of Caliph Ali, Muhammad's son-in-law and cousin, and Muawiya, a member of Uthman's Umayyad family. After Ali was murdered in 661, Muawiya (r. 661–80) became caliph, founding the Umayyad dynasty. Ali's murder led to the most significant schism in Islam. On Muawiya's death, Ali's son Husain tried to seize the caliphate, but was killed in battle with the Umayyads at Karbala in Iraq in 680. Subsequently Islam split into two branches, the majority Sunni, from *sunna* (tradition of Muhammad) and the minority Shi'ite, from *shi'atu Ali* (party of Ali).

Expansion continued under the early Umayyads with the conquest of North Africa, Spain and parts of central Asia. Lacking institutions suited to the government of an expanding world empire, the Umayyads created an administrative system based on the Byzantine bureaucracy. Medina was too remote to be convenient and the capital was moved to Damascus in 661. Arabia's moment of glory had passed. The Umayyads were unsure of the loyalty of the conquered populations, so they settled Arabs in strategically sited *amsars* (military settlements), such as Basra and al-Fustat (Cairo), with easy escape to the desert.

Several factors explain the rapid rise of the Arabs in the seventh century. Among the pre-Islamic Arabs, war played much the same role as it did among the Germanic tribes in providing the opportunity for young warriors to win status and plunder. Inter-tribal feuding was endemic and raids on Byzantine or Persian territory were common. Arabs usually fought on horseback or on camels, giving them great mobility. Because of their ability to strike from the desert quickly and without warning, the Arabs were regarded as a difficult enemy to deal with, but their raids were on a small scale and did little long-term

Muhammad at the Battle of Badr, fought in 624 against the Quraysh, from a devotional Ottoman Turkish manuscript made in 1594. In accordance with Sunni Islamic tradition, to avoid idolatry, Muhammad's face is shown veiled.

The Arab conquests, 633–717

- border at the death of Muhammad, 632
- Arabs practising Islam, 632

Growth of the Arab caliphate:

- at the death of Abu Bakr, 634
- at the death of Uthman, 656
- at the fall of the Umayyad dynasty, 750

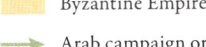

	Byzantine Empire	Kufa	Umayyad cultural centre
→	Arab campaign or raid, with date	✕	Arab victory
	Amsar (Arab military settlement), 638–70	✕	Arab defeat
	Umayyad mosque	✕	battle between Arabs
•	Umayyad palace		

damage. Internecine warfare was suppressed by Muhammad and his successors, but the social need for war remained strong and could now only be channelled outwards. United, the Arabs could field larger and more effective armies than ever before.

The Arabs were fortunate in their timing. The Byzantine and Sasanian Empires had fought themselves to exhaustion in their twenty-year war to the death and neither was prepared for another major conflict. Their traditional way of dealing with the Arabs had been to subsidize friendly tribes and persuade them to attack hostile ones. This would no longer work, and it is unlikely that either the Byzantines or Persians understood the magnitude of the changes that were taking place in Arabia. Both empires had serious internal problems. The defeat by the Byzantines under Heraclius had provoked a civil war in the Sasanian Empire and organized resistance collapsed quickly after the Arab victory at Nehavend in 642. The Byzantines' problem was religious disunity. The largely Monophysite populations of Egypt, Palestine and Syria had suffered years of persecution by the orthodox imperial government and welcomed the Arabs as liberators.

The Arabs cannot be blamed for believing that their enemies' problems revealed the workings of the hand of God. Their morale was high. Arab soldiers were probably motivated as much by the prospect of plunder as by Muhammad's promise of immediate entry to Jannah (paradise) for those who died fighting for Islam but they could feel confident of reward whatever the outcome.

The sieges of Constantinople

The greatest failures of the Umayyad caliphate were its two unsuccessful sieges of Constantinople. The city's successful defence saved the Byzantine Empire from going the same way as the Sasanians and brought a decisive end to the great age of Arab expansion. After the initial shock of the loss of Egypt, Palestine and Syria, the Byzantines stabilized a frontier with the caliphate along the line of the Taurus mountains in Anatolia. The Arabs were unused to fighting in mountain country and they lost many of the advantages of mobility that they enjoyed in more open terrain. There are only a small number of passes through the mountains, which made the Byzantine defenders' job easier. The Anatolian themes supplied the bulk of the Byzantine

THE SIEGES OF CONSTANTINOPLE

Arab horsemen ride into battle, from a French manuscript of the Crusades era. Brightly coloured and highly decorated banners, caparisons and shields played a major role in Arabic warfare long before the Islamic period.

army and the knowledge that they were fighting in defence of their homes no doubt steeled the soldiers' determination.

Though the Taurus were difficult to cross, they could be circumvented by sea. The Arabs were initially reluctant to assemble a fleet, but after a surprise Byzantine attack on Alexandria in 645 they realized that their coasts could not be defended without one. The shipbuilders and sailors of the ports of Egypt and Syria built and crewed the ships, while the Arabs provided the fighting men. At the Battle of the Masts in 655, the new Arab fleet destroyed the Byzantine navy and won unchallenged control of the eastern Mediterranean. Caliph Muawiya stepped up naval operations against the Byzantines, with raids on the Greek islands and Sicily.

In about 672 an Arab fleet penetrated the Dardanelles and established a base at Cyzicus in the Sea of Marmara, a day's sail from Constantinople. Using Cyzicus as a forward base, the Arabs laid siege to Constantinople itself in 672. The Arabs, inexperienced in siege warfare, made little impression on Constantinople's massive walls and their fleet was destroyed by the Byzantines' new secret weapon, an early form of napalm called Greek Fire. The Arabs returned in 674 and, despite continuing to suffer heavy casualties from Greek Fire, maintained the siege for four years. Further Byzantine victories over the Arabs in Anatolia finally forced Muawiya to lift the siege, agree a thirty-year peace, and pay tribute to Emperor Constantine IV (r. 668–85).

The defence of Constantinople, 699–778

→ Arab campaign, 669–77
→ Arab campaign, 717–18
✂ Arab victory
✂ Arab defeat

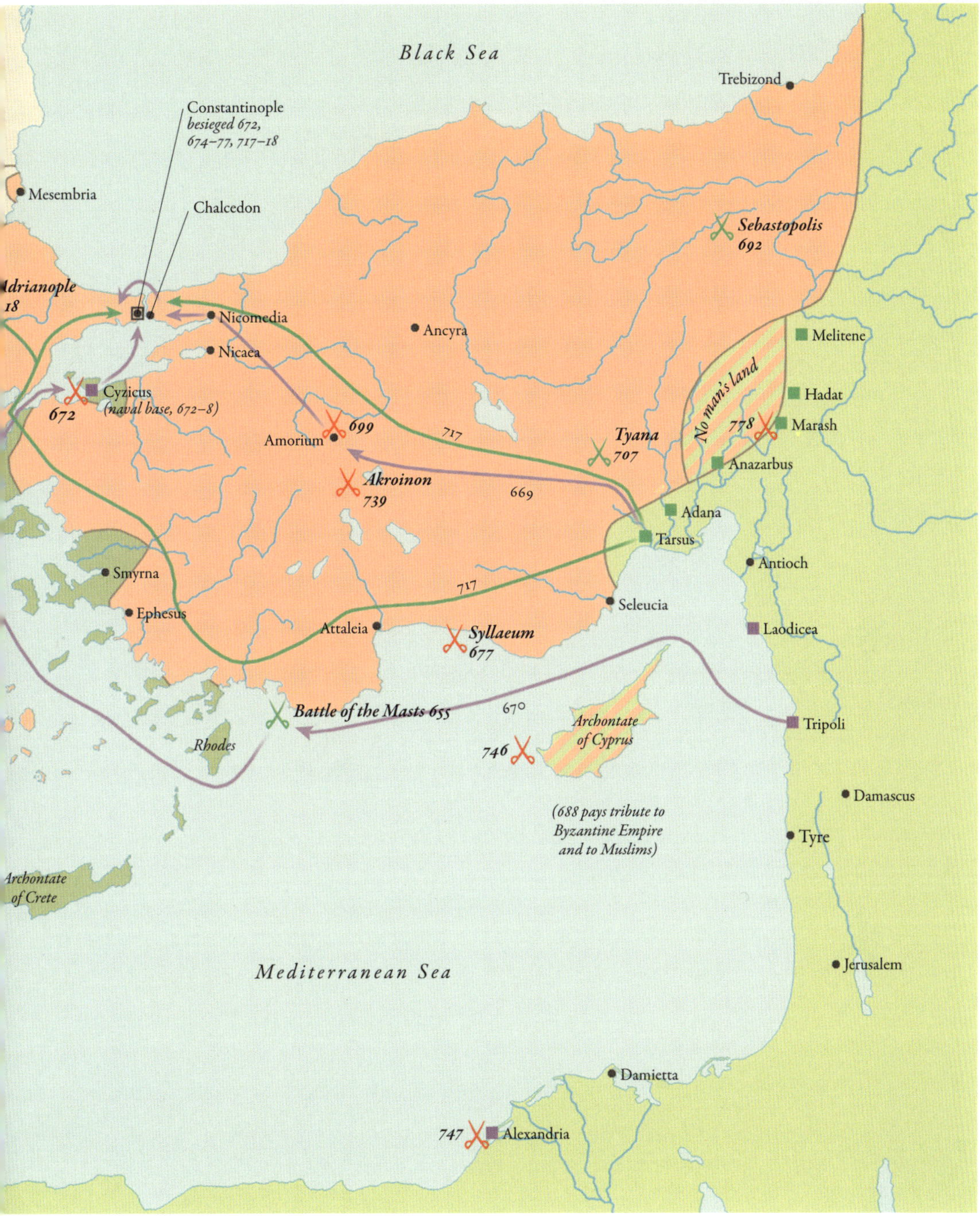

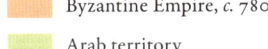

- Byzantine Empire, c. 780
- Arab territory
- temporary Arab occupation, 670–78
- jihad base
- Arab naval base used for raids against the Byzantine Empire

A fresh attempt to capture Constantinople was made in 717, involving three armies said to total around 200,000 men and a fleet of over 1,000 ships. The main force under General Maslama, the brother of Caliph Umar II (r. 717–20), approached Constantinople from the east, while a second army advanced across Anatolia to Chalcedon. The fleet was present to prevent Constantinople being supplied by sea and to secure communications between the Arab armies. Emperor Leo III 'the Isaurian' (r. 717–41), who had won the throne only a few months previously at the end of a civil war, hurriedly prepared the city for defence. Maslama's initial assaults were beaten off and Greek Fire once again caused great destruction. Maslama maintained the siege through a severe winter, but the next summer Leo destroyed the remains of the Arab fleet, then crossed the Bosporus and defeated the Arab army at Chalcedon.

After Leo's Bulgar allies defeated Maslama at Adrianople (possibly in July 718), the Arabs began a desperate retreat through Anatolia. Of the huge Arab force, only 30,000 men were claimed to have made it home. Arab attacks on Anatolia continued for the rest of the eighth century, but they never seriously threatened Constantinople again. Had Constantinople fallen, the full strength of the Arab armies might then have swept into a Europe ill equipped to resist them. Their advance twice blocked at the Bosporus, the Arabs' only route into Europe was through Spain, at the end of a very long chain of communications.

The Abbasid caliphate

The overthrow of the Umayyad dynasty by the Abbasids in 750 marked a major shift in the balance of power in the Islamic world – away from Arabs and into the hands of new converts. The Umayyads followed Muhammad's practice of allowing 'people of the Book' (Jews, Christians and Zoroastrians) to practise their religions, provided they paid the *jizya* tax, a kind of tribute levied on unbelievers according to holy law. For the Umayyads, Islam was a symbol of Arab unity and superiority. They did not make great efforts to convert the conquered populations, because this would have diminished the amount of tribute received. Despite this there were increasing numbers of non-Arab converts, but all were expected to become *mawali* (clients) of the Arab tribes, allowing the Arabs to retain a hegemonic role. Converts were excluded from the highest offices of state, which were reserved for people of pure Arab descent.

Some converted to Islam simply to avoid the *jizya* tax, others did so because they were ambitious and wanted to join the ruling elite, still others because they had married Muslims. Islam was attractive for purely religious reasons. For Christians weary of arcane arguments over the nature of the Trinity, Islam's recognition of Jesus as a prophet was a bridge to the new faith. For Jews, Islam could be presented as a reformed Judaism. Because translation of the Qur'an was forbidden, conversion began to Arabize the conquered populations. Naturally, new converts were resentful of the Arabs' privileged position and became increasingly discontented with Umayyad rule. The caliphate, they believed, had been founded to further the message of Islam, not advance Arab interests. The dynasty's authority was further undermined by Sunnite-Shiite conflict and the re-emergence of feuds between Arab tribes, caused by disagreements over the distribution of tribute.

In 747 a manumitted Persian slave called Abu Muslim led a rebellion against Umayyad rule, which began in Khorasan and quickly spread through Persia and Iraq. In 749 Abu al-Abbas, a descendant of Muhammad's uncle al-Abbas, was proclaimed caliph by rebels in Kufa. After routing the Umayyads at the Battle of the Zab in 750, the Abbasids captured Damascus. The last Umayyad caliph, Marwan II (r. 744–50), fled to Egypt, where he was captured and killed. The Umayyad family was massacred and even the bodies of earlier Umayyad caliphs were disinterred and destroyed. The only significant member of the family to escape the slaughter was Abd al-Rahman, who fled to Spain and set up an independent Umayyad emirate.

The ideal of the caliphate uniting all Muslims in a single religious and political community had suffered its first setback, and the Abbasid victory ended Arab domination of the caliphate. Client converts were freed and government was opened up to Muslims of all nationalities. The new, cosmopolitan caliphate was a cultural melting pot where the influences of Greek science and philosophy and Persian literature could be assimilated to Islamic beliefs.

In 762 the second Abbasid caliph, al-Mansur (r. 754–75), founded a new capital for the caliphate at Baghdad in Iraq. By the end of the century, it had become the world's largest city and its greatest

Rise of the Abbasid caliphate, 763–1071

- border, 763
- Abbasid caliphate, 763
- Abbasid caliphate, 900
- Umayyad emirate, 763
- Byzantine Empire, 763
- Umayyad caliphate, c. 900
- Buwayhid emirates, c. 900
- Fatimid caliphate, c. 990
- eastern border of Byzantine Empire, 1022–71

- • Abbasid-founded city
- ⌂ Abbasid palace
- ☪ Abbasid mosque
- ⌂ Umayyad palace
- ☪ Umayyad mosque
- ✕ Arab victory
- ✕ Arab defeat
- ✕ battle between Muslim states
- → Arab nomadic migration, 7th to 11th centuries

cultural centre. The Abbasid caliphate reached its height under Harun al-Rashid (r. 786–809), whose magnificent court provided the setting for the stories of *The Thousand and One Nights*. Even before the end of his reign, however, power was slipping into the hands of provincial emirs (governors). By 800 the Maghrib and Ifriqiya had become independent under their emirs. In 868 Egypt became independent under the Tulunid emirs and the eastern provinces followed suit shortly afterwards under the Persian Samanid and Saffarid emirs. In 945 the Abbasids even lost control of Baghdad to the Buwayhids, who retained the caliphate as a purely spiritual office.

Abbasid Baghdad

When the second Abbasid caliph, al-Mansur, chose Baghdad in Iraq to be the site of a new capital city for the caliphate it was still a small village. Officially, it was to be called Madinat al-Salam (City of Peace), but it was usually known by its original Persian name of Baghdad ('God gave it'). The site was chosen for political, economic and agricultural reasons. It was situated on the fertile Mesopotamian plain, criss-crossed with canals, so a large urban population could easily be supported without relying on food from external sources. Baghdad was closer to the centre of the caliphate than Damascus and reflected the new importance of Persia, now that converts had equal rights with Arabs. It was close to major east–west caravan routes and was on the navigable River Tigris, giving easy access to Basra and the Persian Gulf. Faster flowing than its twin, the Euphrates, the Tigris was free of malarial mosquitoes which affected much of Mesopotamia.

The city was originally planned as a circle 2.64 km (1⅔ miles) in diameter, surrounded by a wall with 360 towers. The circular plan was probably based on the former Sasanian capital city of Gur, a sign of increased Persian cultural influence under the Abbasids. Baghdad was divided into equal quarters, used to house courtiers and administrators, with the caliph's palace and grand mosque at the centre. Four main roads radiated from the palace to various parts of the caliphate.

Because of its natural advantages, Baghdad flourished and rapidly expanded outside the walled city and onto the east bank of the Tigris. By the early ninth century the population had reached one million, making it the largest, and richest, city in the world

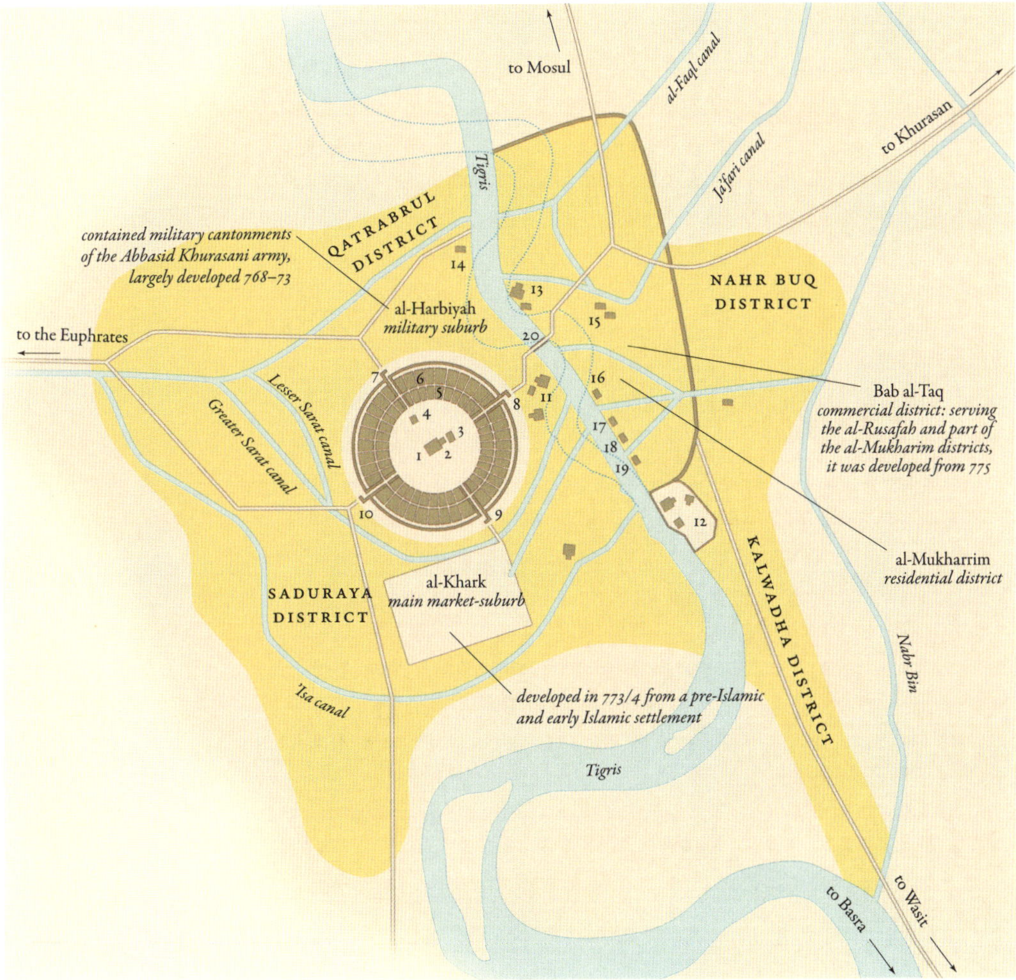

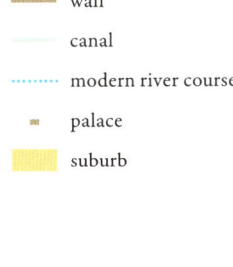

Baghdad under the Abbasids, 773–900

- —— wall
- —— canal
- ⋯⋯ modern river course
- ▪ palace
- ▨ suburb

Dar al-Khilafa, the 'Round City'

1. palace
2. mosque
3. police
4. guards
5. inner ring
6. outer ring
7. Syrian gate
8. Khurasan gate
9. Basra gate
10. Kufa gate

Suburban palaces

11. al-Khuld, al-Mansur's second residential palace, built in 773/4
12. Dar al-Khilafa, third palace complex, built after 892/3
13. al-Rusafah palace complex of Caliph al-Mahdi, built 768–775
14. palace of the Tahirids
15. palace of the Barmekids
16. palace of the Firdaws
17. palace of al-Hassani
18. Taj
19. palace of al-Amin
20. Bridge of Boats

VI ISLAMIC EXPANSION

at that time. The western suburbs were divided into quarters on ethnic and occupational lines. Arabs, Khwarazmians (from central Asia) and Persians had their own quarters, as did soldiers, merchants and craftsmen. Each quarter had its own mosques, shops and markets. There were many specialist markets too, selling meat, fruit, textiles, books, metalwork and flowers, and even one for Chinese goods. The volume of trade made necessary the development of a banking system. Thousands of bath houses were built for the benefit of the population. Just as the Romans had done, Baghdadis went to the baths for social reasons as much as for hygiene. The eastern suburb grew around palaces built for the caliph's heir and the great families, such as the Persian Barmekids. The eastern region eventually became dominant and forms the heart of the modern city of Baghdad.

Under caliphs al-Mahdi (r. 775–85) and Harun al-Rashid (r. 786–809), Baghdad developed into a vibrant and cosmopolitan cultural centre as poets, scholars and artisans flocked there in search of patronage. Many mosques had *madrasahs* (residential Islamic colleges) and there were important law schools, hospitals and many libraries. Under Caliph al-Ma'mun (r. 813–33) a school known as the House of Wisdom opened for the translation of ancient literary works into Arabic. Al Ma'mun also founded an astronomical observatory, and in the tenth century al-Muqtadir (r. 908–32) added a zoo to Baghdad's cultural splendours. The eleventh-century Baghdadi writer Khatib described his home city as having 'no peer throughout the world' and as 'the navel of the universe'.

Civil unrest in the 830s led Caliph al-Mutasim (r. 833–42) to abandon Baghdad in favour of Samarra in 836, but the city continued to flourish. In 892 al-Mutamid (r. 870–92) brought the court back to Baghdad and built several new palaces and a racecourse. The political decline of the caliphate was mirrored in Baghdad's fortunes and in the eleventh century it was overtaken by Cairo as Islam's leading city.

Gold dinar of Abu al-Abbas, the first caliph of the Abbasid dynasty, who overthrew the Umayyads in 750. The coin was struck at Damascus.

Early Islamic civilization

There could hardly be a less appropriate term than 'Dark Age' to describe the Islamic civilization of the early Abbasid caliphate. The Abbasids maintained a court so brilliant that it awed even the Byzantines, while small armies of scholars laboured to translate the science and philosophy of the ancient world. Although at the time of their conversion to Islam the Arabs did not have sophisticated literary, scientific and architectural traditions, they were not barbarians and showed a keen interest in the Christian, Jewish, Hellenistic, Syriac, Persian and Hindu civilizations they had conquered. The Umayyads invited scholars from around the caliphate to their court at Damascus, but the real mingling of cultures took place when new converts from the conquered peoples gained greater equality and influence under the Abbasids.

The Arabs adopted almost wholesale the corpus of ancient Greek science, mathematics, astronomy and medicine. From India, Arab mathematicians learned the decimal system and adopted the Hindu numeral system, which through them was passed on to Europe as Arabic numerals. Building on the achievements of the Greeks and Hindus, the Arabs developed the most sophisticated mathematics and astronomy of the medieval world. The need to fix the direction of Mecca for prayer was a major stimulus to the development of Arab astronomy, as was a strong interest in astrology – despite Muhammad's condemnation of attempts to predict the future.

The work of cultural assimilation was greatly encouraged by al-Ma'mun's House of Wisdom in which Greek, Persian and Hindu works were translated into Arabic. Many manuscripts were supplied by visiting scholars, but the caliphs also sent missions to Constantinople to buy manuscripts for translation. Ironically, the Byzantines showed little interest in the culture of Greek antiquity because of its pagan associations, and many works of ancient science and philosophy would have been lost if not for Arab scholars. It was mainly through Arabic translations of the works of Plato and Aristotle that western Europeans rediscovered Greek philosophy in the twelfth century. Similarly, the work of the Greek astronomer Ptolemy was known in the West by its Arabic name, the *Almagest*.

Al-Ma'mun's motivation was largely religious. He was an advocate of Mu'tazilism, a doctrine which held that faith must be in accord with reason, and sought to justify his position using Greek philosophy. Mu'tazilism held that the Qur'an had been created in a specific place and time and had to be interpreted accordingly. This was out of step with mainstream opinion, which held that the Qur'an existed eternally in the mind of God. Opposition was so strong that Mu'tazilism was suppressed later in the ninth century.

Overleaf: Entrance to the Dome of the Rock in Jerusalem. It was the first great Umayyad monument to be completed after the conquest of Palestine. Built by Caliph Abd al-Malik (r. 685–705).

VI ISLAMIC EXPANSION

A caravan of Muslim pilgrims depicted in an Arab manuscript made in 1237. *Hajj*, the pilgrimage to Mecca, is required of all Muslims once in their life, if they are capable of performing it.

The Persian contribution to Islamic civilization was mainly literary. The Arabs had a well-developed oral tradition of epic poetry and storytelling, which continued to flourish after the conversion to Islam. Persian influences diversified Arabic poetry into songs about love, wine and religious subjects, fired the first Arab historical writing and inspired collections of stories. An ornate literary style became fashionable, again as a result of Persian influence, but religious disapproval ensured that Islam did not develop a tradition of drama.

An Islamic style of art and architecture emerged only slowly. The earliest Islamic monuments, such as the Dome of the Rock in Jerusalem (692) and the Great Mosque at Damascus (705–15), were built of stone in the Byzantine style and decorated with glass mosaics and marble veneers; even the decorative motifs were Byzantine. The only significant Islamic influences were a rejection of figurative art and the introduction of Qur'anic inscriptions in religious buildings. However, secular figurative art continued to be produced under both the Umayyads and the Abbasids. As a result of increased Persian influence under the Abbasids, brick rendered with plaster replaced stone in construction. Stucco (moulded plaster panels) was increasingly used for abstract vegetal ornamentation. Arabic inscriptions became dominant elements in the decoration of buildings and also of textiles, metalwork and pottery.

The most important religious building in the early Islamic period was the hypostyle mosque, designed to accommodate large congregations. They typically had a square plan with a courtyard, hypostyle (large hall with a low flat roof supported by dozens of columns) and a single minaret. Probably the best-preserved example of this type and period is the mosque of Ibn Tulun in Cairo (built 876–79).

Islamic Spain

The fall in 698 of Carthage, the last Byzantine stronghold in Africa, and the conquest of the Berbers in 702 brought Arab armies to the straits of Gibraltar. A short day's sail away was the Visigothic kingdom of Spain. Riven by civil war, it was ripe for invasion. In April 711 the Arab general Tariq led an army of Arabs and Berbers across the straits and seized Gibraltar, the name of which comes from the Arabic Jebel al-Tariq (Mountain of Tariq). Tariq had led a reconnaissance raid on Spain the previous summer and it may be that this was only intended to be a plundering expedition.

King Roderic (r. 709–11) of the Visigoths rushed to meet Tariq, but was defeated and killed at the Battle of the Guadalette in July. After defeating another Visigothic army at Ecija a few weeks later, Tariq captured Córdoba without a fight. These spectacular successes persuaded Tariq's superior, Musa ibn Nasayr, governor of Ifriqiya (Tunisia), to bring a second army to Spain in 712. Organized Visigothic resistance collapsed completely. Toledo tamely surrendered to Tariq and within two years he had brought the entire Iberian peninsula under Muslim control, except for the Cantabrian mountains in the north, where Basques, Asturians and Visigothic refugees held out. The rapid collapse of the Visigothic kingdom is best explained by their failure, even after ruling Iberia for over 200 years, to instil any sense of loyalty in their Hispanic subjects. When the Arabs invaded, the small, disunited Visigothic ruling elite faced them alone.

As they did elsewhere, the Arabs adapted existing government institutions in what became the province of al-Andalus (hence the

Islamic Spain, 711–750

Settlement of Iberia by:

- Arabs
- Berbers
- Christian or Mozarab
- limit of Muslim conquest, 750
- Christian-controlled territory by c. 750

- ☪ main centre of Muslim culture
- ✝ major Mozarab centre
- ○ substantial Jewish population
- → Arab campaign, with date
- ✂ Arab victory, with date
- ✂ Christian victory, with date

modern name Andalusia). The Arabs came to arrangements with some surviving Visigothic magnates, such as Theodomire of Alicante, who kept their lands so long as they passed on tax revenues to the new rulers. Although most of the Muslim army were Berbers (or Moors, as the Christians called them), their subordinate status is clear from the distribution of confiscated land for settlement after the conquest. The Arabs got the Mediterranean coast and the fertile Ebro and Guadalquivir valleys; the Berbers got the Meseta, the high, dry, hard lands of central Spain. Reflecting the new balance of power, Córdoba, on the Guadalquivir, became the capital of the new province. It became the largest and most prosperous city of western Europe, and remained so for centuries. Genomic studies of the modern Spanish and Portuguese populations are consistent with significant immigration from North Africa to the south and west of the peninsula, where between 7 per cent and 11 per cent of the population have North African ancestry. This genetic imprint diminishes to zero in the north.

Christians and Jews were allowed freedom of worship on payment of the *jizya* tax. Christians remained the majority at least until the tenth century, but their way of life became Arabized. Many even spoke Arabic and their art and architecture were pervaded with Arabic influences. These Arabized Christians became known as Mozarabs, from the Arabic *musta'rib*, meaning one who has assimilated Arab customs. Inevitably some Christians converted to Islam to advance their careers in government, but Christians and Jews were not completely excluded from positions of authority and played a full part in cultural life. The relative tolerance of its rulers allowed al-Andalus to become the most important centre for the exchange of ideas between the Muslim and Christian worlds.

Spain was at the end of a very long chain of command from the Umayyad caliph at Damascus. Rivalry among Arab commanders hampered operations north of the Pyrenees even before Charles Martel's decisive victory at Poitiers in 732. Then in 739 the Berber settlers rebelled against their second-class status, throwing al-Andalus into chaos. The Abbasid revolution in 750 brought more disruption to the province. In 756 the refugee Umayyad prince Abd al-Rahman arrived in Córdoba, seized power and set up an independent emirate. It took Abd al-Rahman several turbulent years to impose his authority throughout al-Andalus, which gave the independent Christians of the north an opportunity to regroup and recover territory.

VII

The Rise of the Franks

Clovis and the Merovingians

Ruthless and energetic, Clovis (also Hlodwig or Clodovech) is regarded as the founder of Frankish power. He united the Franks into a single kingdom and began a period of spectacular territorial expansion which made them a major European power. Still a pagan at the beginning of his reign, Clovis's conversion to Catholicism helped persuade his Gallo-Roman subjects to accept the Franks as the heirs to Rome.

When Clovis (*c*. 465–511) succeeded his father Childeric as king of the Salian Franks *c*. 481, rule of the Franks was spread among numerous petty kings. Clovis's kingdom was confined to part of the old Roman province of Belgica Secunda, but his 486 victory against Syagrius, the independent Roman ruler of Soissons, led to his takeover of the whole of Gaul north of the River Loire. This newly conquered area became known as Neustria, the 'new lands'. Subsequently, Clovis moved his capital to Soissons and then to Paris, which became the centre of Frankish power. In 491 Clovis extended his influence east of the Rhine by conquering the Thuringians, cementing his position as the most powerful of the Frankish kings.

Though he was still a pagan, in 493 Clovis married the Burgundian princess Chlothild. She was a Catholic but failed to persuade Clovis to convert, possibly because he was considering converting to Arianism, as two of his sisters had done. Clovis finally did choose Catholicism, but it is not clear when or why he did so. According to the Gallo-Roman

The baptism of the Frankish king Clovis in 496 by St Remigius, the bishop of Reims, from a 14th-century French manuscript. Clovis expanded Frankish territory from its traditional heartland in the Rhineland and Flanders as far south as the Pyrenees.

chronicler Gregory of Tours (538–94), who wrote a monumental history of the Franks in the 590s, Clovis converted in 496 to show his gratitude to God for his support in a campaign against the Alamanni, and was baptized with 2,000 of his warriors on Christmas Day by Bishop Remigius of Reims. Other evidence suggests that Gregory placed the Frank's conversion a decade too early. In reality, Clovis may have announced his conversion in the buildup to his campaign against the Arian Visigoths in 507, when it would have had great propaganda value.

Clovis's crushing victory over the Visigoths at Vouillé (or Voulon) near Poitiers brought the whole of Aquitaine under his control, including the Visigothic capital Toulouse. He was only prevented from extending his kingdom to the Mediterranean by the intervention of the Ostrogothic king Theodoric the Great (r. 471–526). Traditionally, it has been claimed that hostility between Catholic Gallo-Romans and their Arian rulers was a major factor in Clovis's victory at Vouillé. It is possible that this hostility has been exaggerated, as a large Gallo-Roman contingent fought loyally for the Visigoths there. However, Clovis's conversion brought many benefits, not least the support of the Catholic Church, which was happy to overlook the unsavoury side of his character. It also won Clovis the support of the eastern Roman emperor Anastasius (r. 491–518), who awarded him the title of consul, doing much to legitimize his rule in the eyes of his Gallo-Roman subjects. With the major religious and political obstacles removed, the Gallo-Romans increasingly identified with their prestigious Frankish rulers. The exemption from land tax enjoyed by Franks no doubt helped persuade many to switch their ethnic allegiance.

Clovis spent his last years eliminating competing Frankish kings, notably his main rival Sigibert the Lame, king of the Ripuarian Franks (the 'river people', who lived along the Rhine). Clovis incited Sigibert's son Chloderic to murder the disabled ruler and take the kingdom for himself, then had one of his men split Chloderic's head with an axe. Clovis returned from a sailing trip arranged as an alibi and offered the kingless Ripuarian Franks his protection. They gratefully accepted. Lesser rival kings were murdered at Cambrai and Le Mans.

Towards the end of his reign, Clovis bewailed the fact that he had no living relatives, but Gregory of Tours thought this was a ruse to lure any survivors into declaring themselves so that he could have them murdered too. Clovis died at Paris in 511, aged 45.

Gold *solidus* of the eastern Roman emperor Anastasius II. Anastasius's support helped Clovis legitimize his rule over his Gallo-Roman subjects.

Conquests of Clovis

- Frankish territory, 481
- conquered by Clovis by 497
- conquered by Clovis by 508
- ✂ battle, with date

VII THE RISE OF THE FRANKS

The sons of Clovis

In the half-century after Clovis's death, the Franks under the Merovingian kings (the dynasty is named for Clovis's probable grandfather Merovech) extended their power and influence over much of western Europe, despite the division of the Frankish kingdom. When Clovis died, his hard-won kingdom was split between his four sons: Theuderic I, Childebert I, Chlodomer and Chlothar I. It is assumed that this was in line with the Frankish custom of partible inheritance, but this was the first time the principle had been applied to kingship. Clovis's decision may have come in response to Chlothild's determination that her three young sons by Clovis were not disinherited by Theuderic, his adult son by an earlier relationship. Whatever the reasons, Clovis set a precedent that was followed by all future Merovingian kings.

The division was accepted by all his sons, even Theuderic, who had most cause to feel aggrieved. However, any respect the brothers may have had for each other did not extend to their nephews. When Chlodomer died in 524, his lands ought to have been shared between his sons, but they were murdered by Childebert and Chlothar. They sought to do the same when Theuderic died in 534, but his son Theudebert had already proved himself as a warrior by defeating a Scandinavian pirate raid *c.* 528. Theudebert held onto his throne and, on his death in 548, passed it on to his son Theudebald. When Theudebald died without heirs in 555, however, Chlothar seized his lands unopposed. He did the same when his last surviving brother Childebert died without a male heir three years later. For the last three years of his reign, Chlothar ruled a reunited Frankish kingdom. He was survived by four sons, so on his death in 561 the whole process of division began again.

These dynastic machinations did not interfere with the expansion of the Merovingian kingdom. The southern border with the Visigothic kingdom was in a state of flux. Childebert conquered Gascony in 531, but his attempts to take Septimania (roughly equivalent to modern Languedoc) and drive the Visigoths completely out of Gaul were abandoned after an invasion of Spain in 541 went disastrously wrong. The Visigoths blockaded the Pyrenean passes, cutting off the Frankish army's retreat. Few of the Franks survived.

A Frankish silver-gilt bow-headed fibula inlaid with garnets and other precious stones.

The most important territorial acquisition by Clovis's sons was the kingdom of Burgundy. Chlodomer invaded Burgundy in 523, hoping to take advantage of a political crisis caused when King Sigismund (r. 516–23) murdered his son and heir Sigistrix for plotting to seize the throne. Chlodomer captured and killed Sigismund and his family. His generosity to monasteries ensured that Sigismund became the first royal saint of the Middle Ages. Burgundian resistance continued and Chlodomer was ambushed and killed in 524. Burgundy was finally conquered by an alliance of Childebert, Chlothar and Theudebert in 532–34.

The emperor Justinian's invasion of Italy gave the Franks the opportunity to expand their kingdom to the Mediterranean. In 537 the hard-pressed Ostrogothic king Witigis offered to give up Provence in return for military aid. The Franks sent an army into Italy in 539, but when it entered Pavia, the Ostrogothic capital, it turned on its hosts and massacred most of the population. However, the Franks found campaigning in Italy difficult because of the length of their supply lines and prevalent disease; they were driven out by the Byzantine general Narses in 554.

By the 540s Frankish conquests had made the Merovingian kingdom the greatest power of western Europe. The influence of the Merovingians extended far beyond their borders and they were able to present themselves as overlords of the Saxons, Frisians, Jutes, Danes, Bretons, Basques and Visigoths. When Childebert sent an embassy to Constantinople *c.* 550, he even brought along some Angles to back up his claim that he ruled Britain. This was a boast too far: the Romans were not fooled.

Dividing the kingdom

The reign of Chlothar I represented the apogee of the Merovingian kingdom. Under his successors, the kingdom was rent by fratricidal civil wars that began to undermine the dynasty's authority. Events in the years after Chlothar's death were driven by the ambitions of his son, King Chilperic I (r. 561–84). Chilperic was well educated, wrote Latin verse, dabbled in theology and showed his respect for Roman culture by restoring the amphitheatres at Paris and Soissons. He wanted to be seen to be civilized. Yet the chronicler Gregory of Tours, who knew him personally, dubbed Chilperic 'the Nero and Herod of our time' for the ruthless way in which he, and his equally calculating wife Fredegund, eliminated relatives who stood in their way.

On his father's death, Chilperic seems to have attempted a coup to take over the whole Frankish kingdom. His brothers Sigibert, Guntram and Charibert united against him and he was forced to accept the smallest of the four kingdoms. Hemmed in on all sides by his brothers' kingdoms, Chilperic could only expand his territory at their expense. Chilperic harboured a deep sense of injustice and the Merovingian kingdom was divided and re-divided several times over the next forty years as civil wars and murderous plots took a heavy toll on the royal family. Sigibert and Chilperic were only the most prominent victims of assassination. The family feud worked itself out in 613 when the sole survivor, Chilperic's son Chlothar II (r. 613–29), reunited the kingdom once more.

The divisions of the kingdom may seem arbitrary but they were not intended to reflect geographical or cultural divisions, instead evenly distributing its resources between heirs. The most significant division was between Neustria and the old homeland on the Rhine, known as Austrasia. The Franks who settled in Neustria were a small minority among the Gallo-Roman population. While the Gallo-Romans adopted the ethnic identity of their rulers, the Neustrian Franks adopted their subjects' romanized culture and Latin dialect. The Austrasian Franks remained Germanic-speaking. Though both continued to call themselves Franks, their cultural and linguistic identities increasingly diverged in the following centuries.

The basic territorial units of the Merovingian kingdom were the Roman *civitates*. Each was governed by a count (*comes*) responsible for collecting taxes, administering justice and raising troops for the royal army. Counts were appointed from local aristocratic families, but their positions were not yet hereditary. Groups of *civitates* were placed under the power of a duke (*dux*), a military office derived from the late Roman army. Counts also supervised their local bishops. The Church, with its literate personnel, was very much an arm of government: its bishops were appointed by the king and kept under tight royal control.

The centre of government was the royal palace, organized as a household. The most important offices were those of the constable or count of the stable, who was responsible for the king's horses; the steward or *seneschal*, responsible for provisioning; and the

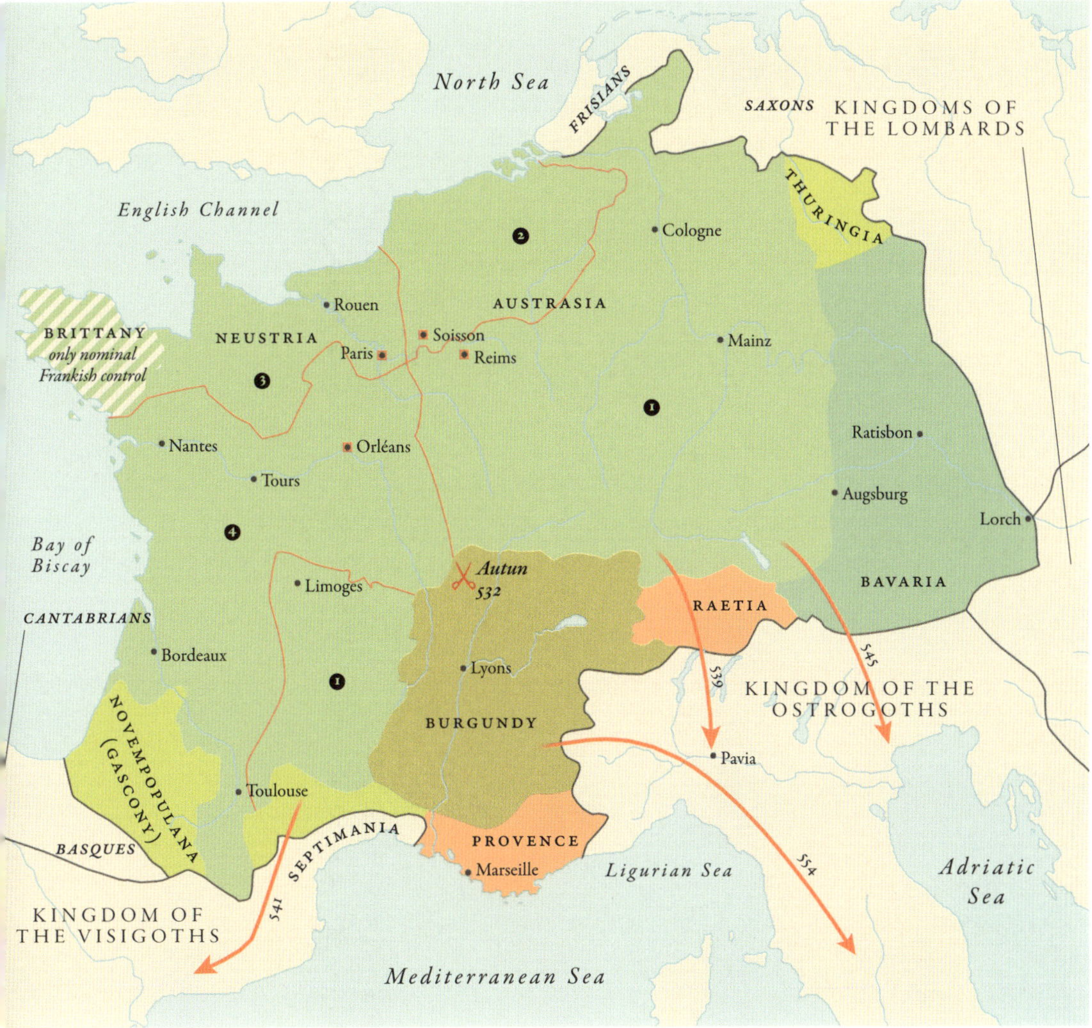

Frankish expansion to 561

— partition of the kingdom, 511	❶ Theuderic	Frankish territory, 511
❋ royal residence	❷ Chlothar	added 531/2
⚔ battle, with date	❸ Childebert	added by 534
	❹ Chlodomer	added by 537
		added later

Divisions of the Merovingian kingdom

1. on the death of Chlothar I, 561 (with royal residences)
2. on the death of Charibert, 567
3. in 583
4. by the Treaty of Andelot, 587

- Sigibert
- Guntram
- Charibert
- Chilperic
- Childebert II
- Chlothar II

mayor of the palace (*major domus*), who managed the royal estates and supervised the other officers of state. Though kings had their favourite residences, the palace was not a building so much as a mobile court. A 'palace' was wherever the king and his household were in residence. The counts found the frequent divisions of the kingdom disruptive and in 614 they forced Chlothar II to establish palaces for Neustria, Austrasia and Burgundy, each with its own mayor, to provide administrative continuity.

The period of Merovingian history from 639 to 751 is characterized by what have become known as *les rois fainéants* (the do-nothing kings), a succession of monarchs who ascended the throne as children and died in their twenties before they could establish their authority. Inexorably, real power began to pass into the hands of the mayors, who controlled the appointments to all significant offices of state.

The Frisian North Sea

As the Roman Empire entered its terminal decline, northern Europe experienced a long economic recession. Greater political stability under the Merovingian hegemony stimulated a modest revival of trade which, thanks to their strategic position at the mouth of the Rhine, the Frisians were quick to exploit.

The Frisians are first recorded living on the lower Rhine and the North Sea coasts of the modern Netherlands and Germany in the first century AD, where they reared livestock on the coastal marshland and built villages on artificial platforms called terps to protect them from flooding. Their homeland made them natural seafarers – between the third and seventh centuries they were active as pirates, preying on merchant ships plying the sheltered waters of the Waddensee wetland on their way between the Rhine and Jutland. The great disturbances of the Migration Period (*c.* 400–600) seem to have left the Frisians unaffected, though a few may have joined the Anglo-Saxons in Britain.

One of the effects of the collapse of the Western Roman Empire and the rise of the Germanic kingdoms was to isolate the North Sea region from the Mediterranean. The achievement of Clovis and his successors in creating a powerful Frankish kingdom and Justinian's reinvigorated eastern Roman or Byzantine Empire stimulated a revival

VII THE RISE OF THE FRANKS

in trade with the Mediterranean. Luxury metalwork and other prestige goods began to reach the North Sea via the Po valley in northern Italy and over the Alpine passes directly into the Rhine. Around 600 another route reached the Rhine via the Rhône valley.

Because they were settled across the mouth of the Rhine, the Frisians were ideally placed to take control of the onward trade to Britain, northern Germany and Scandinavia, where Rhineland products such as glass and lava quernstones were in demand. The Franks sought to control the lion's share of trade by founding *emporia* (market centres) at Dorestad on the lower Rhine and at Quentovic, close to Boulogne, which became important revenue-gathering centres for the Merovingian kings. The Frisians also controlled *emporia* on islands off the North Sea coast, such as Domburg on Walcheren. Other kingdoms around the North Sea set up their own *emporia* to attract and to tax trade.

The relationship between the Frisians and the Franks was uneasy. While Anglo-Saxon writers usually described the leaders of the

The Frankish king Dagobert I (d. 639), shown in this 14th-century manuscript, was the last monarch of the Merovingian dynasty to rule the kingdom in his own right. After his death, real power passed to the mayors of the palace.

The Frisian North Sea

— division between Frisian (east) and Frankish (west) dominated trade routes based on pottery distribution

→ trade route

Frisians as kings, Frankish chronicles only afford them the title of *dux*, implying that they were regarded as subordinates. Frankish kings tried to exert influence over the Frisians by encouraging Christian missionary activity. Evangelization began in 678 when bishop Wilfrid of York met King Aldgisl at Utrecht to seek his permission to preach to the Frisians. Wilfrid's work was continued by two other Anglo-Saxons, Willibrord, active *c*. 700, and Wynfrith, better known as St Boniface, who began preaching in Frisia in 716. The Frisians were resistant to Christianity – they killed Boniface at Dokkum in Friesland in 754 – and it was not until Charlemagne's time that their conversion was forcibly completed.

The declining authority of the Merovingians in the seventh century gave the Frisians an opportunity for expansion, and in *c*. 650 they seized Dorestad, which had become northern Europe's most prosperous trade centre. The loss of Dorestad and the dues which were levied on its trade must have been a painful blow for the Frankish kingdom. Pippin II, the Carolingian mayor of Austrasia in Germany, launched two unsuccessful campaigns to recover Dorestad in the early 680s, but was successful in 689. Dorestad was defended by a Frisian army under King Radbod (r. 680–719), who was forced to take refuge in the marshes after his battle line broke under a ferocious Frankish assault. The Franks also captured Utrecht, which became their main military and ecclesiastic base for the conquest and conversion of Frisians.

The Frisians did not succumb easily to the Franks. Frisia's low-lying marshy terrain, broken by fens, creeks, rivers and lakes, was favourable for defence. In 716 Radbod even mounted a counteroffensive, taking a fleet up the Rhine, ravaging Frankish settlements as far south as Cologne. Frankish control of the Rhine estuary was not secure until 734, when Charles Martel mounted a major naval expedition against the Frisians, and their conquest was finally completed by Charlemagne in 784–85.

Scandinavia before the Vikings

In the Merovingian period, Scandinavia was only just emerging from its prehistoric Iron Age. A process of political centralization that had begun in the Migration Period led to the emergence of the

A 5th- to 7th-century Scandinavian gold bracteate. While this example was worn as a pendant, they could also be sewn onto clothing. Many bracteates feature images of Germanic kings or gods, in this case the Norse god Odin.

first Scandinavian kingdoms and a warlike society with a tradition of piracy. During the late Roman period, the Scandinavians were still divided into tribes, each dominated by a warrior aristocracy that maintained its status with raiding. Because of its indented coastline and many islands and lakes, travel in Scandinavia was easiest by water. Shipbuilding and seafaring skills therefore developed early, as did piracy. Most of this was probably local in nature, but at the end of the third century the Heruls from Jutland joined the Saxons in raids on the Roman Empire. Much of the loot was cast into bogs as votive offerings. One of the most spectacular of these was at Nydam in Jutland, where hundreds of weapons were interred, along with two ships and a boat. The Nydam ships showed many of the characteristics of the longships that carried the Vikings on their terrifying raids in the ninth century.

Fortresses proliferated across Scandinavia during the Migration Period and the semi-legendary traditions recorded by the medieval Danish historian Saxo Grammaticus (c. 1150–1220) hold that it was a time of intense conflict between competing tribes. As had happened in Germany 200 years earlier, tribes formed alliances and merged or were conquered and assimilated by stronger rivals. In this way the Danes emerged as the dominant people of southern Scandinavia during the sixth century. Successful leaders concentrated more and more wealth and power in their own hands; society became increasingly militarized and predatory. Piracy was so rife that some coastal areas of Scandinavia became depopulated.

Scandinavia largely escaped the wider disruptions caused by the Germanic migrations: it was a place people migrated out of, rather than into. Many Germanic peoples, including the Goths, Burgundians, Vandals and Lombards, believed (incorrectly as far as the Goths were concerned, according to new genetic evidence) that they had originated in Scandinavia but been forced to emigrate because of overpopulation and a shortage of good farmland. In the fifth century, Angles and Jutes from Jutland migrated to Britain and the Heruls were hired as mercenaries for the Byzantine Empire, launching pirate raids as far afield as Spain. The earliest named Scandinavian ruler, Hygelac, was also a pirate. He was a king of the Geats (probably the Götar of southern Sweden) who made an unsuccessful raid on the lower Rhine c. 528. His death in battle against the Franks was recorded by Gregory of Tours and in the Old English epic poem *Beowulf*.

Pre-Viking Scandinavia

Roman Iron Age, c. AD 1–400:
- warrior grave
- votive ship
- other votive offering

pre-Viking ship burials:
- royal or aristocratic
- other
- votive ship

Migration Period, c. 400–600:
- migration from settled area
- dense concentration of fortresses
- SVEAR main Scandinavian peoples, c. 500
- FINNS non-Scandinavian peoples, c. 500
- early runic inscription

Late Germanic Iron Age, c. 600–800:
- unsettled areas, c. 700
- chief's residence and religious centre
- seasonal trading place
- the Danevirke

Archaeological evidence points to the development of several small kingdoms in Scandinavia by 750. One of these was in the Vestfold of Norway, where the pagan cult centre and impressive burial mounds at Borre are evidence of a royal dynasty. Rich warrior burials, some of them in ships, at Vendel and Valsgärde near Uppsala point to the emergence of a dynasty among the Svear, the people from whom Sweden takes its name. The Svear kings probably controlled the cult centre and seasonal market on the island of Helgö (Holy Island), which had trade links with the Mediterranean and perhaps farther afield. The most exotic find from the site was a statuette of the Buddha, made in northern India *c.* 600.

Jutland was the centre of the most impressive early Scandinavian kingdom, evidence for which comes from large-scale public works. In 726 a canal was dug across the island of Samsø, probably to regulate shipping, and in 737 a rampart – the Danevirke – was built across the neck of the Jutland peninsula as a defence against the Saxons. Such major projects could only have been ordered by a ruler who commanded the labour and resources of a wide area.

Around the same time, a well-planned trading place was founded at Ribe. Large quantities of Frisian coins, evidence of leatherworking and huge quantities of cattle dung suggest that Ribe was exporting hides to the Frankish kingdom. The ruler responsible for all these works was probably Angantyr, the earliest historical Danish king, whom the Anglo-Saxon St Willibrord (658–739) met on the first Christian mission to Scandinavia *c.* 725.

Charles Martel and Poitiers

In the seventh century, the Merovingian kings became mere spectators to the power struggles between the mayors who supposedly ruled in their name. Two families came to dominate the office, the Wattonids in Neustria and the Pippinids or Carolingians in Austrasia. The Carolingian family – named for its most famous member, Charlemagne – traced its descent to Pippin I (d. 640), mayor of the palace of Austrasia under Chlothar II. Pippin I's grandson, Pippin of Herstal (Pippin II), who became mayor of Austrasia in 679, extended his influence to the whole kingdom after he defeated Berchar, the Wattonid mayor of Neustria, at the Battle of Tertry in 687. Ever since

VII THE RISE OF THE FRANKS

Charles Martel's victory over the Arabs at the Battle of Poitiers (also known as the Battle of Tours) in 732, from a 13th-century French manuscript.

Clovis had established his capital at Paris, Neustria had been the politically dominant region of the Frankish kingdom; Pippin's victory marked a shift of power back to the Franks' Germanic heartlands.

By the time Pippin II (sometimes rendered as Pepin) died in 714, the office of mayor had become hereditary, but his sole male heir was an illegitimate son, Charles, better known as Charles Martel ('the hammer'). Charles's accession was opposed by the Neustrians, who chose their own mayor, and Pippin's widow Plectrude, who tried to establish her five-year-old grandson as mayor. Despite strong support in Austrasia, it took Charles five years to see off the opposition. As the authority of the Merovingian kings had withered, so too had the Frankish kingdom. As mayor, Charles energetically reasserted Frankish power, campaigning continuously against breakaway states in Aquitaine and Bavaria and against the Frisians, Saxons and Arabs who had seized or raided Frankish territory during the years of decline.

Charles Martel is best remembered for his victory over the Arabs and their Moorish allies at Poitiers, where he earned his nickname. Within a year of invading Spain, Arab raiding forces had begun probing north of the Pyrenees. In 719 the Muslims captured Narbonne and used it as a base to bring the rest of Septimania under their control and launch further raids into Aquitaine and Burgundy in the 720s. In 732 Abd er-Rahman, the governor of Spain, led the largest Arab invasion of Aquitaine so far and defeated Duke Eudo at Bordeaux, forcing him to flee to Austrasia and beg Charles for help. Charles responded rapidly. The threat to the Frankish kingdom was clear enough, but it also gave Charles a welcome opportunity to force Eudo to recognize Frankish overlordship as the price of his support.

Abd er-Rahman had advanced as far as Tours when he learned that the Frankish army was trying to cut off his line of retreat. He began a withdrawal but was slowed by a wagon train loaded with booty, so was forced into battle near Poitiers. The Muslim cavalry repeatedly charged the Frankish infantry's shield wall but it held firm, according to the Spanish *Mozarabic Chronicle,* as if 'it was frozen to the earth like a rampart of ice'. Abd er-Rahman was among those slain and the Muslim army fled during the night, leaving its booty for the Franks.

French historians have often been accused of exaggerating the importance of Charles's victory for patriotic reasons. It is true that the immediate consequences of the battle were not great. Charles faced further Arab raids and his attempt to drive them out of Septimania in 737 failed. Nor was Frankish control of Aquitaine restored – Eudo forgot his promises to Charles as soon as the battle was over. However, all previous Arab conquests had begun only after raids had revealed the weakness of the enemy; Charles's victory had shown that the Franks were not weak. By the time Charles's Merovingian puppet king Theuderic IV died in 737, his control over the Frankish kingdom was such that he did not feel the need to appoint a successor and he ruled alone until his death in 741. His son, Pippin III, would take the next logical step and overthrow the Merovingian dynasty to become king.

Fall of the Merovingian dynasty

Charles Martel was survived by two sons, Pippin III the Stout (sometimes Pepin the Short) and Carloman. Following Merovingian custom, the kingdom was shared, Carloman becoming mayor of Neustria and Burgundy, Pippin becoming mayor of Austrasia. The brothers' accession appears to have been unpopular as they had to suppress several rebellions. It was probably to legitimize their position that they made Childeric III king in 743, filling a throne which had been vacant since 737. That they felt the need to do this suggests that the Merovingian dynasty was, even then, not so lacking in authority as later Carolingian chroniclers implied.

There is no obvious evidence of discord between the brothers, but in 747 Carloman abdicated to become a monk in the monastery of Monte Cassino in Italy, leaving Pippin III in control of the whole kingdom. Events in Italy offered Pippin the opportunity to usurp the throne. Rome was officially part of the Byzantine Empire, but the popes often engaged in doctrinal disputes with the emperors, who saw themselves as leaders of the Church. Problems elsewhere meant that emperors paid little attention to Italy and the papacy felt constantly exposed to attack by the aggressive Lombard kings. The popes had urgent need of an alternative protector. The activities of Anglo-Saxon missionaries in the early eighth century had increased Frankish respect for the papacy, which made it possible for Pippin to seek permission to depose Childeric III, asking if 'it was good or not that the king of the Franks should wield no royal power', as was the case at the time. Pope Zacharias replied that 'it was better to call him king who had the royal power than the one who did not' and commanded that Pippin be made king.

It was over a century since the Merovingians had ruled as well as reigned over the Frankish kingdom, yet Pippin's decision to depose Childeric III and take the throne for himself was still a bold one. Lacking royal blood, Pippin had to offer a new ideology of kingship to justify his usurpation.

Pippin III became king at Soissons in 751 in a novel ceremony inspired by Frankish custom and the Old Testament. He was first acclaimed king by Frankish nobles and then anointed with holy oil by the Anglo-Saxon missionary St Boniface in the manner of the Old Testament kings. He was lifted onto the throne by the nobles and symbolically put in possession of the kingdom of the Franks. Anointing conferred on Pippin a semi-sacred character that set him apart from other men and replaced the charisma of Merovingian royal blood with kingship by divine grace. The custom was widely adopted by other European monarchies and became a defining mark of legitimate kingship. Childeric III was formally deposed, tonsured and packed off to a monastery, there to pray for the health and success of King Pippin.

The following year, the Lombard king Aistulf (d. 756) captured Ravenna, the main Byzantine stronghold in northern Italy, and advanced on Rome. The new pope, Stephen II, fled to Pippin to seek his help. While with Pippin he repeated the anointing ceremony and

The Frankish kingdom, c. 700

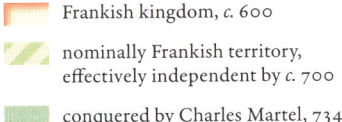

- Frankish kingdom, c. 600
- nominally Frankish territory, effectively independent by c. 700
- conquered by Charles Martel, 734
- Arab/Moorish invasion, 732
- Charles Martel's counterattack, 732
- battle, with date

The Carolingian takeover

- Frankish kingdom border, 741
- other border
- conquered by Pippin, 744
- conquered by Pippin, 759
- conquered by Pippin, 768

also anointed his two sons, Charles (the future Charlemagne) and Carloman, as kings, securing the Carolingian succession. In return Pippin promised to recover lost papal lands from the Lombards.

In a desperate attempt to avoid war, Aistulf ordered Pippin's brother Carloman out of his monastery and sent him to the king to fight the pope's request, but without success. In two campaigns in 755 and 756, Pippin III defeated the Lombards, secured control of Ravenna and other territories and handed them over to the papacy, so creating the medieval Papal State. The remainder of Pippin's reign was taken up by almost annual campaigns against Duke Waifar of Aquitaine. Waifar's death in battle in 768 brought the war to an end, but Pippin fell ill shortly afterwards and died at the monastery of St Denis near Paris. Before he died he made provision for the division of the kingdom between his sons Charles and Carloman. One of the most important reigns in European history was about to begin.

The Anglo-Saxon missionary, St Boniface, anoints Pippin III as king of the Franks at Soissons in 751.

VIII

The Age of Charlemagne

Uniting a kingdom under God

No early medieval ruler has made a greater impression than Charlemagne (r. 768–814). Even within his lifetime he was called Charles the Great, or in Latin *Carolus Magnus*, from which comes the Old French Charlemagne. Within a few decades of his death, he had attained legendary stature, and his court became almost as popular a setting for authors of chivalrous romances as that of the legendary King Arthur. For once the stature is deserved: Charlemagne's achievements have shaped German, French and Italian history down to the modern age. The French and Germans both herald him as a national hero, and a prize for services to European unity has been named after him.

Charles was born in 742, the eldest son of Pippin III, then Mayor of the Franks. Pippin's elevation to kingship in 751 radically changed Charlemagne's prospects. He was given the training of an aristocratic Frank – taught to ride, hunt and fight. Charlemagne's friend and biographer Einhard claimed that he was not taught to write and had little success when he tried to learn later in life. But this does not mean he was a man of limited intellect. Charlemagne spoke Latin as fluently as his own Frankish language and had a keen interest in astronomy and theology. At the age of eleven he began to play a role in public affairs and accompanied his father on campaigns to subdue Aquitaine. It was on his return from one of these expeditions that Pippin fell ill and died in 768.

An idealized silver-gilt bust of the Frankish emperor Charlemagne, made in the 14th century. The emperor's clothing and hairstyle reflect the fashions of the 14th century rather than his own day. The bust is kept in the treasury of Aachen cathedral in Germany, the emperor's burial place.

Charlemagne's early years

— Frankish kingdom

Division of the kingdom on the death of Pippin III, 768:

- Charlemagne
- Carloman

Following the Frankish custom of partible inheritance, Pippin's kingdom was divided equally between Charlemagne and his younger brother Carloman, though Charlemagne received the bulk of the Carolingian family lands in Austrasia. Following Pippin's death, Aquitaine rebelled against Frankish rule. Charlemagne asked for Carloman's help but was refused. Showing the qualities that later made him such a successful leader, Charlemagne gathered what forces he could and moved swiftly and decisively to crush the rebellion. When the leader of the Aquitainians took refuge with Duke Lupus of Gascony, Charlemagne easily cowed him into submitting to Frankish rule. Within a year of his accession, Charlemagne had made his first conquest.

The reasons for Carloman's refusal to help his brother are not clear, but it clearly angered Charlemagne. Much to the annoyance of Pope Stephen III, who feared he would lose his alliance with the Franks, Charlemagne married a daughter of the Lombard king Desiderius (r. 756–74) in 770. He cultivated good relations with Duke Tassilo of Bavaria, who was married to another of Desiderius's daughters. Carloman found himself politically isolated. Charlemagne's intentions towards his brother can only be guessed: the conflict was resolved peacefully by Carloman's death the next year and the Frankish kingdom was reunited under the sole rule of Charlemagne.

Preferring not to rely on Charlemagne's generosity, Carloman's widow took their children and fled to the Lombard kingdom. Charlemagne repudiated his Lombard bride, her usefulness expired, and sent her back to her father. Shortly afterwards Charlemagne married Hildegard, daughter of the duke of Swabia. At a stroke Carloman's death made Charlemagne the most powerful ruler in western Europe. He had already shown considerable military and political skills and was not slow to appreciate the opportunities for territorial expansion that now beckoned. Over the next twenty-five years Charlemagne was to unite a greater area of western Europe under a single ruler than at any time since the fall of the Western Roman Empire, giving substance to his assumption of the imperial title at his Rome coronation in 800.

The conquests begin

Charlemagne's first conquest after he became sole ruler of the Franks was the Lombard kingdom of Italy. Early in 773 envoys arrived from

Conquests of Charlemagne, 784–812

Pope Hadrian I asking for Charlemagne's help against Desiderius of the Lombards. Hadrian claimed that Desiderius had seized papal lands and was demanding that he anoint the exiled sons of Carloman as kings. There must have been Franks who thought that Carloman's kingdom ought to have been divided between the sons: Charlemagne would have been only too aware of how papal anointing would have given credibility to their claims. This was exactly how Charlemagne's father had become king. Desiderius's motive was probably the strengthening of his position against Charlemagne now that the marriage alliance had been broken. Pope Hadrian's biographer claimed that Desiderius wanted to conquer all of Italy, but this is probably exaggeration. The mere threat of excommunication was enough to deter him from seizing Rome in 773, which hardly suggests he was a man of great determination.

Hadrian's request came at a bad time. Only the year before, Charlemagne had embarked on the conquest of the pagan Saxons and was aware of the consequences of leaving his border with them unprotected. He carefully investigated the pope's claims and, finding they were true, tried negotiating with Desiderius. Only when this failed did he invade. Postponing the conquest of Saxony – his real priority – for this intervention in Italy signifies the importance he placed on maintaining a close relationship with the papacy.

Charlemagne split his forces in two – a favoured tactic of his, made possible by the large resources at his disposal – leading one army along the Mont Cenis Pass himself and sending the other via the Great St Bernard Pass. Both armies found their passage through the narrow alpine valleys blocked by Lombard defences. After a brief stand-off, Charlemagne's scouts found an alternative route through the mountains and Desiderius withdrew his forces to the heavily fortified capital at Pavia to prevent himself being outflanked. The Lombards were well used to Frankish invasions and knew from experience that they always withdrew at the end of the campaigning season, to avoid becoming stranded in Italy when winter snows closed the Alpine passes. It was already September when he retreated to Pavia, so Desiderius cannot have expected to be besieged for very long.

Unfortunately for Desiderius, he had misjudged his man. Charlemagne had no intention of withdrawing before winter. With the Lombards blockaded in Pavia, Charlemagne spent the winter taking over the rest of the kingdom unhindered, even finding time to visit Hadrian in Rome. Carloman's wife and her sons were captured at Verona. Their fate is unknown, but it is likely the boys spent their lives incarcerated in a monastery, praying for the success of their uncle.

In June 774 Pavia surrendered. The Lombards submitted to Charlemagne and Desiderius was taken back to Francia as a prisoner. This did not mean that the Lombards became a subject people; the kingdom kept its separate identity and institutions, but Desiderius was deposed and Charlemagne adopted the title King of the Lombards. Franks were given key positions in the kingdom, but Lombard landowners were not dispossessed and there was only one minor rebellion against Frankish rule. Though Charlemagne restored the papal lands seized by Desiderius, he also took the title Patrician of the Romans and made it clear to Hadrian who was now the real ruler of Rome.

The conquest of Italy was an important moment for Charlemagne personally and European history generally. As ruler of most of Italy, Charlemagne was drawn into the complex politics of the papacy and the Byzantine Empire, which still ruled the south and staked a claim on the rest. Without this involvement, Charlemagne's imperial coronation would probably never have happened. The conquest also marked the beginning of northern European involvement in Italian affairs, which remained a decisive factor in the history of the country down to the nineteenth century.

Bringing the Saxons to heel

Of Charlemagne's conquest of Saxony, Einhard said that 'no war ever fought by the Franks was more prolonged, more full of atrocities and more demanding of effort'. It would take dozens of campaigns spread over thirty-three years to extinguish the last Saxon resistance. The Saxons were still a decentralized tribal people, divided into four main groups: the Westphalians, Angrarians, Eastphalians and Nordliudi. Despite some Anglo-Saxon missionary activity, they were still wedded to paganism.

There was no love lost between the Saxons and the Franks. Cross-border raids by the Saxons were common; the Franks retaliated by invading and imposing tribute, which the Saxons stopped paying as soon as they thought they could get away with it. Charlemagne decided that the only way to reach a lasting settlement was to conquer the Saxons and convert them to Christianity by whatever means necessary. The conquest began in 772 by capturing the fortress at Eresburg. From there he advanced to the most important of the Saxons' pagan shrines (probably at Lippespringe), plundered it and provocatively destroyed the Irminsul, its great idol, as a demonstration of God's superior power. Trouble in Italy prevented Charlemagne following up this campaign until 775, and by 777 he felt his control of Saxony was secure enough to hold the kingdom's annual assembly at Paderborn. But Charlemagne's celebrations were premature. While he campaigned in Spain in 778, the Saxons revolted, destroying Frankish garrisons, attacking churches and ravaging the Rhineland. More campaigns followed.

Pitched battles were rare in the Saxon wars. The Saxons preferred to avoid battle against the better-equipped Franks and employed guerrilla tactics instead. The main Frankish strategy was to establish a camp deep in Saxon territory and send out cavalry units, called *scaras*, to ravage the surrounding countryside and wear down the Saxons' resistance. By 780 Saxon resolve seemed to be crushed. Charlemagne divided Saxony up into counties, the normal unit of local government in Francia, and severe measures were introduced to suppress paganism. But again he was premature. In 782 a new rebellion broke out under Widukind and a Frankish army was virtually wiped out in battle in the Süntel mountains. In response, Charlemagne ordered the execution of 4,500 Saxon prisoners at Verden, but it was not until 785 that Widukind surrendered and accepted baptism.

Saxony was quiet for seven years, but in 792 another widespread revolt broke out, this time while Charlemagne was campaigning against the Avars. Again, churches and the clergy were targeted, but this was the Saxons' last effort. By 797 resistance south of the Elbe had collapsed and it was finally broken north of the Elbe in 805 when Charlemagne deported most of the population and resettled it throughout Francia.

Superficially at least, it seems surprising that Charlemagne was able to conquer the rich and centralized Lombard kingdom in a single campaign and yet take so long to overcome the tribal Saxons. However, centralization was not always an advantage in the early Middle Ages. In a centralized kingdom, where power and leadership are concentrated in few hands, an invader could

The conquest of Saxony, 772–804

extent of Saxon territory, 772

key Frankish fortress

Frankish victory

Frankish defeat

Frankish army camps in Saxony:

772–80

782–85

794–804

forest

NORDLIUDI main Saxon tribe

SORBS Slav tribe

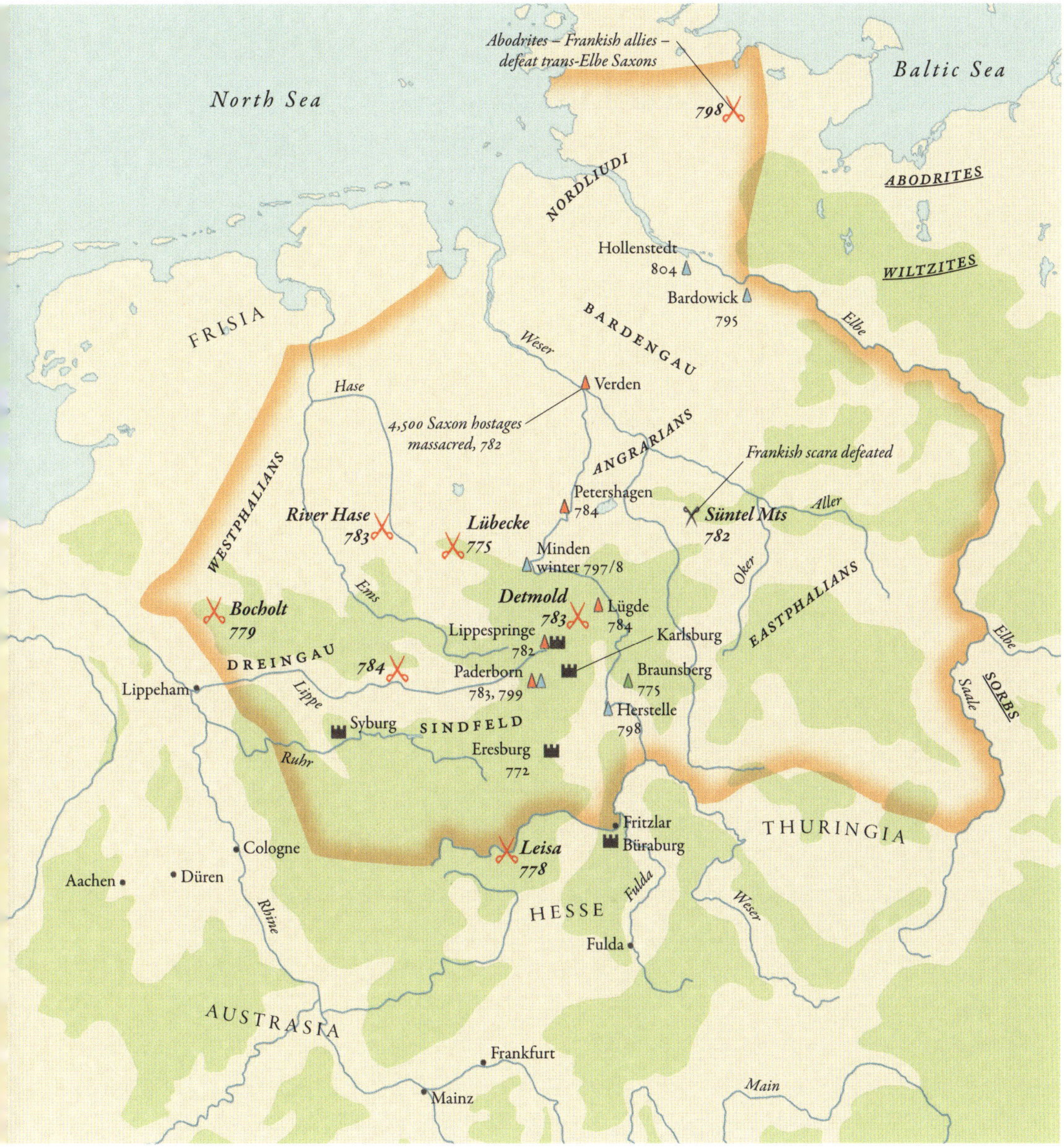

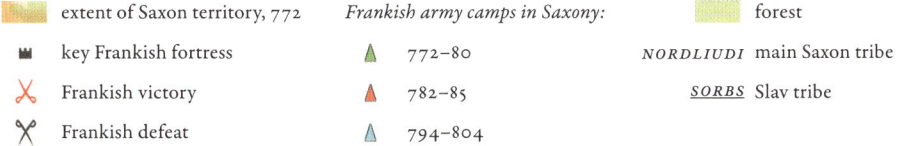

knock out the elite and take over completely, as happened with the Lombards. Another good example is the Norman conquest of England, which hinged on just one battle. Where power and authority are decentralized, as it was in Saxony, this cannot be done. With so many different chiefs, it was impossible to seize control from a single battle: there was no one with whom to negotiate a lasting peace, and no institutions of government to take over and use to control the natives. Decentralization was a hidden strength that allowed the Saxons to renew their resistance time and again.

The campaigns continue

There were very few years in Charlemagne's long reign when he did not lead a military campaign in person and fewer still when a Frankish army was not actively campaigning somewhere on the empire's borders. One such year was 790, when an astonished chronicler wrote simply that 'this year, the Franks were quiet'.

As well as Saxony and Italy, Charlemagne campaigned against the Avars, Spanish Moors, Bretons, Bavarians and Slavs, Venetians and Byzantines. In most cases his efforts were crowned with success, but Charlemagne's most celebrated campaign was a failure. In 777 Ibn al-Arabi, the Moorish governor of Zaragoza (formerly Roman Caesaraugusta in northern Spain) rebelled against Abd al-Rahman, the Umayyad emir of Córdoba, and offered to hand over his territory to Charlemagne. The following year the Franks invaded Spain in massive strength. Charlemagne led one army across the western Pyrenees from Aquitaine to lay siege to Zaragoza, Ibn al-Arabi having already reneged on his offer and turned hostile. A second Frankish army crossed the Pyrenees from Septimania and approached Zaragoza from the east.

After receiving the submission of Zaragoza, Charlemagne returned to Aquitaine over the pass of Roncesvalles, where his rearguard was ambushed and destroyed by Basques. It was a disaster, with several important nobles among the dead, including Roland, the count of the Breton March. The battle was immortalized in the Old French epic *The Song of Roland*, though the Moors are depicted as the enemy in place of the less glamorous Christian Basques, and the campaign itself is portrayed as a prototype crusade.

A gold Avar imitation of a Byzantine goblet, made in the 700s. Decorated with female personifications of the four major ecclesiastical centres in the Byzantine world: Cyprus, Rome, Constantinople and Alexandria.

The expedition produced no lasting results to compensate for this defeat and Charlemagne never again led an expedition to Spain. However, through the efforts of Frankish margraves (border lords) and, later, his son Louis the Pious, the frontier was pushed slowly south. The capture of Barcelona in 801 firmly established Frankish power south of the Pyrenees.

The most ambitious of Charlemagne's campaigns were those he fought in Pannonia against the Avars, who had earned a terrifying reputation in the previous two centuries. Charlemagne's campaigns against them are notable not only for their meticulous planning but also their religious preparation. Charlemagne clearly felt that he needed all the help he could get. The first campaign in 791 involved a total of three armies. He gathered two of them at Regensburg on the Danube. One army under Count Theodoric and Meginfred the Chamberlain, marched along the north bank of the river; the other, under Charlemagne's command, marched along the south bank. A fleet accompanied them on the river, to carry supplies, ferry troops from one bank to the other and outflank Avar defensive positions. On reaching the Avar border, the armies halted and spent three days in fasting and prayer to secure divine support. The third army, a cavalry *scara*, was sent to invade the Avar kingdom from Italy. Seeing the massive forces arrayed against them, the Avars did not put up much of a fight and for several weeks the Franks plundered their territory.

While returning from this expedition, an epidemic broke out killing thousands of horses in the Frankish army, so Charlemagne spent 792 at Regensburg preparing a massive campaign for 793, including the construction of a pontoon bridge, but a rebellion in Saxony meant this was cancelled too. Charlemagne evidently still believed the Avars to be a serious threat because considerable resources were expended in 793 in an unsuccessful attempt to link the Rhine and Danube with a canal to expedite movement of troops and supplies to the front. However, no further intervention from Charlemagne was needed. A civil war broke out among the Avars and a Frankish army under the duke of Friuli met little opposition in 795 when it plundered the Avar capital, a fortress known as 'the Ring' somewhere between the Danube and the Drava. A vast hoard of treasure, looted by the Avars during their centuries of greatness, was carted back to Francia.

The conquest of the Avar kingdom was completed in 796 by Charlemagne's son Pippin, who led another army from Italy to destroy

The Avar campaign of 791

- Frankish territory, 791
- Count Theodoric and Meginfred the Chamberlain
- Danube supply fleet
- Charlemagne
- Pippin
- Avar defensive fortifications

the Ring and remove any remaining treasure. The wealth gained in these two expeditions was so great that Einhard was moved to claim that after the conquest of the Saxons, this was Charlemagne's most important war.

The revival of empire

The culmination of Charlemagne's reign came on Christmas Day 800 when he was crowned Emperor of the Romans by Pope Leo III at St Peter's Church in Rome. The meaning of the ceremony and its significance have been endlessly debated. It was later claimed by his biographer Einhard that Charlemagne had not expected to be crowned emperor and, had he known, he would not have entered the church that day. This is simply the biographer showing that his hero was a modest and humble man. In reality, the coronation was long planned and even the date was chosen so as to be memorable to posterity.

Certainly by the 790s, Charlemagne was ruling as *de facto* emperor, even if he was not one in name. Charlemagne was a sincerely devout man who had a very clear concept of the responsibilities of a Christian ruler. He believed that God would hold him accountable not only for his own conduct, but also that of his subjects. The fortunes of his kingdom depended on God's favour, and throughout his reign Charlemagne's legislation shows his concern to create a just and orderly Christian society. He saw his relationship with the Church in much the same way as the Christian Roman emperors had. Charlemagne was responsible to God for the quality of worship and the clergy, and for the maintenance of religious orthodoxy. Charlemagne condemned the Byzantine emperors for their support for the iconoclast heresy and even overruled the papacy on doctrinal matters.

In 799 Pope Leo III was attacked and imprisoned in Rome by a hostile faction who charged him with various crimes, including perjury and fornication. Rescued by the duke of Spoleto, he was taken to Charlemagne at Paderborn where he cleared himself of the charges on oath. It was probably while he was there that Leo agreed to crown Charlemagne emperor. Leo was taken back to Rome by royal legates, who arrested the conspirators. Charlemagne waited a year before going to Rome in person, suggesting that the date of the coronation had already been fixed.

The divisio regni of 806

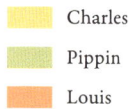

- Charles
- Pippin
- Louis

The *divisio regni* (Charlemagne's plan to divide the empire between his sons) never materialized, since Charles and Pippin died before him.

Later popes claimed that the fact that Leo III had placed the crown on Charlemagne's head showed that an emperor could only be made by papal coronation. This would cause much trouble for the German Holy Roman emperors, who claimed to be Charlemagne's successors. Charlemagne would certainly not have seen it this way. After crowning him Leo performed the *adoratio* (prostration) before Charlemagne in a clear imitation of the practice in the Byzantine Empire, where the Church was subordinate to the emperor. The Byzantines were horrified by the implications of Charlemagne's coronation, which they saw as usurpation of a title only the emperor in Constantinople had the right to use – or in this case, the empress, for in 800 the Byzantine Empire was ruled by a woman, Empress Irene. Her female status meant that, as far as the west was concerned, the imperial throne was vacant.

In any case, by this time most western Europeans thought that the Greek-speaking Byzantines' claims to be Roman were preposterous. As the ruler of Rome and much of the old Western Roman Empire, and a true defender of religious orthodoxy, Charlemagne probably believed that he had a better claim to the title than the Byzantines and that he was, therefore, reviving the Roman Empire. Charlemagne attempted a reconciliation with Constantinople by offering to marry Irene and unite both empires. Her acceptance in 802 appalled the court and resulted in her immediate overthrow; it wasn't until 812 that Charlemagne's title was recognized in Constantinople.

Charlemagne's provision in 806 for the division of the empire between his three sons on his death, in accordance with the Frankish tradition of partible inheritance, has been seen as a sign that he became disillusioned with the imperial title, or that he saw it as a purely personal honour. This is unlikely to be the case. As under the Merovingians, the Frankish realm remained a single polity, even if it was divided between two or more rulers. And had not the Romans also divided their realm? In the event, Charlemagne was survived by only one of his sons, Louis the Pious, who inherited the whole empire.

Government of the Frankish kingdom

Charlemagne's kingdom established the shape of government for much of Europe for hundreds of years to come. At the centre of government was the royal household. The chief officers of state all had duties related to the management of the royal household and estates, but they also advised the king and most had military and diplomatic duties. The chief official was the count of the palace, who supervised the other officials such as the chamberlain (housekeeper), seneschal (responsible for provisions), count of the stable, marshall (who maintained order at court) and chancellor (head of the writing office). This was the nearest the Frankish kingdom came to having a central bureaucracy; most functions of government were devolved to local officials. Aachen was the nominal capital of the kingdom, but the royal household was mobile, constantly moving between royal estates.

The main instrument of public government was the annual general assembly, which only the king could call. These were held in different locations, but were usually near an important royal palace in the Carolingian heartland, such as Aachen, Thionville, Ingelheim, Worms and Frankfurt. Assemblies were called to gather the army for a campaign and to discuss major political or ecclesiastical issues, but legislation was the preserve of the king. Summaries of the legislation announced at assemblies were recorded on 'capitularies', many of which survive. Assemblies passed judgment in important legal cases. Law was generally based on the Frankish Salic code, originally written in the reign of Clovis, but there was no single law code for the whole empire and some peoples, such as the Lombards, retained their national laws.

The main social distinction in the Frankish kingdom was between the free and the unfree (serfs and slaves). Freedom brought responsibilities. All free men were expected to attend the annual general assembly and were liable for military service, for which they were expected to provide their own equipment. These duties were beyond the means of poorer freemen and were not rigorously enforced. In practice, the bulk of armies consisted of military vassals who had commended themselves to the king – that is, they had become his sworn dependents, in return for which they received a *benefice*, usually an estate, so that they could devote themselves to military service. Such agreements were the basis of what has become known as feudalism (from *foedus*, agreement).

The most important method of establishing the relationship between king and subject was the oath of fidelity. This was not required universally until 789, when Charlemagne ordered every freeman over the age of twelve to swear that 'I am and shall be faithful to my lord Charlemagne the king and his sons, all the days

The Palatine Chapel at Aachen cathedral. The chapel, commissioned by Charlemagne in 796, was a consciously imperial building modelled on the Byzantine basilica of San Vitale in the former western Roman capital of Ravenna.

of my life without fraud or evil design'. After his imperial coronation, Charlemagne ordered all free men to swear a new oath with added conditions, including the duty to be obedient. As oaths were the basis of trust in society, those who broke them were severely punished.

The basic unit of local government in the Carolingian Empire was the county; there may have been as many as 600 altogether. Counties were administered by counts, responsible for justice, collecting taxes and tolls, maintaining roads and bridges, and levying troops for the army. In most cases counties were based on bishoprics and counts and bishops worked closely together – there was no meaningful distinction between Church and State in the Frankish kingdom. Secular and spiritual authority were both wielded to the same end: the protection of Christian society. When newly conquered areas, like Saxony, were organized into counties, Frankish counts were appointed, but elsewhere they were usually men with some local standing. The office of count was in the gift of the king and could in theory be withdrawn. However, this rarely happened and a count was usually succeeded by a son or other close relative. As the authority of the Carolingian dynasty declined, the office became a hereditary one.

Administration of the Carolingian Empire

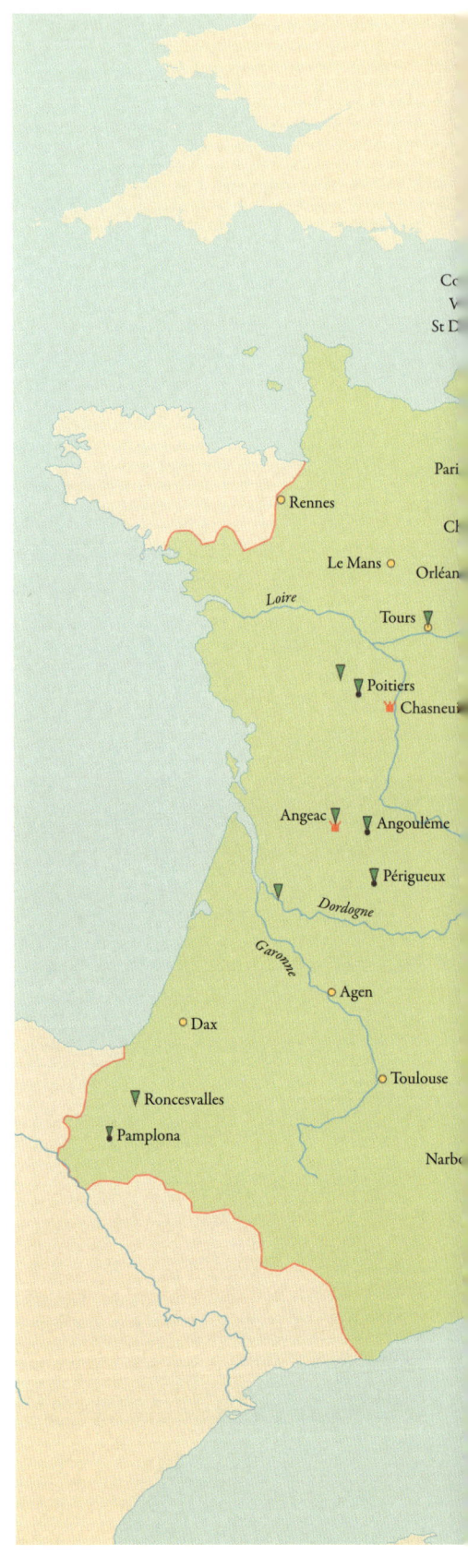

extent of the empire, 812

royal palace or residence

key mint

Rouen key trading place (toll collecting station)

Places Charlemagne visited:

1–4 visits

5 or more visits

VIII THE AGE OF CHARLEMAGNE

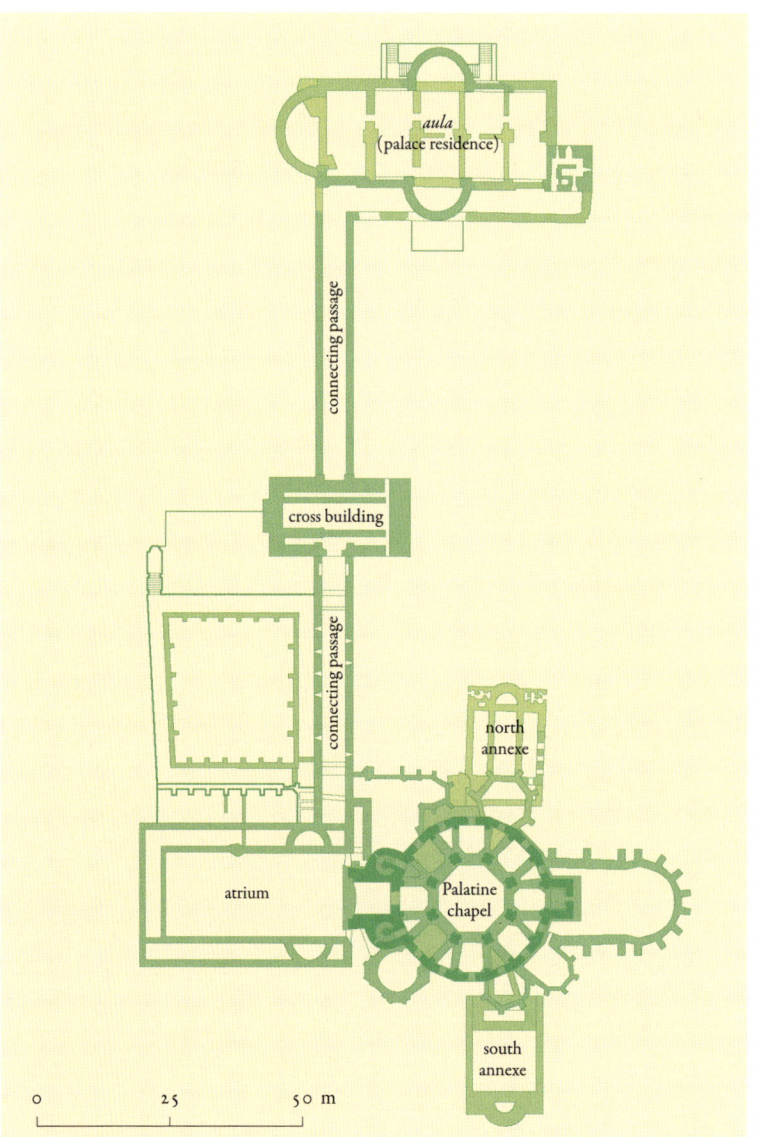

Floor plan of Charlemagne's palace at Aachen.

Counts were sent copies of royal decrees and were duty-bound to make their contents known to the people and oversee their implementation. Each count was assisted by a viscount, who took charge during their absence when they attended court once a year or were on campaign. Counties were organized into larger districts called *missatica*, supervised by two *missi dominici* (royal legates) – one a layman, the other an ecclesiastic – who reported the conduct of counts and bishops to the king. Later in the ninth century, authority was formally devolved, with a number of counties assigned to a duke appointed by the king. In the tenth century these duchies developed into powerful semi-independent principalities that posed a serious challenge to royal authority.

The Carolingian Renaissance

Charlemagne's reign saw a revival of learning which has become known, after him, as the Carolingian Renaissance. The internal peace and prosperity his rule provided was the main factor in this revival but it was actively supported by Charlemagne, who saw it as a means to pursue his goal of reforming society in accordance with Christian doctrine. He invited scholars to his court to educate the Frankish nobility. Charlemagne believed that learning was the key to reform. For the kingdom to prosper it had to be pleasing to God, but how could one know what was pleasing to God without knowledge? As Charlemagne himself put it: 'For although it is better to do what is good than to know it, yet knowing comes before doing.' A well-educated clergy was needed to maintain high standards of worship and teach Christian doctrine to the laity so they would know how to behave as good Christians. Better education for all would benefit the kingdom in other ways, by improving the implementation of legislation and the administration of justice.

Charlemagne could not find enough learned scholars in Francia, so to help him he brought together leading representatives of the three main scholarly traditions of the early medieval west: the Anglo-Saxon, Irish and Italian. Of these it was perhaps the Anglo-Saxon theologian Alcuin who became closest to the emperor. Alcuin was a teacher in the cathedral school at York when he met Charlemagne at Parma in 781 while returning from a mission to Rome. At Charlemagne's invitation, Alcuin set up a school and library, based at the palace in Aachen, stocking it with books from England. The school's main pupils were leading members of the court and their children. It is clear from their correspondence that Alcuin encouraged Charlemagne to adopt a more imperial style of leadership in the 790s and advised him as he prepared for his coronation.

The Carolingian Renaissance

A number of major cultural centres sprang up in the late 8th and the 9th centuries, largely based on religious establishments. They built libraries with the books they produced in their own *scriptoria* and founded schools which principally concentrated on teaching theology.

- extent of the empire, 812
- monastery
- bishopric
- archbishopric
- *scriptorium* (centre of writing)

St Matthew the Evangelist from the Ada Gospels, made in the late 8th–9th century. The book takes its name from a dedication to Charlemagne's sister Ada.

Other significant figures in the circle of scholars close to Charlemagne were the grammarian Peter of Pisa, the Lombard historian Paul the Deacon, Visigoth theologian Theodulf, bishop of Orléans, and Einhard, who was to write Charlemagne's biography. Many of these men were accomplished Latin poets in their spare time. The relations between these scholars, Charlemagne and his family were intimate, sometimes very intimate – the poet Angilbert seduced one of the king's daughters and was packed off to a monastery. The scholars addressed each other using nicknames borrowed from the Bible or Classical history. Alcuin was known as Flaccus Albinus (i.e., the Roman poet Horace); Angilbert was Homer; Charlemagne was, appropriately, David, after the Old Testament king; and his son Pippin was Julius.

Unlike the Renaissance of the fifteenth century, the Carolingian Renaissance did not produce much that was original in art or thought, with the exception of Irish philosopher John Eriugena, who taught at Laon, Francia, in the 840s. But his Neo-Platonist analysis of the evolution of the universe, *On the Division of Nature*, was too out of step with the spirit of his times to be influential. The main aim of the scholars involved in this renaissance was accurate understanding of the scriptures. This explains their seemingly pedantic concern with correct grammar – the word of God should be set down accurately. As it was the main source of Christian knowledge, great effort was put into making copies of the Bible and the works of the Church fathers. Charlemagne was said to be a great admirer of Augustine's *City of God*.

Charlemagne wanted education to be available to all 'those who by the gift of the Lord are able to learn'. In 789 he ordered all monasteries and cathedrals to set up free schools, but is not clear how many complied: the churches in Theodulf's see of Orléans had still not done so in 802. The Carolingian Renaissance ran out of steam before the end of the ninth century, undermined by the decline of the dynasty that had promoted it and the attacks of pagan Vikings and Magyars. However, Charlemagne's reputation created a lasting association between good government and support for intellectual life that later rulers aspired to emulate.

Louis the Pious

The reputation of Louis the Pious (r. 814–40) has suffered by comparison with his father Charlemagne. Louis was a skilled diplomat, but his reign ended in failure and marked the beginning of the long decline of the Carolingian dynasty. In most respects, Louis was a highly able ruler who rose to the challenges of an empire at the natural limits of expansion, confronted by new threats of Viking and Muslim piracy. His problem was that he had too many ambitious sons and wanted to break with Frankish custom and pass on the empire to only one of them.

Louis believed in Charlemagne's project of reforming society on Christian lines, but did not think his father had gone far enough. Louis wanted his empire to mirror the perfect unity that it was believed Christ had intended for his Church. In place of the many local laws and customs, Louis believed there should be only one. In place of the empire's many national identities, there should be only one Christian people. This was an impossible ideal, but Louis made some progress in standardizing the application of law across the empire.

He was more successful in imposing uniformity of practice on the Church. In his reign, the Rule of St Benedict became the basis of

Division of the Carolingian Empire, 829

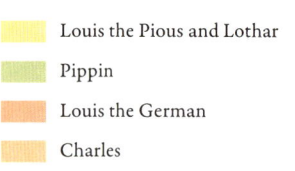

- Louis the Pious and Lothar
- Pippin
- Louis the German
- Charles

monastic life and would remain the most important rule throughout the Middle Ages. Louis respected the popes but did not consider them his equals, describing them merely as his 'helpers' in caring for Christians. Concern for uniformity led naturally to worries over the empire's territorial integrity. Louis did not believe he had the right to divide the empire that God had given him, even out of love for his sons or respect for Frankish tradition. This was something not even Charlemagne had been prepared to do – it had been sheer chance that Louis had been the only son to survive him.

At the time of his accession in 814 Louis already had three sons: Lothar (the eldest), Pippin and Louis the German. In 817 Louis appointed Lothar co-emperor and made Pippin and Louis sub-kings of Aquitaine and Bavaria respectively. But this was as far as he was prepared to subdivide the empire: Lothar would inherit the whole empire and his brothers would remain subordinate to him.

The birth of a son, Charles the Bald, to second wife Judith of Bavaria in 823 was the turning point of Louis's reign. His older sons were not pleased and wanted to cut Charles out of the inheritance. Judith was equally determined that her son should get a fair legacy and there was much sympathy among the Franks for her stance. In 829 Louis granted Alamannia to Charles. Even though Charles was not given the status of sub-king, this provoked Lothar and his brothers to

Charlemagne appointing his son Louis the Pious as co-emperor at Aachen in 813. Louis became sole ruler following his father's death a year later.

rebel in 830, ostensibly to free Louis from the influence of his 'jezebel' wife. The three brothers quarrelled and the rebellion collapsed. Louis abandoned his cherished plans to preserve the unity of the empire and instead provided for its division into four equal kingdoms on his death. This provoked Lothar into another rebellion in 833.

Lothar enjoyed the support of the pro-unity party who were dismayed by Louis's return to the principle of partible inheritance. At the 'Field of Lies' near Colmar in Alsace, Louis met Lothar to settle their differences, but found that his son had been joined by Pippin and Louis the German. Louis was forced to abdicate in a humiliating ceremony, presided over by a reluctant Pope Gregory IV.

Disagreements between Lothar, Pippin and Louis the German quickly allowed Louis to regain his throne, but the abdication had damaged his dynasty's prestige and disorder left the empire prey to Viking attacks. Louis worked energetically to recover his lost authority and when Pippin died in 838 he granted his sub-kingdom of Aquitaine to Charles the Bald, even though this meant disinheriting Pippin's own sons. Nevertheless, the issue of the division of the empire continued to fester. Lothar remained unreconciled to the principle and in 839 Louis had to put down another rebellion by Louis the German. When Louis the Pious died in June 840 no one expected a smooth succession.

The Treaty of Verdun

Louis's task had been simplified by the death of Pippin of Aquitaine in 838 and the unsuccessful rebellion of Louis the German in 839. Lothar was to inherit all of the empire except for West Francia, which would go to Charles the Bald, and Bavaria, which Louis the German would be allowed as his sole inheritance. In return for receiving the lion's share of the empire, Lothar swore that he would uphold this settlement and secure West Francia for Charles, who was still in his teens. Keeping oaths had never been Lothar's strong point. As soon as his father was dead, he went back on his word and attempted to seize the whole empire in a coup against his brothers who, despite their animosity, united against him. Success would be determined by the protagonists' ability to command the loyalty of the counts and dukes, a situation they used to increase their authority at the expense of the monarchy's.

Division of the empire under the Treaty of Verdun, 843

- Charles the Bald
- Lothar (emperor)
- Louis the German
- tributary to the Frankish Empire
- Byzantine Empire
- ✕ battle, with date

Lothar felt that he was in a strong position. He argued that the whole empire was his by right of the agreement of 817, which had made him co-emperor with his father. Having been king of Italy since 822 he was already an experienced ruler with a substantial following of military vassals and could count on the support of the unity party. Louis the German had a loyal following in Bavaria and was a better soldier than Lothar. Charles the Bald's position was the weakest. Still in his teens, he had little experience of leadership and, though his inheritance was a generous one for a younger son, he did not control all of it because, out of loyalty to the memory of Pippin, Aquitaine had chosen his son Pippin II as their king. However, both younger brothers had the sympathy of Frankish traditionalists who saw Lothar's actions as profoundly unjust.

Lothar's hopes of a quick victory were crushed when he was defeated by Charles and Louis the German at the Battle of Fontenoy in June 841. His rivals presented Lothar's defeat as a judgment of God. Charles and Louis strengthened their alliance at Strasbourg in 842. The wording of the oaths sworn by their supporters was preserved and reveals the cultural and linguistic divergence of the East and West Franks: Louis's supporters swore in Old High German, Charles's in the oldest recorded form of French.

The dispute was finally settled by the Treaty of Verdun in 843. The biggest winner was Louis, who received most of Germany. Charles was confirmed in his possession of West Francia (though it was 848 before he could get rid of Pippin II), and Lothar kept the title of emperor but had no sovereignty over his brothers. This division was carefully drawn up by 120 commissioners, 40 from each party, to take account of 'the affinity and convenience of everybody', rather than the economic value of the land as had been the case when the kingdom had been divided by the Merovingians. No lord's lands were divided by an arbitrary border and no king had an enclave in another kingdom. A king could not have vassals in any of his brothers' kingdoms.

The Treaty of Verdun was a decisive defeat for those who believed in the vision of a single united Christian empire, but it is possible to exaggerate its significance. The treaty did not create France or Germany, nor did it mark the disintegration of the Carolingian realm. The Carolingians were Franks and, just as the Merovingians had done before them, they saw the empire as family property. Over the next half century, it was divided and redivided according to the accidents of dynastic survival before it was reunited for the last time under Charles the Fat in 884–87.

Towns, trade and farming

The rise of the Carolingian Empire brought peace and stability to a wide area, helping the modest economic recovery of Merovingian times gather pace. Trade and agriculture developments helped restore the population of western Europe. Economic recovery was strongest in northern Europe around the main centres of Carolingian power. This marked the beginning of the shift of Europe's economic centre from the Mediterranean, where it had been throughout Classical times, to the countries around the lower Rhine and the southern North Sea, where it remains to this day.

Following the fall of the Western Roman Empire, most of the towns that survived in western Europe did so mainly because they were the seats of bishoprics. The presence of bishops made them attractive to such secular officials as counts, who had to work closely with the Church, and as centres of power they continued to attract a certain amount of trade. However, they were shadows of their former selves, with populations numbering in the hundreds rather than thousands. Aachen, the nominal capital of the Carolingian Empire, was little more than a village to which the king and his court were only occasional visitors.

The most important urban settlements of the ninth century were the *emporia* (or *wics*, as they were called in Anglo-Saxon England), which had begun to develop as trade centres in Merovingian times near the mouths of navigable rivers around the North Sea. The most successful *emporium* was Dorestad on the lower Rhine which, with a population of perhaps 2,000, may have been the largest town in northern Europe in 800. Like other known *emporia*, Dorestad was an unprepossessing place, with wooden houses, warehouses and craft workshops clustered around the wharves, as well as a long suburb of smallholdings, which supplied the craftworkers and merchants with food. Textiles, metalworking, jewelry, basket-weaving, bone-working and shipbuilding were the main trades. The town was a major centre for the export of Rhineland products such as lava quernstones and glass,

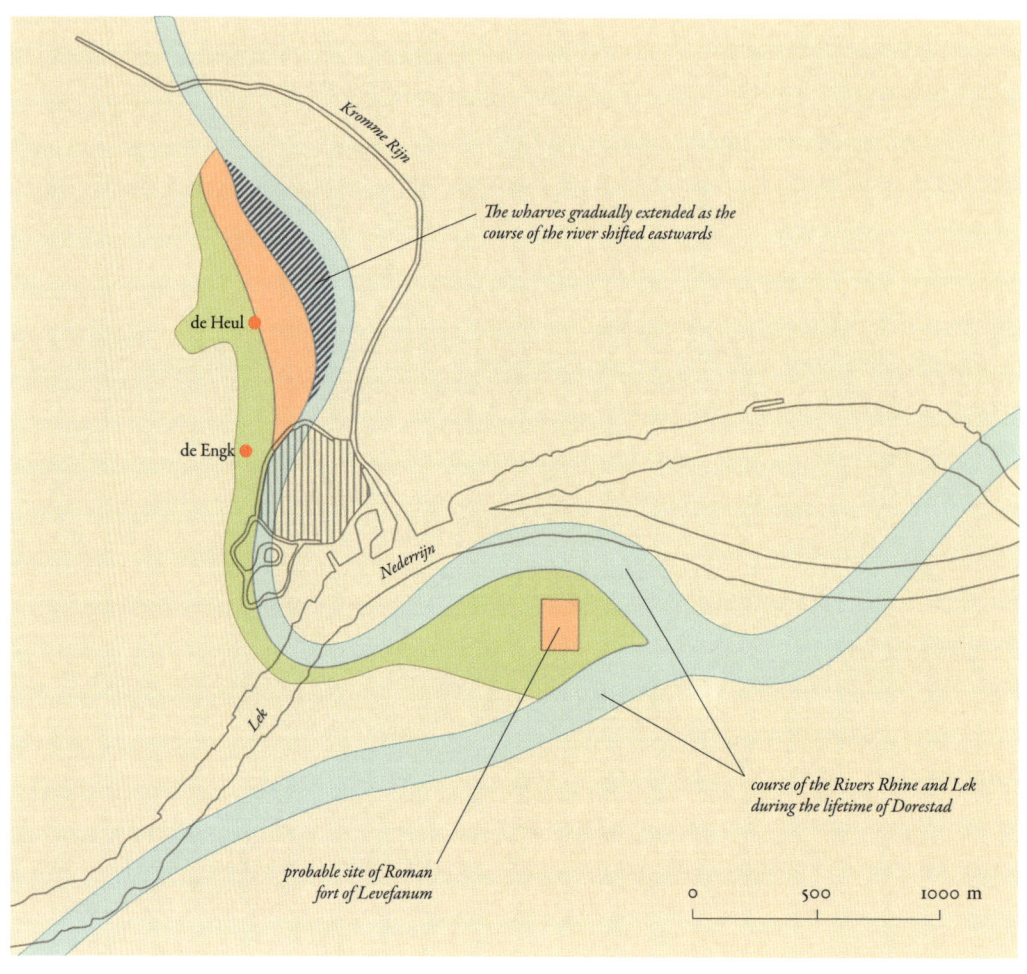

The emporium of Dorestad

- northern harbour (wharves)
- northern *vicus* (main commercial/industrial zone)
- agrarian zone (occupants mainly engaged in farming)
- medieval Dorestad
- cemetery
- present course of Rivers Rhine and Lek

This was the most important trading centre in northern Europe during the Carolingian period, although it was little more than a small village surrounded by landholdings.

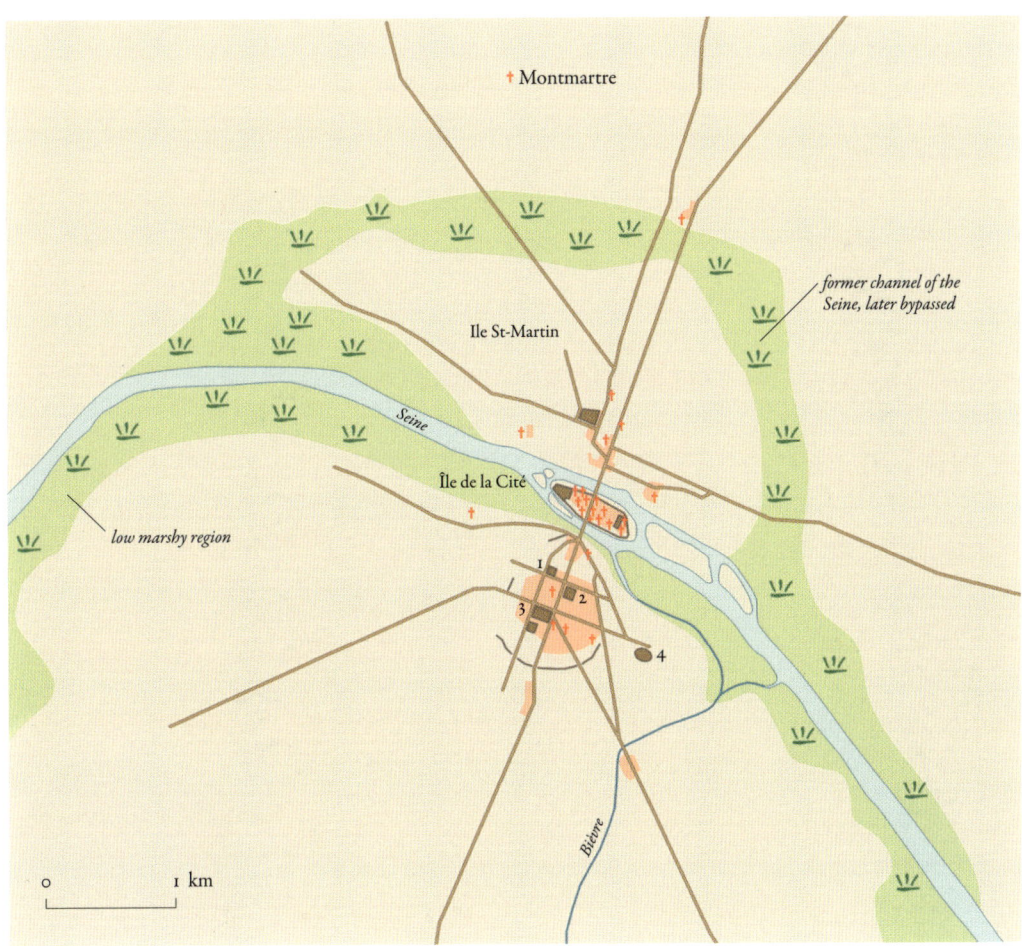

Paris in the Carolingian era

† church or other religious building

1 Cluny baths
2 Roman *thermae* (baths)
3 site of Roman forum
4 site of Roman amphitheatre

Paris first became politically important under the Merovingians when Clovis chose the former Roman town as his main residence. Under the early Carolingians, whose main centres were towards the Rhineland, Paris declined but its importance was restored after the Treaty of Verdun when it became the main centre of the West Frankish kingdom, later France.

and perhaps bulk commodities like grain, to Scandinavia and England. No doubt these were exchanged for perishable imports, such as furs, hides and slaves.

At Quentovic, an *emporium* of comparable size to Dorestad sited on the Canche near Étaples, a similar range of trades was practised. Archaeological finds indicate that its trade was mainly with England. Both towns had prolific mints in Charlemagne's reign. Used to pay foreign merchants, these coins helped promote the image of Charlemagne as a great ruler abroad. Charlemagne founded a number of *emporia* on the eastern frontier to promote and regulate trade with the Slavs. A downside of the increased economic activity was that it attracted pirates. Dorestad and Quentovic were both sacked several times by Vikings in the ninth century but recovered quickly.

The volume of trade around the North Sea is hard to judge. Many merchants must have been little more than travelling tinkers. Charlemagne complained to King Offa of Mercia that Anglo-Saxon merchants were posing as pilgrims to avoid paying tolls on their goods. No Carolingian trade ships are known, but Scandinavian vessels of the period could carry cargoes of nearly 40 tons, so some merchants operated on a large scale. Trade only marginally impinged on the lives of most Europeans, who were free or servile peasants engaged in subsistence agriculture. In most of Europe at the beginning of the Middle Ages, farmers practised the two-field system of crop rotation which had been introduced from the Middle East thousands of years earlier, along with farming itself. In this system, one field was cultivated, while the second was left fallow and grazed by livestock whose dung helped replenish the fertility of the soil.

In the Carolingian period this immemorial system began to be replaced by the three-field system, which originated in the area between the Loire and the Rhine and spread to the rest of northern Europe and Britain. The three-field system had the advantage of allowing more arable land to be cultivated, since only a third was left fallow. Of the two fields under cultivation, one was usually planted with grain, the other with legumes or root crops, alleviating the danger of complete crop failure inherent in the two-field system. Further improvements in productivity came from the introduction of the heavy wheeled plough. As a result of agricultural improvements, Europe's population began to bounce back from the depopulation that had accompanied the decline of the Roman Empire.

A silver *denarius* of the emperor Charlemagne, struck in 812–14 with the inscription KAROLVS IMP AVG (*Karolus Imperator Augustus*).

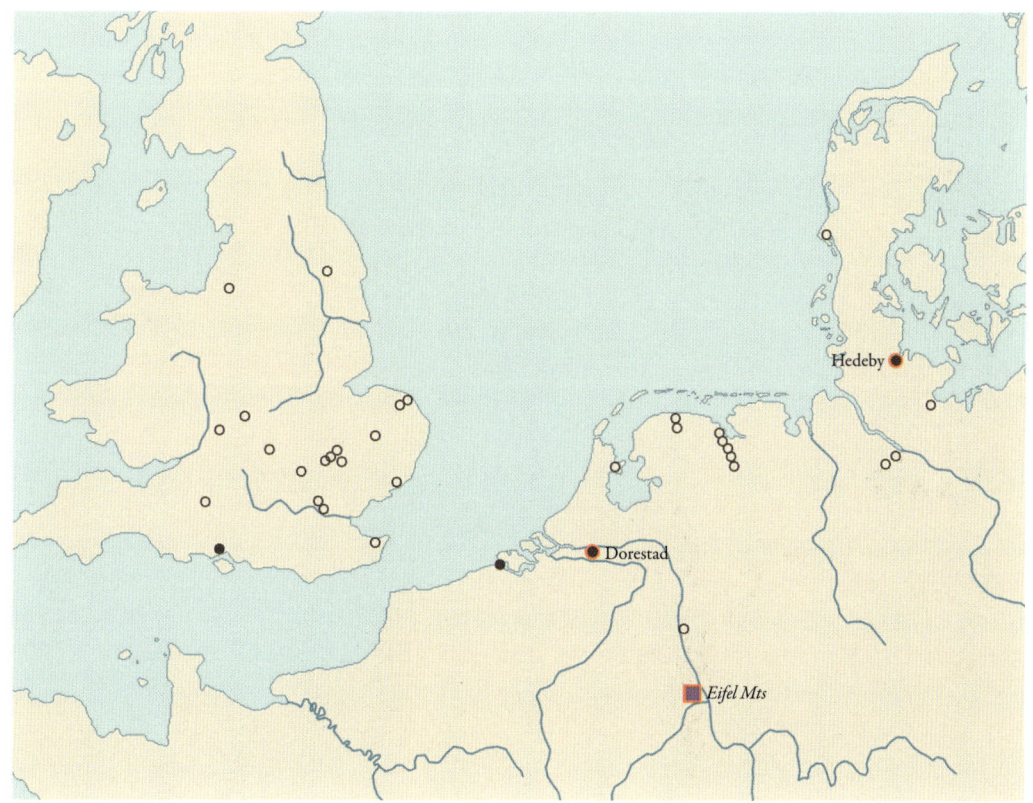

Distribution of Eifel mountain quernstones

- major site
- minor group, individual finds
- lava quarries
- finishing site

The Carolingian Empire was successful at stimulating international trade in prestige items, such as the 'black stones' (*petrae negrae*) mentioned in a letter of Charlemagne's to King Offa. The lava quernstones quarried in the Eifel mountains to the north of Koblenz – used in milling grain – were highly prized.

IX
Saints and Scholars

Educating hearts and minds

Though Christianity was already established in Europe by AD 313, Constantine's edict of toleration in that year gave it a great boost. Thanks to imperial patronage, it was the majority religion in the Roman Empire by the early fifth century. Large parts of Britain and Gaul reverted to paganism as a result of Germanic invasions, but this setback was short-lived. Despite the loss of Spain to Islam in the eighth century, the vast majority of Europeans were Christian by the year 1000. And by that time, the most important institution in Europe was the Christian Church. It provided continuity with the institutions and learning of the Roman world, preserved the Latin language, provided secular rulers with most of their literate administrators, patronized artists and scholars, and offered salvation for the common people.

In the early Middle Ages, missionary activity was not centrally directed. The evangelization of Ireland was launched by the Church in Gaul and Britain, and the Irish Church later launched missions to the Picts, Anglo-Saxons and Franks. Augustine of Canterbury's mission to the Anglo-Saxons in 597 was the papacy's first major initiative, but despite its claimed leadership of the Church, it never controlled the missionary effort. The Greek Orthodox Church was also active in evangelization and competed with the Roman Catholic Church for influence in central Europe.

The cover of the Codex Aureus (Golden Book) of St Emmeran, a richly illuminated gospel made in 870. Made of gold, the cover is set with emeralds, sapphires and pearls and has the figure of Christ in Majesty at its centre.

The conversion of Europe to AD 1000

- Christian area, 600
- converted to Christianity, 600–1000
- pagan area, c. 1000
- area largely Muslim in religion, 1000
- approximate border between Roman Catholic and Greek Orthodox Christians, 1000
- border of Roman Empire (effective limit of Christianity, c. 400)
- patriarchate
- British and Gaulish mission, 5th century
- Irish mission, 6th–7th centuries
- Anglo-Saxon mission, 8th century
- German mission, 9th–10th centuries
- Byzantine mission, 9th–10th centuries

Missions were frequently an extension of diplomacy and imperialism. Carolingian rulers sponsored missions to the Frisians and Saxons as a way of extending their influence. Tenth-century German emperors did the same for the Slavs who, recognizing the imperialist intent, called Christ 'the German god'. Christian rulers regarded hostility to Christianity as justification for war; for Charlemagne, conquest of the pagan Saxons went hand in hand with forced conversion. As polytheists, many pagans initially accepted Christ as just one more god to be worshipped; Kjartan, a tenth-century Viking, agreed to become Christian so long as he could still worship Thor. Once the basic belief had taken root, missionaries could eliminate the remnants of pagan beliefs.

A decisive moment in any mission was the conversion of a king, as many of his subjects would follow suit, for political expediency if not out of conviction. The attraction of Christianity for the warlike kings of the Dark Ages may seem obscure, but they would have identified with much in the Old Testament and its many warrior kings. They were aware of the advantages of the powerful ideology of rule by divine grace, which placed kings far above their subjects. Diplomatic considerations were also a factor. For the Rus' prince Vladimir, conversion was the price of an advantageous marriage alliance with the Byzantine Empire. For the Danish king Harald Bluetooth, it meant one less point of conflict with the Holy Roman Empire.

Recognizing the insincerity of forced conversion, missionaries were often surprisingly sensitive to pagan sentiment and tried to ease the transition in various ways. Pagan festivals were Christianized – from around 336, for example, the birth of Christ was celebrated on the day of the Roman pagan festival of *Dies Natalis Solis Invicti* (Birthday of the Sun of Righteousness), 25 December. Pagan deities were sometimes adopted, rather spuriously, as Christian saints. The popular Irish saint Brigid was originally a pagan goddess and her feast day, 1 February, matched a pagan fire festival.

Again in Ireland, missionaries founded churches in close association with important pagan sanctuaries, such as St Patrick's see of Armagh, within sight of the ancient cult centre of Emain Macha. Pope Gregory I (p. 590–604) forbade Augustine and his missionaries in England from destroying pagan temples, instructing them to eradicate the idols and purify the buildings with holy water. Gregory's hope was that people would more readily come to listen to Christian teachings at familiar places. This relatively tolerant attitude ensured that many pagan beliefs survived the conversion process and passed into European folklore.

Rise of the papacy

By the eleventh century, the bishop of Rome, better known as the pope (meaning 'father'), was recognized as the spiritual leader of western Christendom. The idea that the pope should exercise supreme authority over the Church was developed in the third century and adopted as official policy by Pope Damasus I in 381. The papacy's claim to supremacy was based on its foundation by the apostle Peter, to whom Christ had said, 'You are Peter and on this rock I will build my church and the gates of hell shall not prevail against it. And to you I will give the keys to the kingdom of heaven, and whatever you bind on earth shall be bound in heaven, and whatever you loose on earth shall be loosed in heaven' (Matthew 16:18–19).

The papacy argued that this was Christ's commission to Peter, and his successors as bishops of Rome, to exercise supremacy over the whole Church as God's representative on Earth, in much the same way as the divinely appointed emperor exercised supremacy over the Roman state. At that time the bishop of Rome was recognized, along with the bishops of Constantinople, Antioch, Jerusalem and Alexandria, as one of the patriarchs of the Church. Patriarchs had superior dignity to other bishops, but only had authority over those in their own provinces. The papacy's grand claims were therefore denied not only by the other patriarchs but by most other bishops as well, who adhered to the early Church's consensual tradition of decision-making.

The first steps to making papal supremacy a reality were taken by Gregory I when he organized the evangelization of Anglo-Saxons. Gregory maintained papal control of the Anglo-Saxon Church by insisting that newly appointed archbishops go to Rome to receive the *pallium* (the strip of white cloth signifying the office of archbishop) from the pope.

No archbishop could take up his post without papal approval or without acknowledging the pope's ultimate authority. Out of gratitude for the central role it had played in its creation, the Anglo-Saxon

Growth of the Papal State, 756–962

- duchy of Rome before 756
- donation of Pippin, 756
- territory acquired, 757–74
- territory acquired, 781–89
- Byzantine territory
- ──● land and town under effective papal control, 962
- ● archdiocese
- † important monastery
- ········· border, c. 756

IX SAINTS AND SCHOLARS

Church was intensely loyal to the papacy. When Anglo-Saxon missionaries became active on the continent, they automatically sought papal approval for their missions and introduced the practice of receiving the *pallium* from the pope, as Clement and Boniface did when they founded archbishoprics at Mainz and Utrecht in the early eighth century. This practice soon became universal in the Frankish kingdom, giving credibility to the papacy's claims of supremacy. It triumphantly demonstrated the newfound prestige when Pippin III (r. 751–68) sought papal approval for his overthrow of the Merovingian dynasty in 751.

Another significant factor in the papacy's rise was the Muslim conquest of the Middle East and North Africa, which marginalized the patriarchates of Antioch, Jerusalem and Alexandria. The patriarchs of Constantinople would never accept papal supremacy, but the Byzantine emperors' frequent interference in doctrinal matters meant that claims to equal status with Rome carried little weight in the Latin west. While the popes were also subjects of the Byzantine emperor and were not immune to imperial interference, their distance from Constantinople allowed greater independence. They also gained prestige from Rome's imperial past.

A 9th–10th-century Byzantine reliquary. Usually made of precious materials, reliquaries are shrines for keeping the physical remains or other objects, such as clothing, associated with saints.

The papacy was vulnerable to attack, notably by the Lombards, and it seized the chance to ally with the Franks. In 754 Pope Stephen II used a forged document, the Donation of Constantine, to persuade Pippin to hand over the former Byzantine territories of the duchy of Rome and the Exarchate of Ravenna. In the document Emperor Constantine is purported to grant Pope Sylvester I primacy over the other patriarchs, dominion over Italy, the right of judgment over the clergy and even the imperial crown (which Sylvester modestly refused). Pippin was much in the papacy's debt and happily confirmed its right to these lands, which were not legally his to grant. The Donation of Pippin, as it became known, effectively founded the medieval Papal State.

Dark Age Rome

The early Middle Ages really was a 'Dark Age' for Rome. From around one million at the time of the Visigothic sack in 410, Rome's population had declined to only about 50,000 by the sixth century; large areas of the city had been completely depopulated, largely as a consequence of the wholesale destruction of its aqueducts when Witigis besieged Belisarius within the city's walls. Yet even in ruins Rome continued to awe its visitors.

As the seat of the papacy and home to innumerable holy relics, Rome was a place of immense spiritual power and an object lesson in the transience of earthly glory. The fabric of Rome did not suffer terribly from the barbarian invasions. The sack of the city by the Visigoths in 410 was a strangely respectful affair, and if the sack by the Vandals in 455 was more destructive, the damage was insignificant compared to that done by the Romans themselves. As early as the mid-fifth century the emperor Majorian deplored 'the detestable process which has been going on, whereby the face of the venerable city is disfigured'. Countless public buildings were stripped of their marble veneers, sculpted columns and other materials for re-use, often in churches that were being built to honour the martyrs of imperial persecutions.

Under Ostrogothic rule from 489, life continued much as before. The Roman Senate still met, there were chariot races in the circus and King Theodoric even provided an annual corn dole for the poor. The real disaster was Justinian's reconquest of Italy. Repeatedly besieged, Rome changed hands between imperial and Ostrogothic forces three times. By the end of the wars, starvation, disease and flight had reduced the population, and the senatorial and consular system collapsed. Rome remained under imperial control after the Lombards invaded Italy in 568, but its defence was a low priority for the hard-pressed empire.

In the political vacuum, the popes emerged as the city's *de facto* rulers, organizing public works, food supplies and defence against the Lombards. As papal influence grew in the seventh century, increasing numbers of pilgrims began to visit Rome, both for the spiritual merit of the journey itself and to see the miracle-working bodies of the holy martyrs, neatly stacked and labelled in the suburban catacombs. The needs of pilgrims were served by guesthouses, souvenir sellers and even guidebooks, while scholars had places of study. People migrated to Rome from as far away as Greece, Syria and northern Europe, causing tensions with the native population, who felt they were being marginalized.

Under the popes, the focus of the city shifted away from the Forum to the Lateran palace, home of the popes, and across the Tiber to

Rome in the early medieval period

- —— principal road
- inhabited area, c. 500
- inhabited area, 10th century
- ⌁⌁⌁ Aurelian wall (built 270)
- ☿ Christian church, c. 500
- ☩ church, c. 500–600
- ☩ church, c. 600–700
- ☩ church founded after 750
- ⚵ major Latin monastery to 700
- ☧ major Eastern monastery to 700
- ⊕ catacomb
- ancient Roman ruin
- ancient building in reasonable condition

Ancient Roman bridges crossing the Tiber still in use or in ruins:

1. Aelian bridge
2. Bridge of Nero (ruin)
3. Bridge of Agrippa
4. Aurelian bridge
5. Pons Fabricius
6. Pons Cestius
7. Aemilian bridge
8. Pons Sublicus (ruin)
9. Bridge of Probius

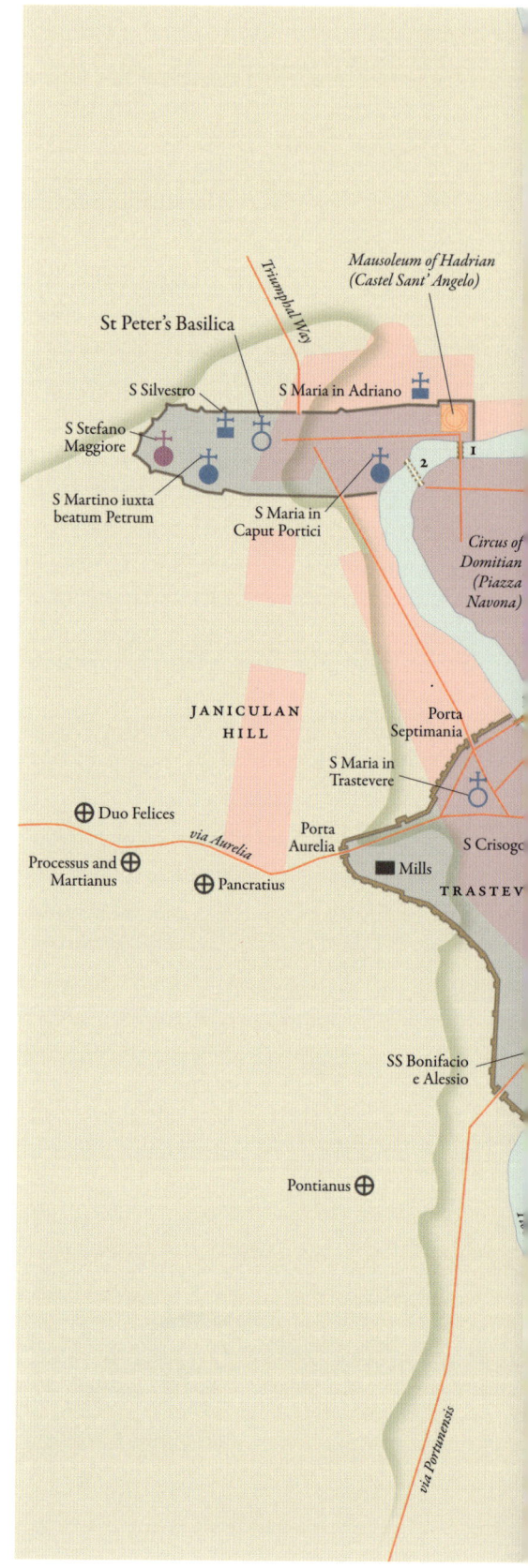

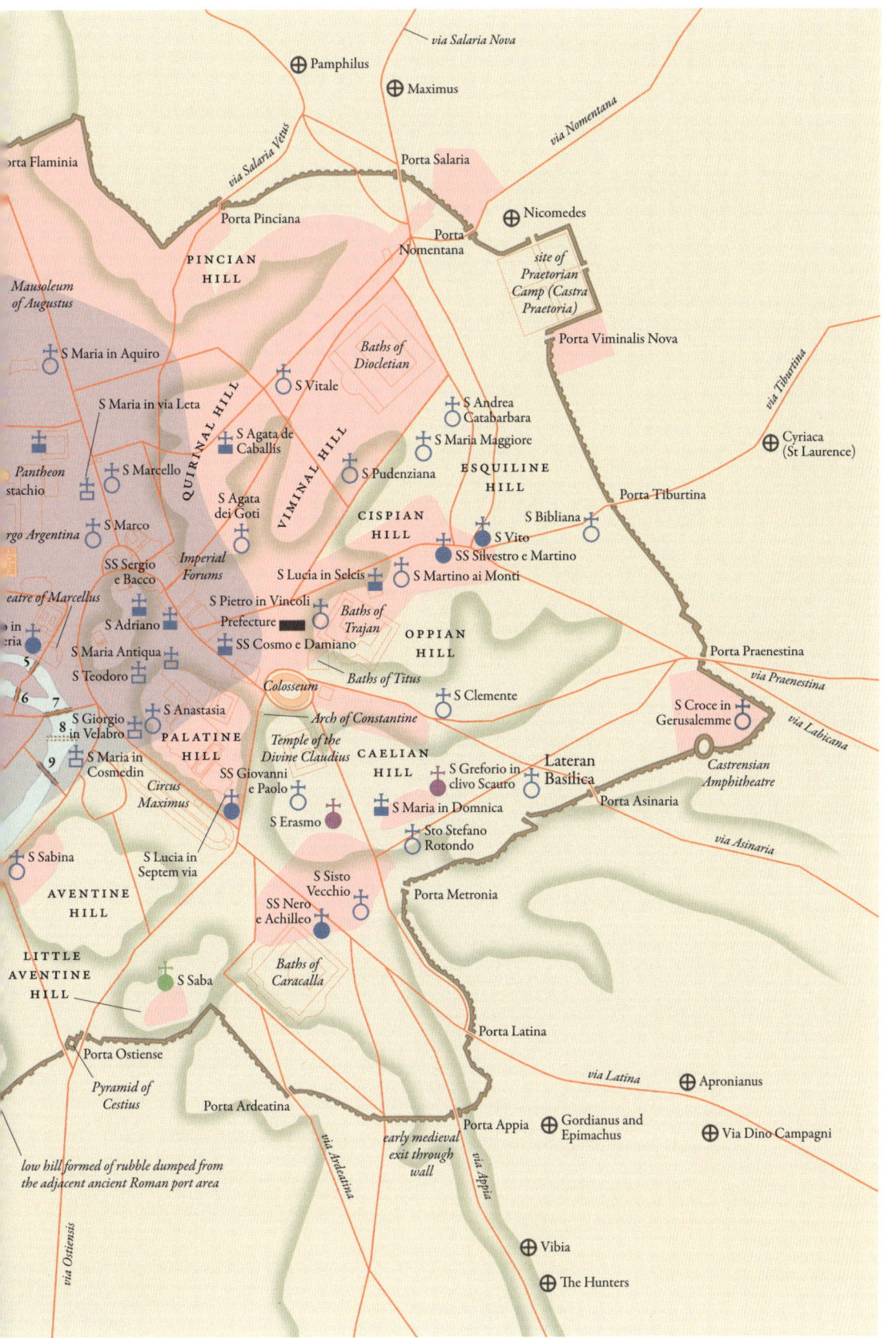

IX SAINTS AND SCHOLARS

the complex of churches and monasteries around St Peter's basilica. Most of the great public buildings of Classical times fell into decay, especially in the old Forum. The modern visitor may look up at the church of San Lorenzo, erected inside the scaffold of columns that once supported the temple of Antonius Pius and Faustina, and note that the church's doorway appears to be halfway up the wall – an indication of how high the rubble of the Forum had risen by that time. However, a few buildings found new uses. In 609 Boniface IV converted the Pantheon into a church dedicated to the Virgin Mary, while Hadrian's mausoleum became a fortified refuge for the popes, the Castel Sant' Angelo.

By allying with the Franks in the 750s, the papacy effectively declared independence from the Byzantine Empire. After his conquest of the Lombards in 774, Charlemagne lavished gifts on the popes. The late eighth and early ninth centuries was a time of vigorous church building and restoration in Rome. With the coronation of Charlemagne as emperor in 800, Rome felt like an imperial city once more.

The decline of the Carolingian dynasty in the ninth century left Rome unprotected, and in 846 St Peter's was sacked by Muslim

An 18th-century replica of a now lost 9th-century mosaic in the papal Lateran Palace in Rome showing Christ and the Apostles. On either side are scenes symbolizing the secular ruler's responsibility to protect the Church.

pirates. In response, Pope Leo IV (p. 847–55) built a wall around the Vatican, creating what came to be known as the Leonine City. By the late ninth century the papacy had fallen under the corrupting control of Rome's noble families, who manipulated the office in their own interests. Only the intervention of the German emperors saved it from being totally discredited. Rome's population continued to fall and by the eleventh century its 30,000 inhabitants occupied only a quarter of the land within the walls.

Monasticism

Christian monasticism was born in the Egyptian desert in the early fourth century, spreading to other wild areas like the Judaean desert and the badlands of Cappadocia in Anatolia. Many Christians, dismayed by the way the Church was becoming a part of the Roman state, chose an austere, celibate, ascetic life over wealth and comfort. Some, like St Anthony (d. 365), became anchorites (solitary hermits); others, like his contemporary Pachomius, created a cenobitic mission, which is an enclosed self-supporting community devoted to prayer and recreating the simple life of the apostles. Egyptian-style monasticism was spread to the West by the eastern monk John Cassian (Johannes Cassianus, 360–435) at the end of the fourth century, and in the fifth century it became the basis for Celtic monasticism, which emphasized an ascetic way of life and physical endurance.

The first rule for monastic living – setting out a daily routine of prayer, study and manual work – was written by the Greek theologian Basil the Great (330–379). This still forms the basis of monastic life in the Orthodox Church. The most influential rule in the West was written by St Benedict of Nursia, who founded the monastery of Monte Cassino in the mid-sixth century. Benedict rejected the extreme eremitic austerity of Egyptian monasticism – he wanted ordinary men to be able to follow his rule. Rather than extreme self-denial, Benedict emphasized life-long commitment to a cenobitic way of life in a single monastery and obedience to its abbot. This mirrored the papacy's authoritarian and hierarchical approach to Church government. Benedictine monasticism was introduced to England in the late seventh century, where it quickly supplanted Celtic monasticism. Under the influence of Benedict of Aniane,

Overleaf: Carved directly into soft volcanic tuff, the 11th-century Karanlık Kilise ('Dark Church') at Göreme in Cappadocia is one of several rock-cut monastic churches in the area, known for their vivid Byzantine frescoes.

IX SAINTS AND SCHOLARS

Emperor Louis the Pious tried to enforce Benedictine rule on all monasteries in the Carolingian Empire; by the tenth century its dominance was unchallenged.

Despite the ideal of withdrawal from the world, most monasteries were intimately engaged with secular society. They depended on donations of land and money from lay benefactors, who in return expected spiritual benefits, such as Masses for the salvation of their souls and prayers for the protection of their land and subjects. In a very real sense support for monasteries was part of the defence budget: soldiers fought human enemies with weapons, monks fought the Devil with prayer.

As the leading cultural centres of early medieval Europe, monasteries were the main providers of education. They also provided respectable homes and careers for the younger sons and unmarried daughters of the nobility; entering a monastery was rarely an option for the poor. Monasteries had duties of hospitality to their benefactors and were often visited by kings and nobles. Irish kings had such confidence

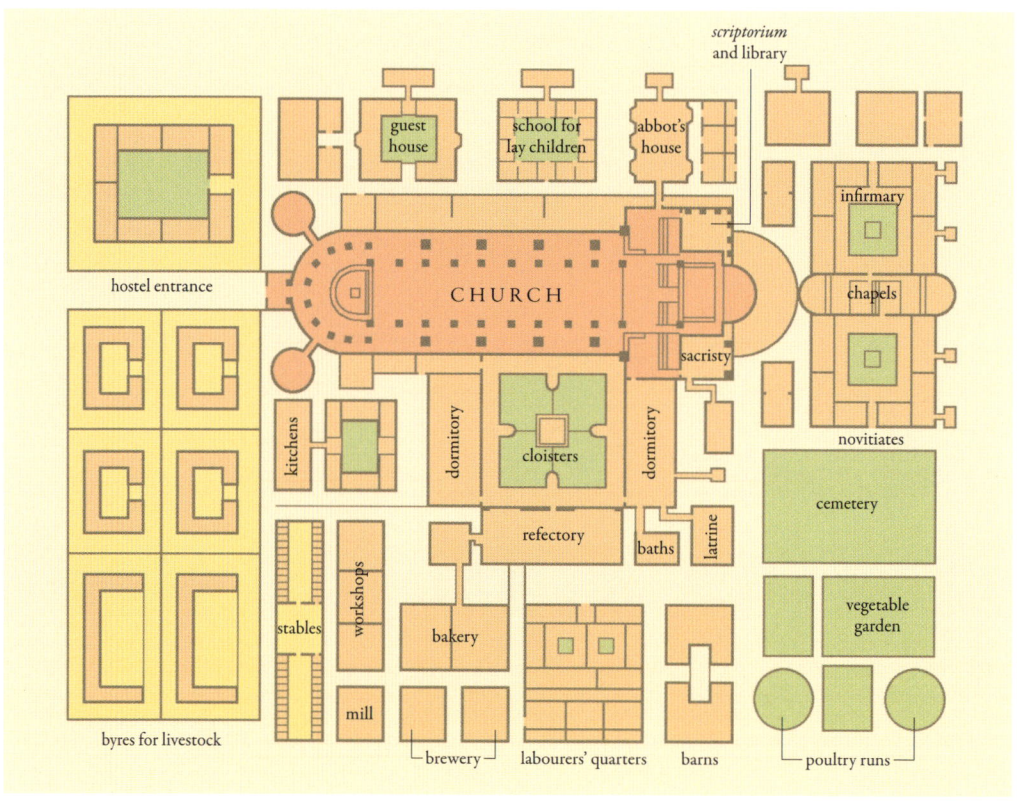

This plan shows the idealized layout of a Benedictine monastery, based on St Gallen, Switzerland.

in the protection of the saints that they often had their treasuries in monasteries. For Carolingian rulers monasteries served as a relatively humane gulag where political prisoners could be supervised and put to useful work praying for the good of the kingdom.

Monasteries also had an important economic function as major landowners and centres of consumption. A monastery needed hundreds of calfskins to produce enough parchment for a single gospel book, precious metals and jewels to decorate its cover, and exotic pigments to illuminate its pages. Outside great monasteries like Monte Cassino, small settlements called *vici* (after the Roman settlements that housed camp followers of a permanent military fort) developed where craftsmen in stone, wood, metals and glass plied their trades and merchants could sell their wares.

Their wealth made monasteries attractive targets for Viking and Muslim pirates and Magyar marauders. The monastery of Luxeuil in Burgundy was sacked by all three between 886 and 924, but managed to survive. Many other monasteries were abandoned. The disruption led to a decline of monastic standards. It became common for laymen to be given abbacies and some monks even married. A vigorous reform movement developed in the tenth century, beginning with the foundation of the monastery of Cluny in Burgundy in 909. Famous for its strict observance of the rule of St Benedict and the beauty and magnificence of its services, Cluny became a model for other reformed monasteries, and inspired the papal reform movement of the eleventh century.

Christianity and civilization in late antiquity

The greatest intellectual and artistic achievements of the early Middle Ages were inspired by Christianity. Religion's dominance began with the education system. Early medieval education was based on the 'seven liberal arts' defined in the *Philologia*, an encyclopaedia by Martianus Capella, a fifth-century North African pagan writing in Carthage during Vandal rule. The curriculum was divided into two parts: the Trivium (grammar, rhetoric and dialectic), which was taught first, and the Quadrivium (arithmetic, geometry, music and astronomy). The obvious difference between this and modern curricula is that it does not attempt to convey

IX SAINTS AND SCHOLARS

a body of knowledge but concentrates on intellectual and literary skills, the point being that, to the medieval mind, a student needed to know how to think and express himself (or more rarely, herself) in order to learn effectively.

In the Classical world the main purpose of education was secular: to equip students for a role in public life. Though the curriculum was based on that of Classical times, the main purpose of education throughout late antiquity and the Middle Ages was to acquire Christian knowledge and understanding. For this reason education was mostly provided by the Church, either at monasteries or, from the tenth century, at cathedral schools. Most educated people stayed in the Church as monks or secular clergy, for there

A page from the Book of Kells depicting the symbols of the four Evangelists, decorated in the Hiberno-Saxon style which blended Celtic geometrical motifs with Anglo-Saxon animal interlace. The book was created *c.* 800, probably at the Scottish island monastery of Iona.

were few opportunities for them to use their education elsewhere. Because of the essentially religious outlook of the times, the majority of early medieval literary output was theological, especially biblical commentaries and hagiography, but encyclopaedias and books on history, grammar, poetry, philosophy, mathematics, law and music were also written. Many monasteries kept annals of contemporary events. Little attention was paid to the natural sciences, the most notable work of the period being a treatise on the tides by Bede, which was not to be surpassed until Newton's time.

There was little emphasis on originality of thought. The two most original thinkers of the period, the ninth-century theologians John Eriugena and Gottschalk, were both criticized for their heterodox conclusions. Nevertheless, it was the plodding scholarship of the early Middle Ages that finally exposed the inconsistencies of the scriptures, which in turn fuelled the search for new intellectual tools that characterized the so-called 'twelfth-century renaissance'.

Latin was the accepted language of learning in western Europe, but there were undoubtedly traditions of orally transmitted vernacular literature, such as legendary tales and heroic poetry. However, because of the prestige of Latin, this was rarely committed to paper except in England and Ireland. Book production was a religious as well as a practical activity. The greatest efforts were put into copying the Bible so that reliable texts could be as widely distributed as possible. Books were copied by monks working in monastic *scriptoria* (writing offices) as devotional acts.

The finest books were elaborately illuminated and bound within jewel-encrusted covers. Eighth-century Irish and Anglo-Saxon gospel books, such as the Book of Kells and the Lindisfarne Gospels, are famous for their 'carpet' pages of intricate interlaced patterns. There are also worthy continental rivals, such as the ninth-century Codex Aureus of St Emmeram in Germany, which has covers of gold encrusted with emeralds and gold lettering on pages dyed with expensive Tyrian purple. It is not surprising that illiterate Vikings looted books. Legibility was not sacrificed for decorative effect, however. Early medieval scripts are notable for their clarity, especially the beautiful Carolingian minuscule script which spread across the Frankish Empire during Charlemagne's reign. The practice of leaving distinct spaces between words was an early medieval innovation to make reading easier.

IX SAINTS AND SCHOLARS

Most monumental architecture of late antiquity was based on Greco-Roman models, in particular the basilica, which inspired both churches and palaces. It was not until the Carolingian period that there was any experimentation. New churches were built with imposing west-facing entrances (westworks) flanked by towers, the solid pillars of Classical times replaced by stronger composite piers to support the walls and roof. Changes to the internal layout of churches made them more convenient for worshippers, notably the introduction of the ambulatory, a passage leading around the east end of a church behind its altar, allowing people to move around the building without disrupting services. It was from these innovations that the solid, dominating, Romanesque architectural style of the early Middle Ages emerged in the tenth century.

Culture and religion in Byzantium

The Byzantine Empire had its own counterpart to the west's cultural decline. Military disasters after Justinian's reign brought political and economic decline that left few resources for the arts. While the empire struggled for survival, the literary and artistic traditions of the Roman world were lost. Byzantine patrons lacked the wealth to commission sculptures and artwork. Great public architecture was simply unaffordable. Between the early seventh century and the early ninth century, literary activity almost died out. The dearth of cultural endeavour was reinforced in the early eighth century by the iconoclast controversy, which stifled the production of religious art. The veneration of religious images of Christ, the saints and prophets had always been important to Orthodox Christians, but likewise there had always been those who believed their use was against the Ten Commandments. The spectacular Arab advance in the seventh century strengthened the critics' case, because it seemed plain that the empire had lost God's favour. Moreover, the Arabs' Islamic religion condemned religious images as idolatry.

Taking a spectacular volcanic eruption on Thera in 726 as a final warning from God, Emperor Leo III (r. 717–41) introduced a policy of iconoclasm ('image smashing') and religious paintings and sculptures in churches were whitewashed over, removed or smashed. Clergy who opposed iconoclasm, like the patriarch Germanos, were removed and

Gold *solidus* of the Byzantine emperor Leo III, whose policy of iconoclasm caused division in the Orthodox Church for a century.

persecuted. Pope Gregory II (p.715–31) condemned iconoclasm as heretical, but Leo was powerless to carry out his threat of deposition. Iconoclasm became just one more issue driving east and west apart. Leo's successes in battle made iconoclasm popular in the army, but following military reverses later in the century, opinion shifted and veneration of icons was restored by Empress Irene after the second Council of Nicaea in 786. Significantly, this was the last truly ecumenical council of the Church. The iconoclasts regained power in 815 and a second period of iconoclasm followed. The final overthrow of iconoclasm in 843 is still celebrated in the Orthodox Church as the Feast of Orthodoxy.

The end of iconoclasm led to a revival of Byzantine art as the imperial court sponsored the redecoration of churches on an even grander scale than before. As the political fortunes of the empire revived in the late ninth century there was an increase in private patronage of the arts, which saw a flowering of miniature painting, manuscript illumination, ivory carving and ornamental metalworking. Artists drew their inspiration from surviving examples of Classical art, but modified it to suit Christian tastes. Monumental sculpture was not revived: the Byzantine Empire lacked the appropriate public settings where it could have enhanced its subjects' reputations.

Literature also revived but, in contrast to the west, the most prominent figures were civil servants rather than monks. Like their counterparts in the Carolingian Renaissance, Greek scholars were concerned with grammar for the purpose of correct understanding of religious texts, and had a similar desire to revive the literary forms of late antiquity. The Byzantine revival was more important for its preservation work: the earliest surviving copies of the works of Thucydides, Herodotus, Aeschylus, Sophocles and many other Classical Greek authors date from this period. Constantine VII Porphyrogenitus (r. 913–59) made an enormous contribution to the preservation of ancient literature by commissioning huge compilations of texts on a range of subjects, including agriculture, medicine, zoology, history, veterinary science, foreign affairs, administration and hagiography. Texts were not copied at random, or even simply because they were old, but because they were considered to contain useful information or were examples of good literary style. This has to a large extent determined what we know about ancient Greek culture, because what the Byzantines did not think was useful or stylish has not survived.

Impressive though its achievements were, the Byzantine revival was almost entirely confined to Constantinople and never extended beyond an elite circle of a few hundred people. This was largely because the high cost of books put them out of reach of all but the richest individuals and institutions. Archbishop Arethas of Caesarea (d. *c.* 932) kept records of the cost of the manuscripts he commissioned. His copy of Euclid's *Elements* cost fourteen gold pieces, while his 471-folio (942 pages) copy of Plato's works cost thirteen gold pieces for copying and eight for parchment. In comparison, the average salary for a court dignitary was seventy-two gold pieces per year.

The Jews and Europe

In most of Christian Europe, Jews were the only significant religious minority during the early Middle Ages. Prejudice was widespread among Christians but, with few exceptions, Jews did not face the violent anti-Semitism so prevalent later in the Middle Ages and were grudgingly tolerated for the role they played in international trade. Despite a history of Jewish rebellion, systematic discrimination against Jews in the Roman Empire only began in the late fourth century after Christianity became the official religion. Marriage between Jews and Christians became illegal and Jews who tried to convert Christians faced the death penalty. Synagogues could only be repaired if they were in imminent danger of collapse and could be confiscated for Christian use. Jewish clergy were subject to burdensome fiscal penalties, and the right of Jews to own slaves was curtailed.

It is plain that discrimination and prejudice continued under the Germanic kings in the west, but for the most part it was of a casual, disparaging nature, as when the papal biographer compared the conspirators who tried to overthrow Pope Leo III (p. 795–816) to Jews because of their faithlessness. It was only in the Visigoth kingdom that anti-Semitism was pursued with vigour. In 681 all Jews in the Visigoth kingdom were given one year's grace in which either to convert to Christianity or face flogging, scalping, the confiscation of all property and exile. Celebration of Jewish festivals was forbidden on pain of the same punishments, and local clergy were expected to supervise Jews to make sure they did not celebrate in secret.

King David playing a lyre, from an 11th-century French musical manuscript.

Flogging and scalping were imposed for a range of other Jewish practices, including adherence to Jewish dietary laws. Travel restrictions were introduced: Jews had to report to the local bishop when arriving at a new place and carry letters detailing their travel plans. Failure to stick to a declared route was punished by flogging. Circumcision was punished by castration if male, amputation of the nose if female. Because it was recognized that forced conversions might well be insincere, even baptized Jews were subject to legal discrimination. It was quite beyond the resources of the crown to enforce these harsh laws and Spain still had a large Jewish population when the Arabs invaded in 711. Not surprisingly, Jews saw the Arabs as liberators.

In the Byzantine Empire Jews were usually tolerated but treated with contempt. Active persecution of Jews was rare, the worst being under the ultra-orthodox tyrant Phocas at the beginning of the seventh century. As part of his programme to win back divine favour for the empire, Leo III tried unsuccessfully to convert Jews by force, but Jewish criticism of Christian use of icons was an influence on his policy of iconoclasm. By this time, the empire's largest Jewish communities – in Egypt, Palestine and Syria – had come under Muslim rule as a result of the Arab conquests.

Jews generally welcomed Arab rule. Though treated as second-class citizens, as 'People of the Book' they enjoyed protected status as long as they paid the *jizya* tax. Heavy land taxes forced most Jews into commerce. Jewish merchants, known to the Arabs as Radanites, were active in long-distance trade between Asia and Europe. One such merchant, Isaac, brought Charlemagne an elephant which had been sent as a gift by Caliph Harun al-Rashid (r. 786–809).

There was one European state which, uniquely, had a Jewish ruling class. This was the Khazar khanate, a sprawling nomad empire that dominated the steppes between the Black and Caspian Seas. Judaism does not actively seek converts – to be a Jew it is usually necessary to be born a Jew. However, under circumstances which are extremely obscure, the Khazar khan and his family converted to Judaism sometime around 740. The khans practised complete religious tolerance and seem to have made no attempt to convert their people to Judaism, so the majority remained pagan, with Christian and Muslim minorities. It is thought that some eastern European Ashkenazi Jews may ultimately have Khazar ancestry.

Jews in the Christian and Muslim worlds

Towns and cities shown were important centres of Jewish settlement.

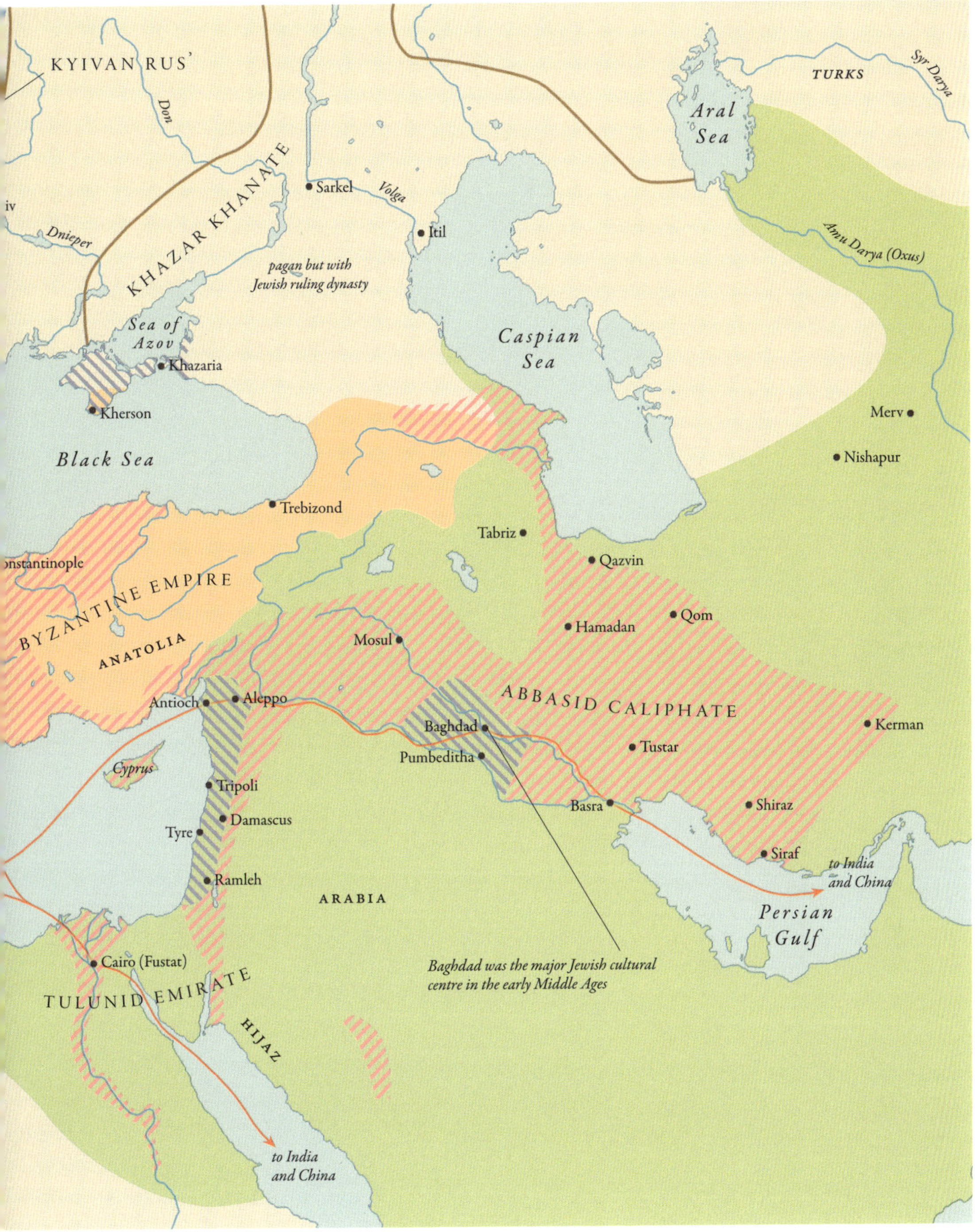

routes of 9th-century Jewish 'Radanite' merchants (al-Radhaniyya)

borders of the Kyivan Rus' state and of the Khazar khanate

area of Christian influence

area of Islamic influence

Area of Jewish settlement:

dense

other

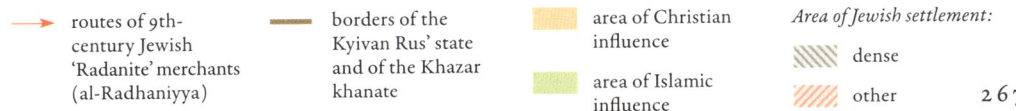

X

Trial By Fire

Viking, Rus, Bulgars and Magyars

By the end of the eighth century, western Europe was more united, prosperous and peaceful than it had been for 400 years. The Muslim advance had been halted and, thanks to Charlemagne's successes in eastern Europe and Spain, Christendom had begun to expand its frontiers. It was not entirely fanciful for Charlemagne to present his imperial coronation in 800 as a restoration of the Roman order. Yet the ninth century was destined to test the resurgent west almost to destruction as it was subjected to assaults by pagan Vikings and Magyars, and by Muslim pirates.

Scandinavian pirates, commonly known as Vikings, had begun to attack the coasts of Britain, Ireland and Francia before Charlemagne's coronation. The earliest securely dated attack was on the Northumbrian monastery of Lindisfarne in 793; the first raids on Scotland and Ireland were recorded in 795 and on Francia in 799. They were the result of the same processes of political centralization and state formation that had transformed the Germanic world in the third and fourth centuries and caused such problems for the Roman Empire.

Viking raids fall into distinct phases. Until around 834 the raids were small – just a few ships and no more than 200 men – and they chose easy targets on the open coast where they could strike without warning and withdraw before forces could gather to oppose them. Monasteries were a favourite target because they were rich

The 8th-century incised picture stone from Stora Hammars on the island of Gotland depicts an early Viking sailing ship and mythological battle scenes.

and unguarded. The cultural impact was devastating. Dozens of monasteries were destroyed or abandoned, their books burned or looted for their jewelled covers, their communities of learned monks dispersed, killed or carried off to be sold as slaves. The failure of the saints to protect them from pagan attack was demoralizing for Christians, as it seemed to be a sign that God was angry with them for their sinfulness.

The 834 sack of the Frankish *emporium* of Dorestad on the lower Rhine marked a significant intensification of Viking activity. Dorestad was 160 km (100 miles) from the sea – the Vikings were showing increased confidence, taking advantage of their ships' shallow draughts to penetrate further and further inland. No doubt they were encouraged by political dissensions in the Frankish Empire. There was also an increase in the size of fleets and, more ominously, Vikings began building bases, as at Dublin in 841 and Noirmoutier Island near Nantes, where they could spend the winter and get an early start to raiding each spring. The raids escalated again after 850, with fleets numbering from around 120 up to 250 ships. Viking ships carried crews of twenty-four to sixty so these fleets carried sizeable armies by early medieval standards.

Now the Vikings were not just interested in plunder. They started seizing lands for settlement, first in the Scottish islands and Ireland, then in the 860s in England and towards the end of the century in Francia. There were rarely more than one or two large Viking armies in the field at a time. The Vikings tended to concentrate in particular places at particular times. When Francia was severely raided in 879–92, England and Ireland experienced a decline; when the Vikings crossed to England in 892, Francia enjoyed a respite.

The Vikings enjoyed great advantages of mobility, using ships or captured horses to keep ahead of defenders. They benefited from the lack of fortifications in most of Europe and also from the limitations of early medieval military systems. Resources were lacking to maintain large standing armies, so it was difficult to mount an immediate response to a raid. By the time local forces had gathered the Vikings had moved on. A bigger problem was the reluctance of troops to serve in defensive campaigns. Charlemagne had no problems raising large armies to conquer new territory because of the opportunities for plunder. Fighting on the defensive offered no such incentives but was just as dangerous. Many were reluctant to leave their families

The death of St Edmund the Martyr, king of East Anglia, from a 12th-century hagiography. According to tradition, Danish Vikings executed King Edmund in 869 after he refused to renounce Christianity.

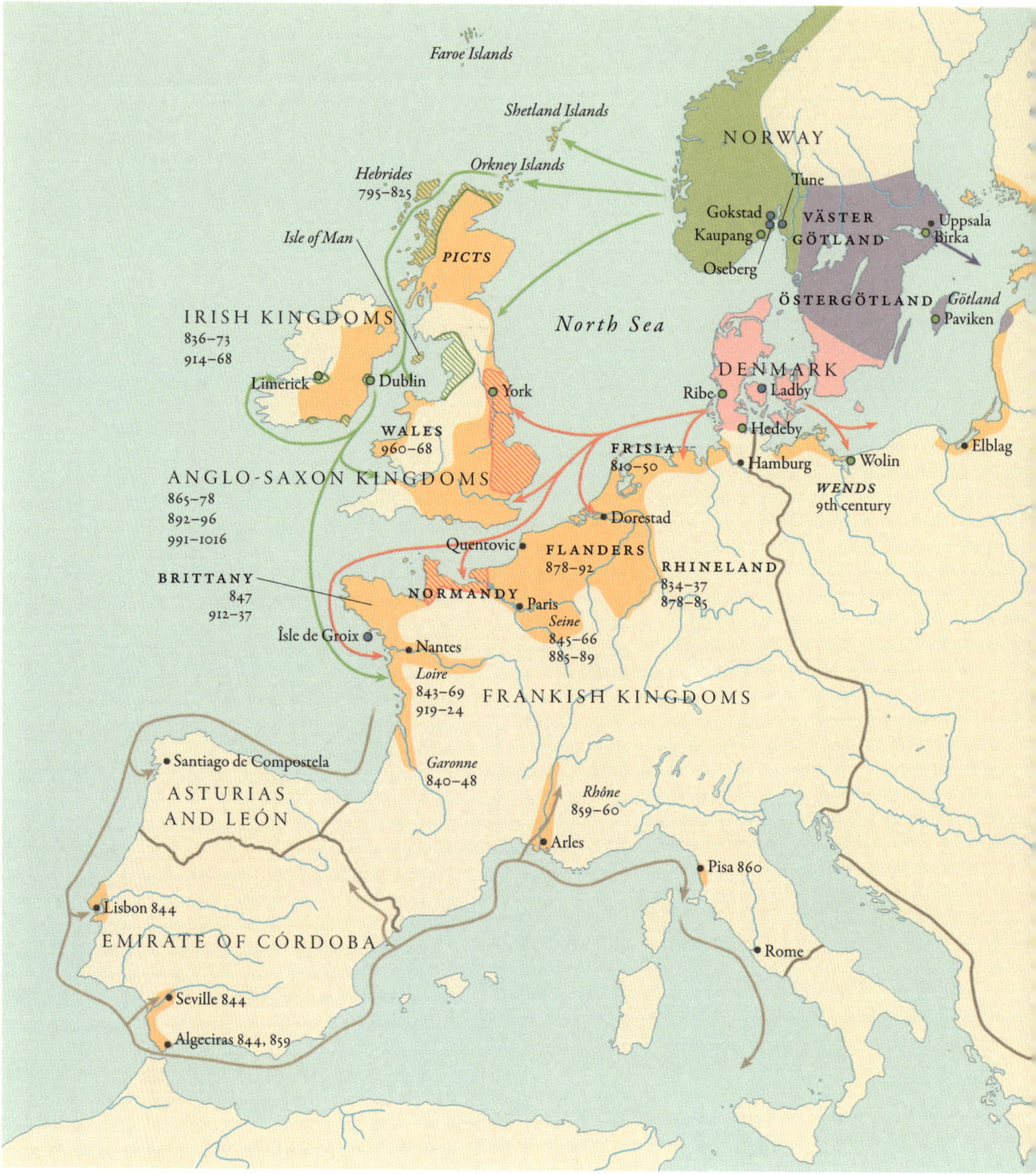

The Viking raids, eighth to eleventh centuries

- Danes
- Norwegians
- Swedes
- areas most intensely raided, with dates
- area of Danish settlement
- area of Norwegian settlement

Viking raids and voyages:

- Danes
- Norwegians
- Swedes (to Kyiv)
- uncertain origin
- Viking-controlled trading centre
- major Viking-age ship burial

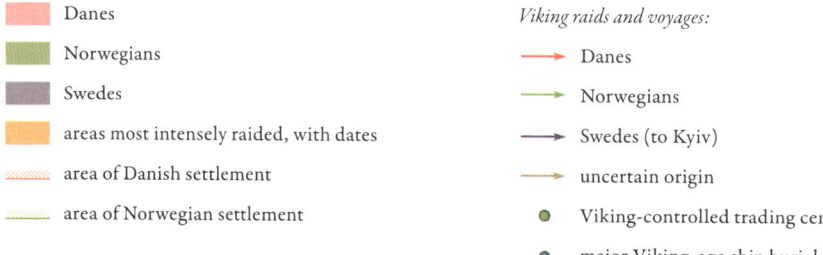

and property undefended in such dangerous times and simply ignored their military obligations.

From raiders to settlers

The Vikings made their most extensive settlements in the British Isles. Most numerous were the Danes, who conquered and settled a wide area of eastern England, which became known as the Danelaw. Smaller numbers of Norwegians settled in Orkney, Shetland, the Hebrides, Ireland and northwest England. The earliest Viking settlements were made in the Orkney and Shetland Islands around the mid-ninth century. The indigenous Pictish inhabitants were probably exterminated by the newcomers; genetic studies show that the majority of the modern populations of the islands are of Norse origin. Orkney and Shetland became completely Norse in language and culture and kept this character long after the end of the Viking age. Norwegian settlers also took control of the Hebrides and much of Scotland's west coast, though in these areas the native Gaelic-speaking population survived and gradually assimilated the settlers through intermarriage and conversion to Christianity.

Initially the impact of Viking raids fell hardest on Ireland. Because of its highly devolved power structure, there was no attempt at a united defence and the Vikings raided almost at will, travelling far inland on Ireland's navigable rivers. By the 840s the Vikings had founded fortified bases called *longphorts* so that they could raid all year round. Most were not occupied for more than a few years, but the most successful ones – such as Dublin, which became an important slave-trade centre, Limerick, Waterford and Wexford – developed into Ireland's first towns.

Attempts by the Vikings to conquer territory outside these towns failed. The same decentralized power structures that made raiding easy also made it impossible to hold territory securely, because there was no one with whom to negotiate lasting peace and because, once they settled down, the Vikings became vulnerable to Irish counterattack. The Vikings were even temporarily expelled in 902. Many of the refugees settled in northwest England; others went to Iceland. Re-established in force in 917, the Vikings were soon confined to their fortified towns once more and by the end of the century maintained their independence only by paying tribute to Irish kings.

Danish settlement in England began with the arrival of a 'great heathen army' in East Anglia in 865. The Danes seized horses and invaded Northumbria, which was indulging in a badly timed civil war. The kingdom was soon occupied between the Humber and Tees rivers. In 869 the Danes conquered East Anglia and the following year they invaded Wessex. Since overthrowing the Mercian hegemony in 825, Wessex had been the strongest Anglo-Saxon kingdom, but it repulsed the Danes only with difficulty. East Mercia was conquered in 873. The following spring the Danish army split up, part of it going to settle the rich lands they had won around York, others to east Mercia, and the rest under Guthrum (d. 890) invaded Wessex, now under the rule of Alfred the Great (r. 871–99).

After initial setbacks, Alfred won a decisive victory over Guthrum at Edington in 878 and then besieged him at Chippenham, forcing his surrender. By the Treaty of Wedmore later that year, Guthrum accepted baptism and agreed to withdraw his army from Wessex to East Anglia, which became a Danish kingdom. Those Danes who did not want to settle crossed the Channel to raid Francia.

With all of Wessex's old rivals eliminated, Alfred was able to assume leadership of all Anglo-Saxons not under Danish rule. Alfred acted vigorously to strengthen his kingdom's defences, building a system of fortresses called *burhs* where the population could take refuge during Viking raids, reforming the army and building a fleet. Alfred's efforts to revive learning were part of his defence; by improving the quality of the clergy, he hoped to win back God's favour.

When a new Danish army landed in Kent in 892, it found the Anglo-Saxons well prepared. Faced with constant harassment by Alfred's forces, the frustrated Danish army broke up in 896, some joining the settlers in the Danelaw, others joining the Viking army on the Seine. Alfred had saved England from a Danish takeover and laid the foundations for a national kingship.

The Vikings in the East

While the Danes and Norwegians were raiding and settling in the west, their Swedish neighbours were forging new trade routes to

Viking settlements in Britain and Ireland

Byzantium and the Abbasid caliphate along the great navigable rivers of eastern Europe. The native Slavs described these Swedish Vikings as Rus'. The presence of seventh-century Scandinavian merchant graves at the trading centres of Grobin and Elblag shows that Swedish expansion to the east of the Baltic got underway long before the first Viking raids in the west. These merchants were probably trying to acquire furs for the west European market. In the later eighth century Arab merchants began trading with the Khazars and Volga Bulgars, introducing high-quality silver coins called dirhams into circulation in eastern Europe. This encouraged the Rus' – whose name is probably derived from *Ruotsi*, the Finnish name for the Swedes which is thought to be a corruption of old Norse *róðr*, meaning 'oarsmen' – to push inland along eastern Europe's navigable rivers and discover their source.

It was often necessary for the Rus' to drag their boats overland between river systems or around rapids. These were dangerous moments in any journey because of the risk of ambush by local tribes and marauding nomads like the Pechenegs. By the 830s the Rus' had established new trade routes down the Dnieper to the Black Sea and Constantinople, and traded with Arabs on the Volga. These routes

The foundations of a Norse longhouse at Jarlshof in the Shetland Islands. Longhouses, in which a family and its livestock lived under the same roof, were the typical Norse dwelling.

would flourish until the exhaustion of the Islamic world's silver mines in the late tenth century. By that time huge amounts of Arab silver had passed to Scandinavia. Though trade may have been their aim, most of the commodities the Rus' sold to the Arabs were acquired by violence, or at least the threat of violence. During the ninth century the Rus' captured Slav towns, including Novgorod and Kyiv, and used them as bases to subjugate neighbouring tribes and force them to pay tribute in slaves, furs, honey, wax and other commodities.

Around 860, Rurik, the ruler of Novgorod, created a Rus' state that covered much of modern northwest Russia. The capital of the state was moved south to Kyiv after it was captured by Rurik's kinsman and successor Oleg *c.* 883. In 907 Oleg launched an attack on Constantinople. Though defeated, Oleg was able to negotiate a trade treaty with the Byzantines that gave the Rus' from Kyiv preferential treatment compared to Scandinavians from other settlements. The Byzantines clearly remained suspicious. Although the Rus' were allowed to stay in Byzantine territory for up to six months, they were not to live within Constantinople's city walls, could not carry weapons and had to be escorted by Byzantine officials. In a second treaty of 911, terms were agreed for Rus' who wanted to join the Byzantine army. This is seen as the origin of the emperor's elite Varangian Guard of Scandinavian mercenaries. Among other clauses, the Rus' agreed not to plunder Byzantine ships. These treaties began the close relationship with Byzantium that was to have such a great influence on the development of the early Rus' state. Oleg disappeared from history around 913, the same year that Muslim chroniclers record the destruction of a Rus' raiding fleet by the Khazars.

The Scandinavian presence in Russia and Ukraine is well attested from archaeological evidence, most of it from cemeteries. There are a large number of female burials containing characteristic Scandinavian artefacts, suggesting the early Rus' settlers travelled in family groups. The same cemeteries show that the Scandinavians were a minority among a Slav population, even in towns – and there is no evidence of Scandinavian settlement in the countryside. From this it is clear that the Rus' were a military and merchant elite. Although memorial inscriptions on Swedish rune stones indicate that Scandinavian migration to Russia and Ukraine continued until the eleventh century, in the course of the tenth century the Rus' became increasingly assimilated to the native Slavs, with whom they allied and intermarried.

The Vikings in the east

- Bulgar
- probable centre of Rus'-Arab trade
- Volga
- Ural
- Rus' carry their ships from Don to Volga, 912
- Aral Sea
- Sarkel
- Khazars ambush and destroy Rus' fleet, 913
- Itil
- 500 Rus' ships, 912–13
- Caspian Sea
- Rus' defeat Muslim fleet, 912
- KHAZAR KHANATE
- ABASGIA
- Kura
- ARMENIA
- Ardebil
- Abasgun
- 16 Rus' ships plunder Persian coast, 910
- ALID EMIRATE
- ABBASID CALIPHATE
- sacked by Rus', 864–84

Legend:
- Slavs, c. 800
- area under Rus' control by 912
- centre with substantial Scandinavian population
- main route of Swedish penetration
- Askold and Dir, c. 860
- Oleg, 907
- Rus' fleet, 912–13
- portage
- place sacked
- battle, with date

279

The Atlantic adventure

The only permanent expansion of the Scandinavian world in the Viking age came as a result of the settlement of the Faroe Islands and Iceland. The first visitors to the Faroes and Iceland were Irish *peregrini*, who may have discovered them in the late seventh or early eighth century. These monks used the islands as a retreat but did not found permanent settlements. Norse settlement of the Faroes probably began before *c.* 825, when the Irish monk Dicuil complained that they had scared away his brethren. It was possibly that the Norse learned of the islands from the Irish, as the first Norse settler, Grímur Kamban, had an Irish surname and so had probably spent time in the Hebrides or Ireland.

New archaeological evidence indicates that the Norse first began visiting Iceland around the same time as the Faroes, probably to hunt seals and walrus. The first, and unsuccessful, attempt at permanent settlement was made, probably in the 860s, by Floki Vilgerdarson, who gave the island its name after being trapped by sea ice for nearly two years. Other members of Floki's party gave more promising reports and by around 872 settlers had begun to arrive. Most of Iceland's settlers came from the western fjords of Norway. The leaders of the settlements were chieftains who brought their families, personal retinues and slaves. Most of the latter, according to genetic evidence, came from Ireland and Britain and they made up nearly half the population. The chieftains took personal possession of the land, kept some to farm themselves and settled their retainers on the remainder as tenant farmers.

Late ninth-century Norway developed a more powerful monarchy so it is likely that the leading emigrants were attracted by the idea of settling new lands, far from the reach of royal power, where they could maintain their traditional autonomy. Their followers, however, were mostly landless men with poor prospects of ever owning a farm at home. Though Iceland is bleak and treeless, it has a mild climate for the latitude and good grazing; this would have made it attractive to settlers from western Norway, where pastoralism was the basis of the agricultural economy. The early settlements were lawless and in 930 the first annual all-Iceland assembly, the Althing, was held to settle major disputes and establish common laws. Iceland was divided into quarters, each with equal voting rights in the Althing. Often described

A small bronze figurine of the Norse thunder god Thor clutching his hammer Mjölnir. Thor was popular with farmers and sailors, who prayed to him for good weather.

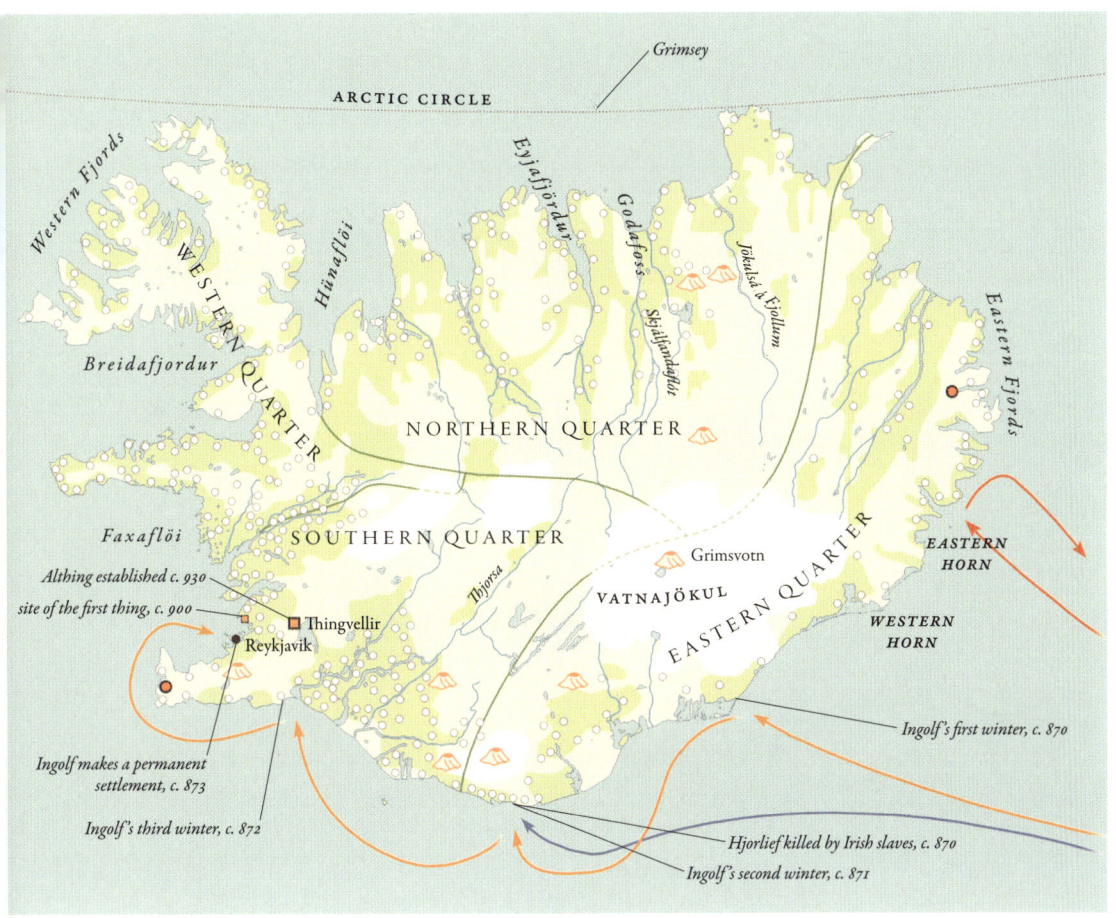

The settlement of Iceland, c. 870–1263

- → Ingolf and Hjorlief, late 860s (pioneer settlers in saga traditions)
- → Hjorlief, c. 870
- → Ingolf, c. 870
- ○ settlement first established by 930
- — regional boundary
- area of pasture
- active volcano
- ⦿ evidence of Norse presence before c. 870

Discovery of the New World

Norwegians
Swedes
Danes

as a democracy, the Althing was actually an oligarchic form of government: although all free men had the right to attend and speak, only the thirty-six paramount chieftains could vote.

The next stage in the Vikings' route across the Atlantic was the settlement of Greenland. The inhospitable glaciated east coast was first sighted *c.* 900, but around 983 Erik the Red rounded Cape Farewell and discovered an uninhabited ice-free region with sheltered fjords and good grazing. To attract settlers, Erik gave his discovery its optimistic name. A couple of years later Bjarni Herjolfsson was blown off course while sailing from Iceland to join Erik in Greenland and made a chance sighting of land to the west: he had become the first European known to have sighted the North American continent. Around 1000 Erik's son Leif set out to investigate Bjarni's sighting. Sailing west from Greenland he discovered a rocky glaciated land he called Helluland ('Slab Land'), which was probably Baffin Island. Sailing south he came to a low-forested land, which he called Markland ('Wood Land'). This was probably Labrador.

Pressing further south, Leif spent the winter in a land with a mild climate where wild grapes grew and the rivers teemed with salmon. He called this Vinland ('Wine Land'). The exact location of Vinland has been much debated but it was probably somewhere on the Gulf of St Lawrence. There were follow-up voyages and attempts to settle – clear evidence of a Viking community has been discovered at L'Anse-aux-Meadows in Newfoundland – but the distances were too great, and the natives too hostile, for this farthest medieval European outpost to succeed.

Breakup of the Carolingian Empire

The Treaty of Verdun (843) that ended the civil war following the death of Louis the Pious three years earlier did not end the rivalry of his sons Lothar, Louis the German and Charles the Bald. As emperor, Lothar was nominally the senior of the three brother kings, but his title gave him no authority over Charles and Louis, who ruled independently. Lothar ruled his straggling kingdom with some ability until 855 when he abdicated to become a monk. His domain was divided between his sons, Louis II (r. 855–75) getting Italy, and Lothar II (r. 855–69) getting the northern half of the kingdom,

The Cross of Lothar II, the Carolingian king of Lotharingia (835–869), takes its name from the engraved rock crystal portrait of the king near its base. However, the cross was probably made for the Holy Roman Emperor Otto III, over a century after Lothar's death.

which became known as Lotharingia (from which comes Lorraine). Louis the German was perhaps the most able of the three brothers and had the least trouble retaining the loyalty of his vassals.

Charles the Bald had to contend not only with the hostility of his brothers but also with rebellious vassals and Viking raids. Charles's main concern was to defend his throne; he regarded the Vikings as an unwelcome distraction from the more important business of putting down rebellions and repelling invasions by his brothers. Although its long coastline left Charles's kingdom vulnerable to Viking raids, he refused to allow the building of castles and town walls, fearing that his rebellious vassals would use them against him as much as against the Vikings. Rather than fight, Charles preferred to buy the Vikings off with tribute, which bought time but only encouraged more raids in the long term. Even when he was prepared to fight, his plans were often undermined by rebellion. For example, in 858 Charles was forced to abandon the siege of a Viking base, because rebel vassals had invited his brother Louis the German to invade and depose him.

After Lothar II died childless in 869, the empire was redivided by the Treaty of Mersen and Charles acquired Lotharingia. This made him ambitious to try to reunite the whole Carolingian Empire under his sole rule. Charles was crowned emperor in 875 by the pope in Rome, but his attempt to seize the kingdom of his brother Louis, who died in 876, failed and the ultimate prize eluded him. Charles died of dysentery the following year and another confusing round of divisions ensued.

The empire was finally reunited under Louis the German's younger son, Charles the Fat. On his father's death in 876 Charles became king of Swabia. When his brother Carloman abdicated in 879 Charles became king of Italy and was crowned emperor in 881. Charles the Fat inherited Saxony on the death of his last surviving brother, Louis the Younger, in 882 and, when Charles the Bald's grandson Louis III died two years later, he gained West Francia too, reuniting the whole empire under a single ruler (excepting only Provence, which was held by a rebel).

Charles the Fat was surely the most uninspiring Carolingian ruler. As the king of Italy, he failed absolutely to quell Muslim pirate raids and was equally ineffective against the Vikings. Despite forcing the Vikings to lift their siege of Paris in 886, which had been defended heroically by its count Eudes (or Odo) for a full year, Charles failed

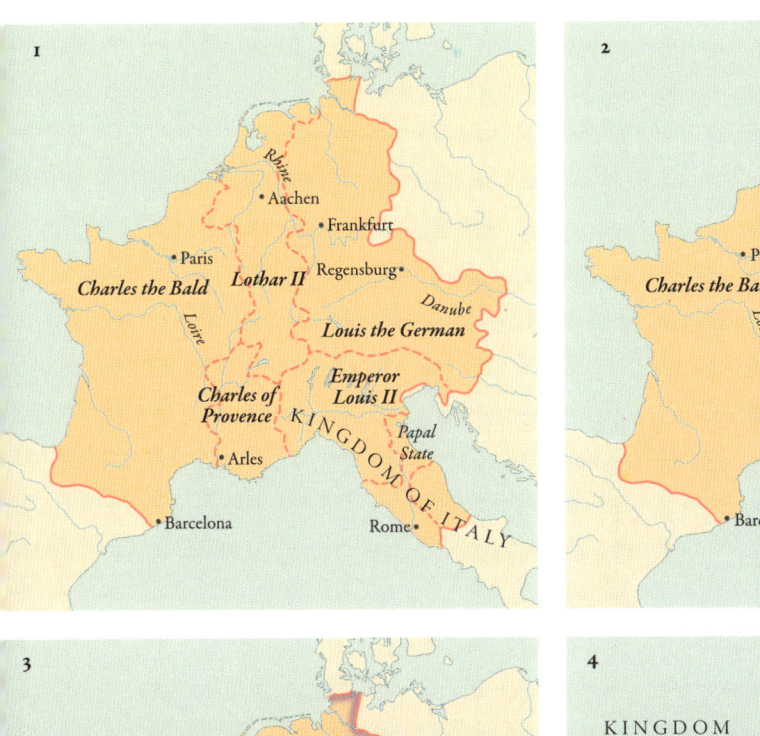

Break-up of the Carolingian Empire

1 Division of the Carolingian Empire, 855

2 Division of the Carolingian Empire, Treaty of Mersen, 870

3 Division of the Carolingian Empire, 880

4 Break-up of the Carolingian Empire, 911

kingdoms under Carolingian rule

Charles the Fat, 885–87

to capitalize on this success and simply paid the Vikings tribute and gave them permission to sail past Paris and ravage Burgundy. This punished the Burgundians for a rebellion but, after all their efforts to defeat the Vikings at Paris, the Frankish nobility was outraged and in 887 Charles was deposed by his nephew Arnulf. Charles's death – probably murdered in January 888 – began the final breakup of the Carolingian Empire. Arnulf was elected king by the East Franks but his authority was not recognized in Italy, nor by the West Franks who chose count Eudes as their monarch, the first Frankish king who was neither a Merovingian nor a Carolingian.

The kingdom of Brittany

The Vikings and the Frankish nobility were not the only ones to benefit from the declining authority of the Carolingian dynasty. It was also an opportunity for the Bretons to assert their independence from the Franks. Although the Merovingians claimed overlordship of Brittany, they rarely intervened in the region so, in practice, it remained independent. The Bretons were not politically united but remained separated into small principalities ruled by counts. Conflict between Bretons and Franks increased with the accession of the expansionist Carolingian dynasty. Charlemagne and Louis the Pious tried several times to conquer Brittany, but apparent success was always followed by successful rebellion.

In 831 Louis tried diplomacy instead of war and appointed a Breton noble, Nomenoë (d. 851), as *missus imperatoris* (imperial legate) for Brittany. This required Nomenoë to become an imperial vassal, for which he was rewarded with the county of Vannes. This was a mutually advantageous arrangement: Nomenoë gained Louis's support in subjugating the other Breton counts, while Louis gained title to lands which he did not control. Brittany as a united political entity was their joint creation.

In the civil wars that followed Louis's death, Nomenoë supported Charles the Bald, king of West Francia, but in 843 he and Charles became embroiled in a dispute over the county of Nantes. Charles invaded Brittany but was defeated by Nomenoë at Ballon near Redon. A truce was agreed, but in 849 Nomenoë dismissed the Frankish bishops of Alet, Dol, Quimper, St-Pol-de Léon and

Kingdom of Brittany, 778–939

- Brittany, c. 778
- territory acquired by Nomenöe, 831–51
- territory acquired by Salomon, 863–67
- approximate border of Frankish-Breton March, c. 778
- approximate eastern limit of Viking occupation, 914–37
- → Alain Barbetorte's reconquest of Brittany, 936–39
- ◉ bishopric
- ◻ Viking fort/camp
- ✠ monastery or church sacked or abandoned, 936–39
- ✂ Breton victory, with date
- ✗ defeat, with date

❶ Landévennec was an important book production centre in the later 9th century

❷ Erispöe's victory over the Franks at Jengland-Beslé established Brittany as a kingdom

❸ A 10th-century Viking chief was cremated in his longship with a human sacrifice, weapons, jewelry, tools and gaming pieces

Vannes and replaced them with native Breton-speakers. In effect, this amounted to a declaration of independence. Nomenoë seized the counties of Rennes and Nantes but in March 851, at the height of his power, he died while campaigning in Frankish territory.

Charles the Bald recognized that Nomenoë's death presented an opportunity to regain control of Brittany. He invaded but was decisively defeated in a gruelling three-day battle at Jengland-Beslé by Nomenoë's son Erispoë (r. 851–57). Charles had no choice but to make peace on Erispoë's terms, granting him regal status as a vassal king within the Frankish Empire and recognizing his possession of all of Nomenoë's conquests: Brittany had become a kingdom.

The Vikings were an important factor. From the early ninth century Brittany suffered numerous raids, but the rich Seine and Loire valleys were always much more attractive to the Vikings, who were therefore much more of a headache for the Franks. Between the Vikings and his dynastic problems, Charles the Bald was usually too busy to focus on Brittany. The Bretons even allied with the Vikings sometimes, as in 865 when they attacked Le Mans together. In 866 Salomon, Erispoë's successor, joined the Vikings to defeat the Franks at Brissarthe, killing Robert, the count of Angers. Faced with this disaster, Charles the Bald ceded the Cotentin peninsula and made Salomon (r. 857–74) the symbolic gift of a crown.

The Vikings were also the downfall of the Breton kingdom. Changed circumstances made Brittany more attractive to the Vikings in the early tenth century. Strong rulers meant England and Ireland were unattractive for raiding, while the settlement of Rollo and his followers in Normandy in 911 (see p. 291) had closed the Seine. In 913 the important monastery of Landévennec was sacked, provoking a general flight of monks to seek refuge in Francia. In 919 Breton resistance collapsed, the nobility fled to Francia or England, and by 921 Nantes was the capital of a Viking state that dominated Brittany. Supported by the English king Athelstan (r. 924–39), Alain Barbetorte (Twistbeard, d. 952) began a campaign of reconquest in 936. Nantes was recaptured in 937 and the last Vikings were expelled from a fort at Trans near Dol in 939. The effect on Breton independence, however, was disastrous. Alain was unable to impose his authority on the Breton nobility and he ruled only as a duke, not a king. After Alain's death in 952 there was no obvious successor and Brittany slowly came under Norman domination.

The foundation of Normandy

The foundation of Normandy by Viking chieftain Rollo (Hrolf) was to have a major impact on the histories of France, England, Italy, the Byzantine Empire and the Middle East in the eleventh century. The origins of Nordmannia, or 'Northman's Land', can be traced to the arrival of a large Viking fleet on the Seine in 885. When most of the force moved on to plunder in Flanders in 890, some remained behind to settle. After he was defeated at Chartres in 911, their leader Rollo reached a peace agreement with the West Frankish king Charles III the Simple (r. 893–923) at St Clair-sur-Epte. In return for his homage and conversion to Christianity, Rollo was made count of Rouen (it was not until 1006 that Norman rulers adopted the title 'duke').

Charles's hope was that Rollo would stop any other Vikings sailing up the Seine to raid his kingdom and, in this respect, the agreement was a great success, effectively ending the Viking age as far as the Franks were concerned. However, because of the weakness of the Frankish monarchy, the Normans were dangerously independent and expansionist. In 924 Rollo was granted more lands around Caen

Idealized 13th-century effigy of Rollo, the first count of Rouen and founder of Normandy, on his tomb in Rouen cathedral.

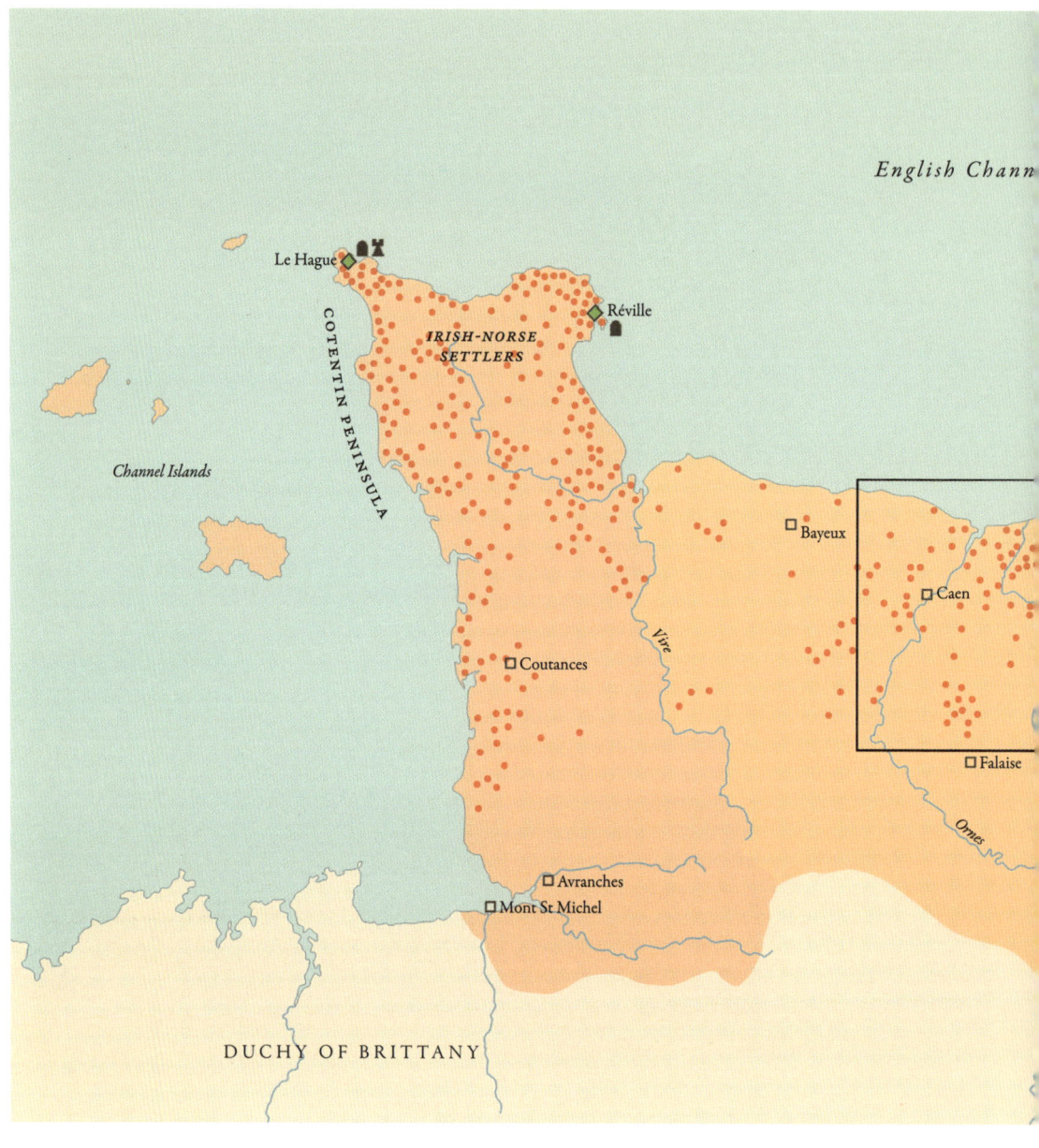

Duchy of Normandy, 911–933

Land granted by Carolingians:
- 911
- 924
- 933
- site of archaeological find

Type of find:
- burials
- fortification
- weapon
- site with Scandinavian place name

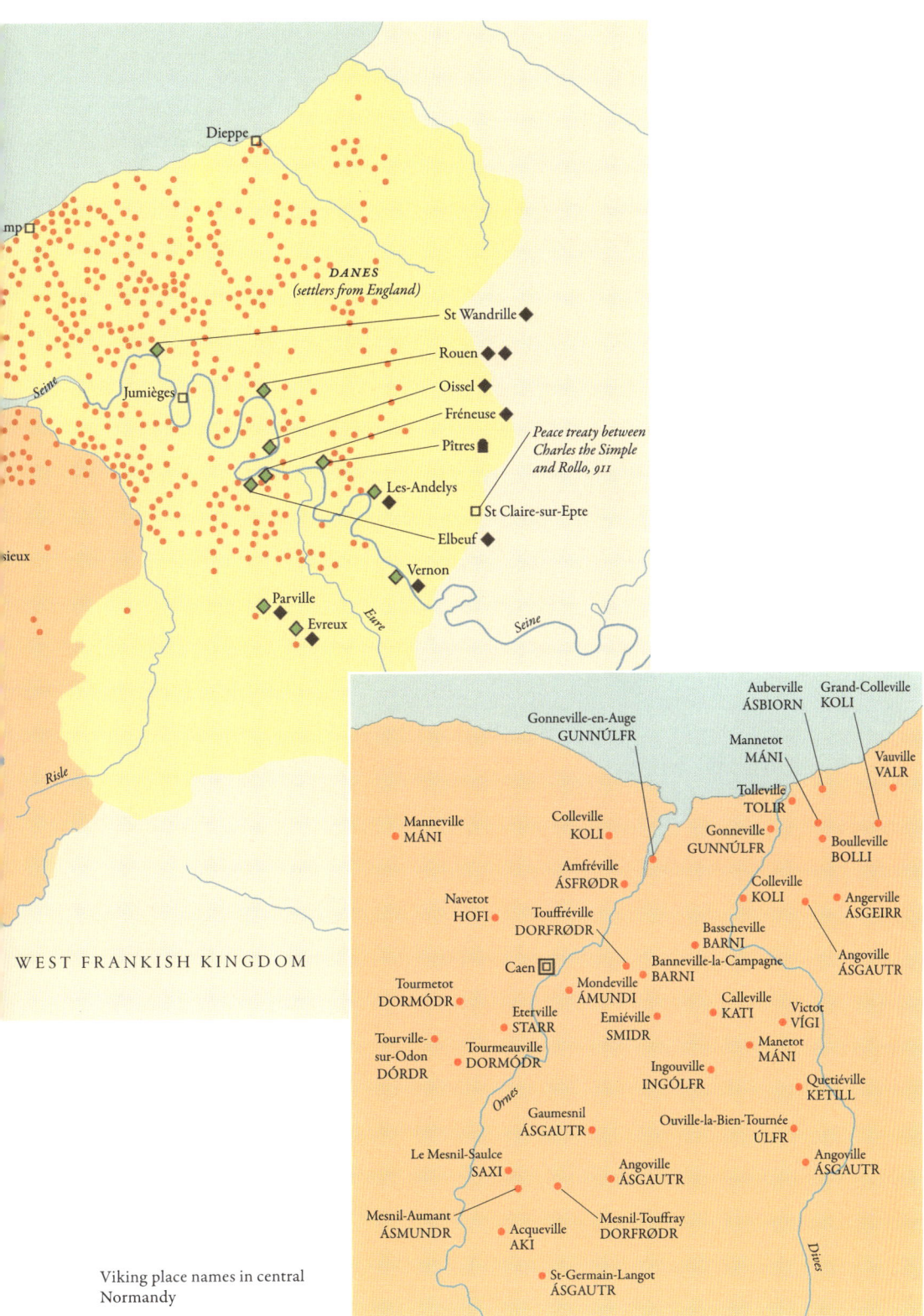

Viking place names in central Normandy

and Bayeux, and in 933 his son William Longsword (d. 942) won control of the Cotentin peninsula. Further expansion was blocked by the powerful counts of Flanders and Anjou, rather than the Frankish kings. Under William's son Richard the Fearless (r. 942–96), Normandy developed into a feudal principality and was progressively assimilated into the normal political and cultural life of the West Frankish kingdom.

The most important evidence for the Viking settlement of Normandy comes from the distribution of Scandinavian place names. These show that there was dense Viking settlement around Fécamp, Rouen, Caen and the Cotentin, but it was sparse elsewhere. Probably nowhere did Scandinavians form a majority of the population. The place names suggest that the majority of settlers were Danes, some of whom had lived previously in England, but there were Norse-Irish settlers in the Cotentin. The settlers have left little archaeological evidence for their presence, a sign that they quickly adopted Frankish material culture and burial practices.

A new wave of pagans arrived around 942, but by this time most of the original settlers had already converted to Christianity and Richard the Fearless helped restore many monasteries which had been abandoned because of Viking raids. A last influx of pagan settlers arrived around 960 (refugees from the kingdom of York) which had recently been conquered by the Anglo-Saxons. After that, Scandinavian influence faded fast. Trade links with Scandinavia, which had never been very important, appear to have been abandoned by the early eleventh century, since from that time Norman coins are absent from Scandinavian hoards.

The last evidence for Scandinavian cultural and political influence in Normandy dates to the reign of Richard the Good (996–1026). Duke Richard allowed the Danish king Svein Forkbeard (r. 987–1014) to use Normandy as a base to attack England, recruited Vikings to fight in wars with rival counts, and sent Norman soldiers to support the Dublin Vikings against the Irish. The presence of a Norwegian poet at the ducal court in 1025 presupposes that there were still people there who could understand his native language, but this is the last evidence of Scandinavian cultural influence in Normandy. Long before William the Conqueror invaded England in 1066, Normandy was culturally, linguistically and politically a French principality. Some have seen evidence of a continuing Viking spirit in the Normans'

wide-ranging conquests, but this was a result of strict primogeniture, which ensured a surplus of landless sons.

A Muslim lake – the Mediterranean in the ninth century

At about the same time that the first Viking raids began to affect the northern coasts of the Frankish Empire, its Mediterranean coasts came under attack by Muslim pirates from Spain and North Africa. After the disastrous failure of the Arab sieges of Constantinople in 672–77 and 717, Muslim naval power collapsed. Because good building timber was in short supply in most of the Middle East, it was impossible for the Arabs to make good their losses quickly, and so control of the Mediterranean passed back to the Byzantine navy. The only real challenge the Byzantines faced in the eighth century came from the Franks under Charlemagne. There were sporadic hostilities from 788 to 815 and though the Byzantines defeated a Frankish attempt to seize Venice, they lost control of Corsica and the Balearic Islands.

The resurgence of Muslim sea power was heralded by a raid on the Balearics by Spanish Moors in 798. The Franks were ready for the Moors when they returned the next year and the Muslims suffered a heavy defeat, but this did not discourage raids from Spain and Africa on Corsica, Sardinia and Sicily. A vigorous response by both Byzantine and Frankish naval forces virtually ended the raids by 813 – but it was only a respite.

In 815 there was a resurgence of iconoclasm in the Byzantine Empire and in the early years of Michael II's reign (820–29) a civil war broke out over the issue. The Byzantine Aegean fleets were destroyed while the fleet defending the western Mediterranean defected to the Aghlabid emir of Tunis. The consequences were immediate: by 826 Malta, Crete and Cyprus had been invaded and occupied by the Muslims, and in 826 they occupied Sardinia and began the conquest of Sicily. Though most of Sicily was in Muslim hands by 878, the last Byzantine strongholds did not fall until 963. The Franks countered with an attack on Tunisia in 828, but after the civil wars of the 830s Frankish naval power declined rapidly.

The Balearic Islands were raided repeatedly from the 830s and in 849 they became a protectorate of Umayyad Spain before being

A high-quality Scandinavian or Frankish sword with a hilt and pommel decorated with silver inlay. Swords were high-status weapons in the early Middle Ages, affordable only for the wealthy.

Muslim dominance of the Mediterranean, ninth century

- Byzantine Empire, 888
- Carolingian kingdoms, 888
- Muslim states, 888
- Muslim conquests, with dates
- Muslim raids, 800–900
- Muslim pirate base

1. Luxeuil was sacked successively by Vikings, Muslims and Magyars between 886 and 924
2. Fraxinetum was a Muslim pirate base between 890 and 972
3. Rome was sacked by Muslim pirates in 846
4. Bari was a Muslim pirate base between 840 and 871

annexed in 903. Raids on the coasts of France and Italy became all too common. Marseille was raided in 838, Arles in 842, Rome in 846 and Marseille again in 848. In 840 Arab pirates from Tunisia seized Bari on the Adriatic coast as a permanent base and in 860 established another at the mouth of the Rhône, raiding upstream as far as Burgundy. By the end of the ninth century they had established a base at Fraxinetum near St Tropez, from which they attacked travellers crossing the Alpine passes between France and Italy. Their most distinguished victim was Maiolus, abbot of the great Burgundian monastery of Cluny. Unlike the Vikings, who were just pirates out for what they could get, many of the Muslim pirates were religiously motivated and considered their raids as part of a *jihad* against unbelievers.

Despite its long coastline, Italy suffered less than might be imagined because its mountainous terrain and lack of navigable rivers made quick inland raids difficult. Under the competent rule of Louis II (r. 855–75), royal authority remained strong and defences were well organized. In alliance with the Byzantines and the Venetians, Louis recaptured Bari in 871, much reducing the Muslim threat in the Adriatic.

However, just as conflicts within Christendom had opened the doors to Muslim piracy, conflict within the Muslim world eventually enabled the Christian states to regain the initiative at sea in the second half of the tenth century. Their control of the Mediterranean sea ways would not to be seriously challenged again by a Muslim power until the sixteenth century.

The Bulgar khanate

The greatest challenge to the security of the Byzantine Empire in the ninth century came from the Bulgar khanate, a powerful state centred on the lower Danube. These Turkic nomads settled on the Ukrainian steppes in the fifth century in the wake of the collapse of the Hun Empire. Under Kubrat (r. *c.* 605–42) the Bulgars were welded into a short-lived khanate known to the Byzantines as Great Bulgaria. On Kubrat's death the khanate split into five hordes under his sons. Three hordes were soon absorbed by other peoples but two had a longer future. One migrated north to the confluence of the Volga and Kama rivers, surviving until the Mongol invasions of the thirteenth century.

The second, under Asparuh, migrated west and took advantage of Byzantium's struggle with the Arabs, crossing the Danube and seizing Lower Moesia. Unable to expel them, Emperor Constantine IV (r. 668–85) recognized their possession in 679. Asparuh and his successors established their court at Pliska and lived on tribute gathered from their mainly Slav subjects and plunder from raids on Byzantine territory. The Bulgars tried to preserve their identity by founding separate settlements, but in the eighth and early ninth centuries the two populations assimilated, the Slavs accepting Bulgar identity and the Bulgars adopting the Slavic language.

In the face of effective Byzantine counterattacks, Bulgar power waned in the eighth century, but they benefited greatly from Charlemagne's destruction of the Avar khanate in the 790s. The Franks did not occupy the former Avar lands, leaving a power vacuum which the Bulgars were quick to fill. Under Khan Krum (r. 803–14) the Bulgar khanate emerged as the great power of the Balkans. In 809 Krum captured the Byzantine fortress of Serdica (Sofia) and massacred its garrison.

The Orthodox monastery of St Ivan at Rila in Bulgaria was founded in the 9th century by the hermit St Ivan, who lived in a nearby mountain cave. The monastery was substantially rebuilt after a catastrophic fire in 1833.

The Bulgar khanate

- Kyiv
- Dnieper
- Magyar migration
- Pecheneg migration
- Dniester
- CRIMEA
- Kaffa
- Kherson
- Danube
- Lower Moesia
- Bulgar capital
- Pliska
- Black Sea
- Verbitza 811
- 817 Mesembria
- Besieged by Bulgars, 813–14
- Visinica 813
- Adrianople
- Sinope
- Constantinople
- BYZANTINE EMPIRE
- ANATOLIA

Legend:
- Bulgar khanate
- Bulgarian territory lost to Pechenegs, Magyar and Rus' by 927
- East Francia (Germany)
- kingdom of Italy
- Byzantine Empire
- Russian attacks
- Byzantine enclave in Italy and Sicily
- battle, with date

301

X TRIAL BY FIRE

The Bulgar king Simeon I defeating the Byzantines at the Battle of Boulgarophygon (now Baebeski, Turkey) in 896, from a manuscript of the chronicle of John Skylitzes.

Emperor Nicephorus (r. 802–11) retaliated by burning Pliska, but on a second campaign in 811 his army was trapped and annihilated at the Pass of Verbitza in the Balkan mountains. Nicephorus was among the dead: Krum was said to have made his skull into a drinking cup. Nicephorus's feeble successor, Michael I, was unable to stem the Bulgar tide and by July 813 Krum had laid siege to Constantinople. Michael was deposed and replaced by one his generals, Leo V the Armenian (r. 813–20). After Leo tried to murder him at a peace conference, Krum laid waste to the countryside around Constantinople, but as winter approached he was forced to lift his siege. Krum had returned to besiege Constantinople a second time in 814 when he died suddenly of a brain haemorrhage. Leo's victory over Krum's son Omurtag at Mesembria in 817 brought the war to an end with a thirty-year peace treaty, but the Bulgars kept the Byzantine territory Krum had conquered.

The Bulgars used the peace to consolidate their Balkan empire, while the Byzantines were distracted by a divisive second round of iconoclasm and wars with the Arabs; a decisive victory in Anatolia in 863 freed the Byzantines to take a more forceful line with the Bulgars. Michael III (r. 842–67), under the influence of his uncle Bardas, sent an army to the Bulgar border to put pressure on Khan Boris I (r. 852–89) to convert to Orthodox Christianity. The Byzantines had recently converted the Bulgars' Moravian neighbours, so to avoid encirclement by hostile Christian powers Boris accepted baptism in 866 and forced his subjects to do likewise.

If the Byzantines thought conversion would make the Bulgars easier to control, they were to be disappointed. Boris's second son Simeon (r. 893–927) waged successful wars against Byzantium in 894–97 and 913–24, extending the Bulgar khanate to the Aegean and the Adriatic. Simeon's real ambition was, however, not mere territorial aggrandizement but the Byzantine throne itself.

Though he forced Byzantium to recognize him as tsar (emperor) of the Bulgars, Simeon found the walls of Constantinople as impregnable as had every other enemy who had confronted them. Moreover, because of his obsession with Constantinople, the Magyars and Pechenegs were able to occupy the Bulgar territories north of the Danube. Simeon's son and successor, Peter, inherited an empire already in decline. In the remainder of the tenth century, Byzantine cultural and political influence over the Bulgars steadily increased.

The Magyars

At the end of the ninth century Europe was invaded by the Magyars, nomads distantly related to the Finns. They settled on the Hungarian plain, and their terrifying raids into western Europe were even more wide-ranging than those of Attila's Huns. The Magyars originated in northern Russia but migrated south onto the Ukrainian steppes sometime before the eighth century, where they became nomad pastoralists. Though divided into independent hordes, the Magyars formed a loose confederation called the On-Ogur (Ten Arrows): it is from the Slavic pronunciation of this name that the Magyars came to be called Hungarians by their neighbours.

In the late ninth century the Magyars, under pressure from their eastern neighbours the Pechenegs, migrated west towards the Danube, where the Byzantines encouraged them to attack the Bulgars. Arnulf, king of East Francia (Germany) 887–99, enticed the Magyars further west by inviting them to join him in attacking the Slav principality of Great Moravia. Under the leadership of Árpád, the Magyars crossed the Carpathian mountains in 896, and by 906 they had driven the Slavs out of the Hungarian plain and begun to launch raids into Bavaria and northern Italy. Though Árpád died in 907, the success of these raids encouraged even bolder raids in the years to come.

The Magyar invasions, 915–55

The Magyars were attracted to the Hungarian plain for the same reasons that had drawn the Avars and Huns to settle there before them. It was the most westerly area of the great Eurasian steppe that had sufficient grazing for the vast herds of horses on which the nomads depended. The plain's westerly position also made it an ideal base for raiding the Frankish kingdoms. The Magyars were typical nomad warriors, light cavalry who, unlike the heavy Frankish cavalry, relied on speed and mobility rather than armour for protection; their principal weapon was the bow. As far as possible they avoided hand-to-hand combat, preferring to shower arrows on their opponents from a distance until casualties, exhaustion and frustration opened gaps in enemy formations. They kept slower-moving opponents off balance by making frequent and unexpected changes of direction, making it difficult to predict where they would strike next.

The Holy Crown of Hungary, the coronation crown of the Hungarian kings, was made in the Byzantine Empire in the 1070s as a diplomatic gift for King Geza I.

In 910 the Germans under Louis III the Child (r. 900–11) were defeated by Magyars at the Battle of Augsburg after falling for the oldest trick in the nomad book of war. Confronted by heavy German cavalry, the Magyars pretended to flee, only to turn and annihilate their pursuers once they had become thoroughly disorganized and exhausted. For the next thirty years Italy, Germany and France were intensively and repeatedly raided. In 921 Magyar raiders reached Otranto on the heel of Italy and in 924 they reached as far as the foothills of the Pyrenees. In 942 a Magyar army reached Constantinople before it was bought off by the Byzantines.

The intensity of Magyar raids gradually declined from the 930s because of widespread construction of fortresses in western Europe. The German kings Henry I the Fowler (r. 919–36) and Otto I (r. 936–73) were particularly active in fortifying the eastern border of Germany against the raiders, and Henry inflicted the first serious defeat on the Magyars at the Battle of Riade in 933. This hardly dented Magyar power. The greatest raid of all came in 954, when a force of Magyars, claimed to be 50,000 strong, rampaged through Germany, France, Burgundy and Italy before returning to Hungary. When the Magyars tried to repeat the feat the following year, however, they were brought to battle by Otto I at Lechfeld near Augsburg. Otto refused to be panicked by the Magyars' enveloping manoeuvre and concentrated his strength on the main body of their army, routing it. The Magyars fled, abandoning their loot.

Otto's victory was decisive, virtually ending the Magyar threat at a stroke. In 975 the ruling prince Géza I (r. *c.* 970–97) converted to Roman Catholicism, beginning the normalization of the Magyars' relations with their neighbours. Under his son Stephen I (St Stephen, r. 997–1038) Hungary emerged as a strong and stable kingdom.

The Magyar invasions, 915–55

- borders, c. 900
- main area of Magyar settlement
- border of the kingdom of Hungary, c. 1000
- initial Magyar migration
- Magyar raid, with date
- main area devastated by Magyar raids, 899–955

XI
Emerging Europe

Defining a continent

The final breakup of the Carolingian Empire in 888 created five kingdoms: Italy, Burgundy, Provence, France (formerly West Francia) and Germany (formerly East Francia). In the following century Germany and France developed in very different ways. Germany became the core of another revived 'Roman' empire, incorporating much of Italy, Burgundy and Provence. France became a decentralized feudal kingdom under the last feeble successors of Charlemagne.

After Charles the Fat was deposed, the West Franks elected Eudes (or Odo, r. 888–96), the count of Paris, as their king on the strength of his victories over the Vikings. However, he spent most of his reign trying, and ultimately failing, to see off his Carolingian rival Charles the Simple (r. 893–923). Though the crown reverted to Eudes's family on Charles's death, the Carolingians were restored again in 936, but could never re-establish their authority. Much as the last Merovingians had been dominated by their mayors, the Carolingians were dominated by the dukes of the Franks, Hugh the Great and his son Hugh Capet, who became the effective rulers during the reigns of Lothar III (r. 954–86) and Louis V (r. 986–87).

The Carolingians had become victims of decentralizing tendencies inherent in feudalism. Under the Carolingians, counts and dukes were vassals who held royal lands in their areas of jurisdiction as *benefices* from the crown. Theoretically, these magnates served for life;

Imperial Crown of the Holy Roman Empire. Made for the coronation of Emperor Otto I in 962, the crown was used until the dissolution of the empire in 1806.

when they died the office and its *benefices* returned into the gift of the king. In practice, however, they became hereditary. This gradually undermined the centralized authority of the monarchy, diminishing the crown's power of patronage by alienating royal land. A strong king could resist this tendency but, during their fratricidal wars, Louis the Pious's sons were reluctant to do anything that might strain the loyalty of their fickle vassals and instead made concession after concession.

Charles the Bald's son, Louis II the Stammerer (r. 877–79), recognized the problem too late and when he tried to redistribute *benefices* the magnates united and forced him to back down. The situation worsened when Eudes allowed the Carolingian system of government to lapse. Royal legates no longer went out to supervise the counts and ensure that the king's rights were respected. As the royal demesne dwindled, so did the king's retinue of military vassals. By the late tenth century the monarchy lacked the means to enforce obedience. Some of the more powerful magnates, such as the dukes of Normandy and Aquitaine, did not even bother with the formality of homage and had more counts among their vassals than did the king.

Hugh the Great, count of Paris: he was the father of Hugh Capet, the first king of the Capetian dynasty, which ruled France uninterrupted from 987 until 1792.

The surprise is that the monarchy survived at all, but despite its lack of power it was a necessary institution. The idea of a divinely appointed kingship was universally accepted: legitimate power 'descended' from God to the king, who alone could devolve it further to the magnates and legitimize their authority over their own vassals. So it was that when the last Carolingian king, childless twenty-year-old Louis V, died in 987, the nobles elected Hugh Capet as king (r. 987–96), but he was no more able to control the magnates than the last Carolingians had been. Hugh's direct rule was confined to his personal estates around Orléans and Paris; he did not even have the power to punish Eudes, count of Blois, and the bishop of Laon for plotting to kidnap him and hand him over to Holy Roman Emperor Otto III (r. 996–1002).

Despite this, Hugh began the long process of restoring the authority of the monarchy by crowning his son Robert II (r. 996–1031) as heir during his lifetime. This custom, followed by all his successors, ended divisible inheritance and established hereditary succession to a monarchy that was becoming elective.

Robert II enhanced the mystique of monarchy by promoting the Royal Touch, the belief that physical contact with the king could cure scrofula, a disfiguring skin disease. Robert also increased the

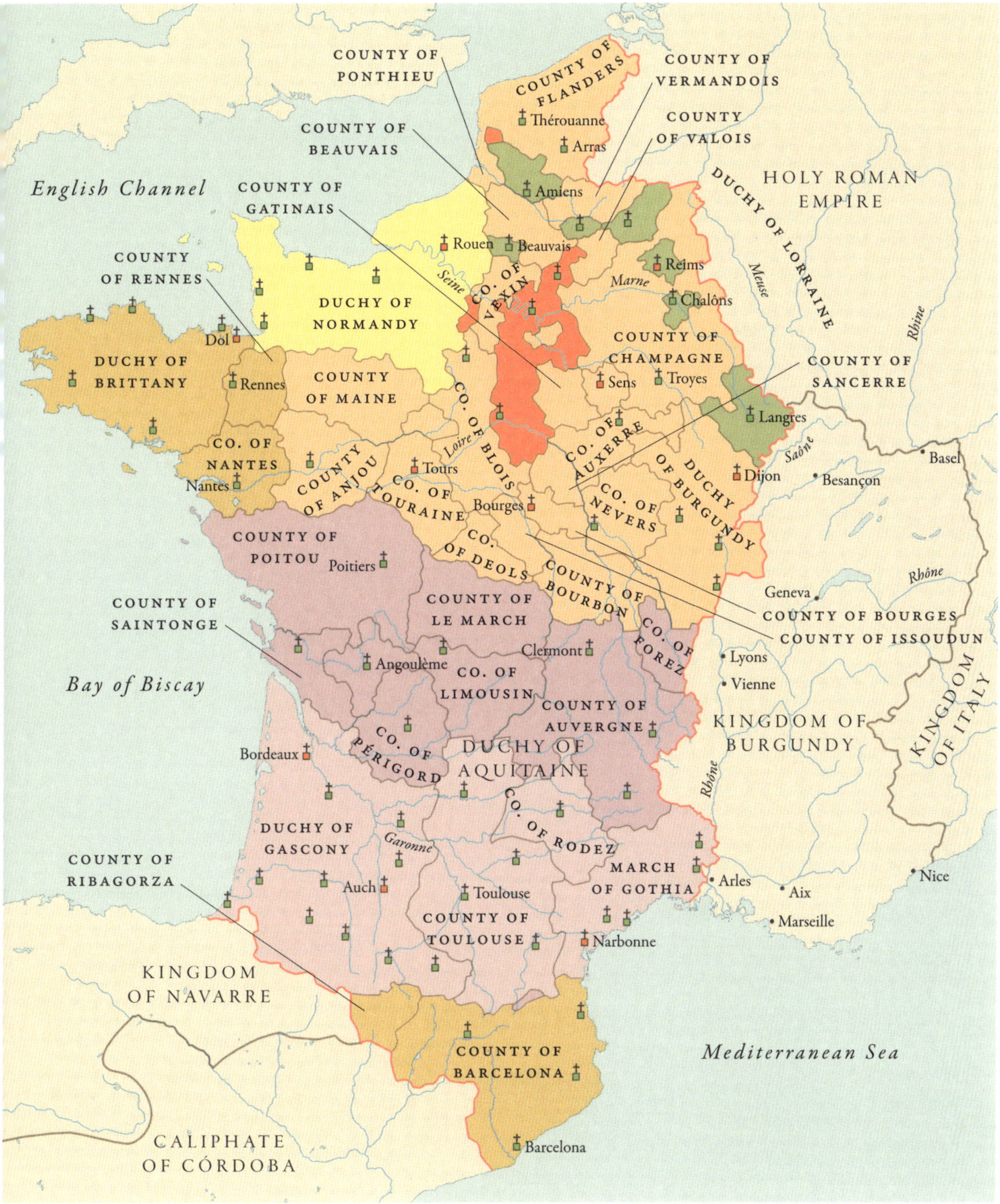

France, c.1000

- boundary of the kingdom of France, *c.* 1000
- French royal demesne, *c.* 1031
- fiefs of the Crown
- duchy of Aquitaine and its fiefs
- Church lands
- other territories owning nominal allegiances to the king
- archbishopric
- bishopric

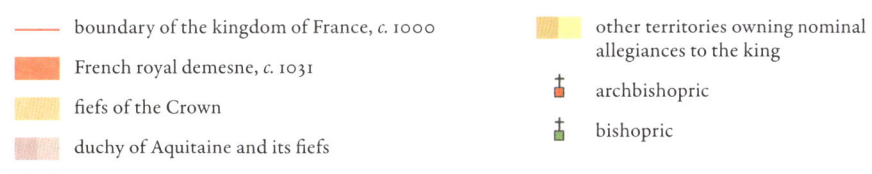

royal demesne by reclaiming lands left vacant through lack of heirs. It was a small beginning but measures like these gradually increased the power of the monarchy. In the twelfth century, the Capetian dynasty was able finally to bring the magnates to heel and become rulers of France in reality as well as in name.

The German Empire

While France was divided into thirty or forty small counties and duchies, Germany in the early tenth century was dominated by the four great 'tribal' duchies of Saxony, Franconia, Swabia and Bavaria, which corresponded roughly to the territories of Germany's main ethnic groups. Germany's duchies had a military origin. From Charlemagne's time, it was customary to call up German contingents of the royal army by 'nation' and the ducal families descended from the leaders of these contingents. Originally royal appointees, the duchies became hereditary principalities under the last Carolingian kings of Germany, Arnulf (r. 887–99) and Louis the Child (r. 900–11). The resources of any one tribal duke rivalled that of the king and made them a grave threat.

When Louis the Child died in 911, aged sixteen and without heirs, the dukes elected one of their own, Conrad of Franconia (r. 911–18), to the throne. The main significance of his reign is that it is usually taken to mark the beginning of the independent history of Germany. However, Conrad was unable to establish his authority and shortly before his death he nominated Henry the Fowler (r. 918–36), duke of Saxony, as his successor. Henry set about restoring authority to the monarchy by reclaiming rights lost in the previous thirty years, including the right to appoint counts and bishops in the duchies, and demanding restoration of royal estates appropriated by dukes. The dukes resisted but Henry's victory over the Magyars at the Battle of Riade in 933 greatly increased his authority. So great was Henry's prestige subsequently that he was able to abandon the Frankish principle of partible inheritance and nominate his eldest son Otto I (r. 936–73) as his sole successor. Otto was crowned at Aachen in a ceremony calculated to revive memories of Charlemagne. The comparison with Charlemagne was justified by Otto's career, in which he conquered Bohemia, Moravia and pagan Slavs between the Elbe and the Oder. His greatest military achievement was his defeat of the Magyars at the Battle of Lechfeld in 955, which broke their power forever. Missionary activity always followed Otto's victories and by the end of the century the Magyars and Poles were Christian.

In 950 the kingdom of Italy was inherited by a woman, Adelaide. Not surprisingly she had many suitors, some of Otto's dukes among them. To forestall them, Otto invaded in 951, married Adelaide himself, and declared himself king of Italy. Otto also demanded the pope confer on him the imperial title but was refused. It was not until 962, when Pope John XII needed Otto's help against a rebellion, that he was crowned *imperator augustus*, founding the medieval German Empire – or, as it was called from the thirteenth century, the Holy Roman Empire.

To limit the tribal duchies' power, Otto deposed all hereditary dukes and replaced them with members of the royal family, an imperfect solution because royals were equally capable of rebelling if they felt their interests were threatened. This led Otto to a novel solution. The Church was given lavish grants of land, in return for which the bishops were obliged to fulfil all the usual feudal duties, such as providing knights for the royal army and hospitality for the king and court. The advantage of this system was that bishops – canonically prohibited from marriage – could not have legal heirs, so there was no danger of land being alienated

The East Frankish king Henry the Fowler's victory over the Magyars at the Battle of Riade in 933, from a 14th-century manuscript.

The German Empire, c. 1000

- boundary of the kingdom of Germany, c. 962
- lands of the German duchies
- German March
- territory lost during the Slav revolt, 983
- state under German influence
- archbishopric
- new bishopric, with foundation date
- important bishopric
- important monastery
- battle, with date

from the crown by becoming hereditary. When a bishop died, his see automatically returned to the gift of the crown, so the king's powers of patronage were permanently being renewed.

This system, known as the Ottonian system after its creator, made the German monarchy the strongest in Europe until, in 1076, Pope Gregory VII successfully challenged the king's right to appoint bishops, dealing a crippling blow to royal authority from which it never fully recovered.

The unification of England

The most important consequence of the Viking invasions of Britain was that they disrupted the existing power structures. It was not ultimately the Vikings who benefited from this but native dynasties who, in the course of the tenth century, forged the kingdoms of England and Scotland.

The only Anglo-Saxon kingdom to survive the Viking invasions intact was Alfred the Great's Wessex. Once he had secured his demesne, Alfred showed that he was aware of the great possibilities created by the demise of Wessex's traditional rivals. He developed a close relationship with the unoccupied western half of Mercia by marrying his daughter Ethelflaed to its ruler ealdorman Ethelred. This paved the way for its formal annexation to Wessex by Alfred's son Edward the Elder (r. 899–924) after Ethelflaed's death in 918. Alfred also showed his ambitions in dealings with Guthrum (d. *c.* 890), the Danish king of East Anglia. When Guthrum broke the peace in 886 Alfred occupied London (then part of Guthrum's kingdom) and forced him to give equal legal rights to the Anglo-Saxons living under his rule. This gave substance to Alfred's claim to leadership of the Anglo-Saxons or, as they had begun calling themselves, Angelcynn or Englisc.

Aided by his sister Ethelflaed, Edward the Elder conquered East Anglia and the Five Boroughs between 912 and 917, bringing all of England south of the Humber under his control. The system of *burhs* begun by Alfred was extended into newly conquered areas to secure Anglo-Saxon control. Then in 927, Edward's son Athelstan (r. 924–39) captured York and deposed the last Northumbrian king, Aldred, bringing all of England under one ruler for the first time.

XI EMERGING EUROPE

Athelstan's growing power united against him a coalition of the Dublin Vikings, the Scots and the Britons of Strathclyde. Athelstan routed this coalition at the Battle of Brunanburh in 937, but his achievement was not yet secure. After his death the Norse captured York, but they could never hold it securely and after its last Viking monarch, Erik Bloodaxe, was killed in 954 it reverted to the kingdom of England. The Vikings had no advantage in military technology over the Anglo-Saxons and fought in a very similar way; their successes were due entirely to their mobility and ability to concentrate their forces on one Anglo-Saxon kingdom at a time. Once they settled down, they lost these advantages and became just as vulnerable to attack as had been their victims.

The Danish settlements had no united leadership and no individual Danish ruler could match the resources of Wessex. The consequences of defeat for the Danes were not serious. The Wessex dynasty was not fighting to liberate England from the Danes but to bring all of England under its sole rule and was quite happy to have Danes among its tax-paying subjects. No attempt was made to expel the Danes from the lands they occupied and the distinct laws and customs of the Danelaw were respected by English

The Alfred Jewel was probably the handle of a pointer for following text in manuscripts. Made *c.* 890, the jewel was probably commissioned by King Alfred the Great.

The unification of England

border of Wessex, 871	kingdom of the Anglo-Saxons, 899	major royal centre
Alfred–Guthrum treaty boundary, *c.* 880	conquered, 912–17	mint
political boundary, 957	conquered, 918–20	English borough
battle, with date	annexed, 927–54	The Five Boroughs of the Danelaw

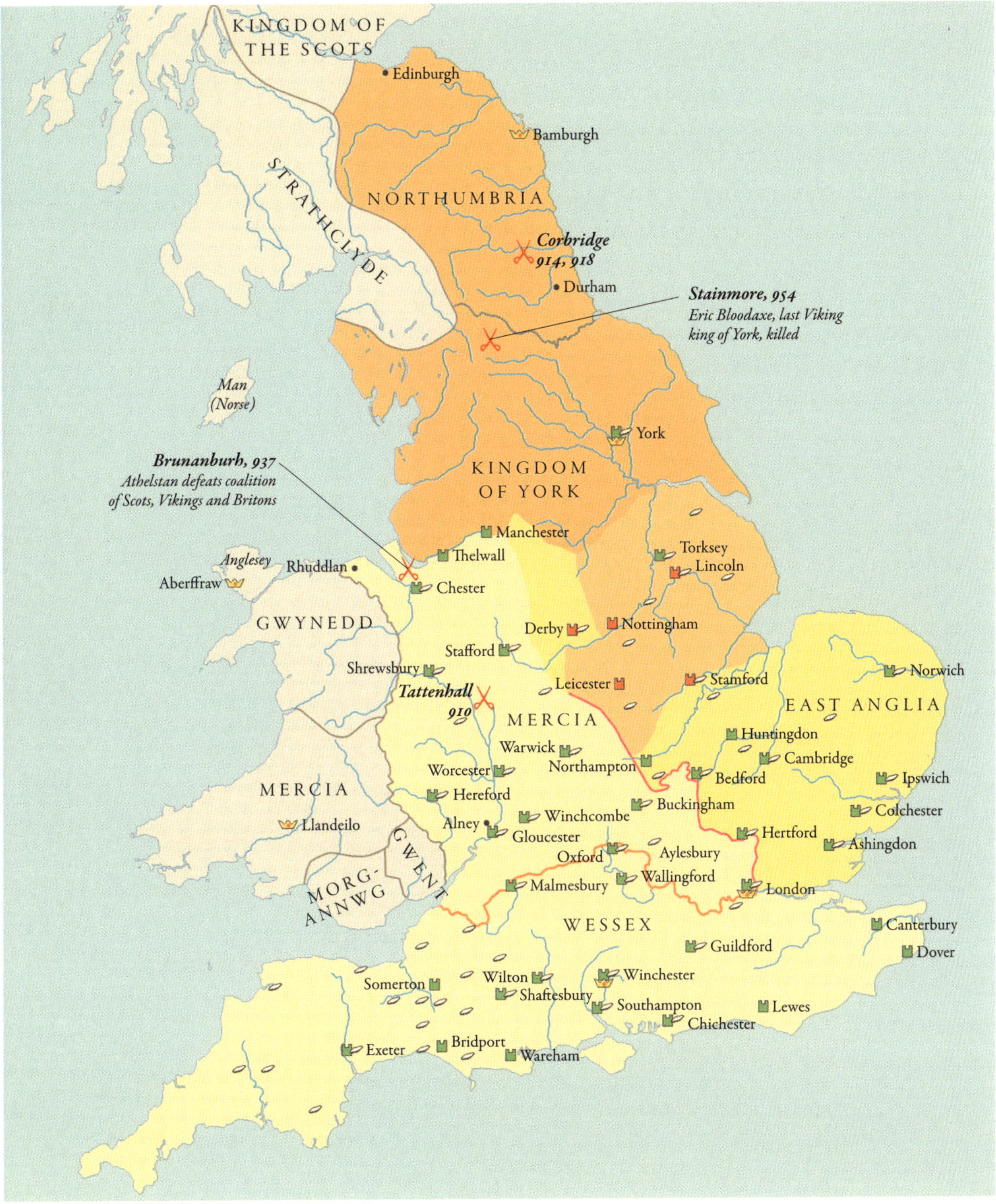

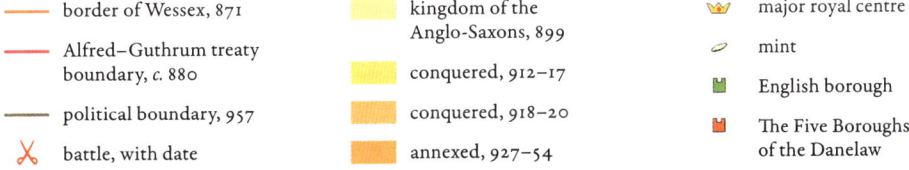

rulers until after the Norman conquest. Many Anglo-Saxons who lived under Danish rule were clear about the Wessex dynasty's aims. They valued their traditions of local autonomy and were willing to fight with the Danes against the Wessex takeover.

Assimilation of the conquered Danes was not difficult. The Anglo-Saxons and Danes had similar ways of life and spoke mutually intelligible languages. Once the Danes had converted to Christianity – few pagan Scandinavian graves have been found, indicating that this was a rapid process – there were no serious obstacles to assimilation. United, England quickly became the dominant kingdom of the British Isles. This dominance was given powerful symbolic expression in 973 when King Edgar (r. 959–75), the strongest of England's Anglo-Saxon monarchs, was rowed on the River Dee at Chester by eight British and Viking kings, while he steered the boat.

Though England was conquered in turn by the Danes and Normans in the eleventh century, these were essentially dynastic takeovers and its unity was never seriously threatened. Neither the Danish Cnut, nor the Norman William the Conqueror, had the slightest interest in dismembering what had become one of the wealthiest and best-governed kingdoms in Europe.

Kingdom of the Scots

Like England, Scotland owes its existence indirectly to the Vikings for breaking up existing kingdoms and altering the balance of power. The Scots kings of Dál Riata proved most adept at exploiting the new opportunities thus created. In 843 Kenneth MacAlpin (r. c. 840–58), king of the Scots of Dál Riata, conquered the Pictish kingdom of Fortriu, whose king had been killed in battle with the Vikings in 839. The presence of the Vikings along the west coast had made their traditional royal centre at Dunadd insecure, so the Scots removed to Fortriu, eventually establishing a new royal presence at Scone.

Kenneth and his immediate successors considered themselves simply as kings of the Scots and the Picts. Kenneth's grandson Donald II (r. 889–900) adopted a new territorial title, King of Alba (from the Irish word for Britain) or Scotia. Scotia was much smaller than modern Scotland; its southern border was at the Forth.

Most of the Hebrides and northern isles were ruled by the Norse and Moray belonged to Scotia more in theory than in practice. It took centuries of aggressive diplomacy and military expansion before Scotland attained its modern borders.

The early kingdom of the Scots was divided into provinces ruled by *mormaers* (stewards). These officers were responsible for leading the men of the province in wartime, collecting taxes and administering justice. Most of the provinces were small but one, Moray, covered most of the northern Highlands. The relationship of Moray to the Scottish kingdom was an ambiguous one, because its rulers were only described as *mormaers* by the kings of the Scots, but considered themselves independent rulers and always described themselves as kings. Thanks to Shakespeare, the most famous ruler of Moray was Macbeth, king of the Scots 1040–57. Moray was only fully integrated into Scotland in the twelfth century.

In the tenth century the Scots began to extend their power south of the Forth. The British kingdom of Strathclyde had been severely weakened when the Vikings sacked its capital at Dumbarton in 870, which allowed the Scots to bring its royal dynasty under their control through marriage alliances. The English reacted by launching several expeditions against Strathclyde, as in 945 when King Edmund I (r. 939–46) defeated Dunmail, the British sub-king of Cumbria. After its last king, Owen the Bald, was killed fighting the English at Carham in 1018, a fatally weakened British Strathclyde was fully annexed by Scotland.

The Scots also put pressure on the English. King Indulf held Edinburgh in 954–62 and in 973 King Edgar, realizing that it would be difficult to defend this distant part of his realm, ceded Lothian to Kenneth II (r. 971–95) in return for his submission to English overlordship. Malcolm II's victory over the English at Carham in 1018, won while England was under Danish rule, established the Tweed as Scotland's southern border, where it has more or less remained to the present day.

Though the Hebrides and northern isles were still under Norse rule, and would be for hundreds of years to come, the kingdom of the Scots in the early eleventh century was a close territorial approximation to modern Scotland. However, it was still a kingdom without a nation. While the English had recognized a degree of common identity even before they were united by the Wessex dynasty,

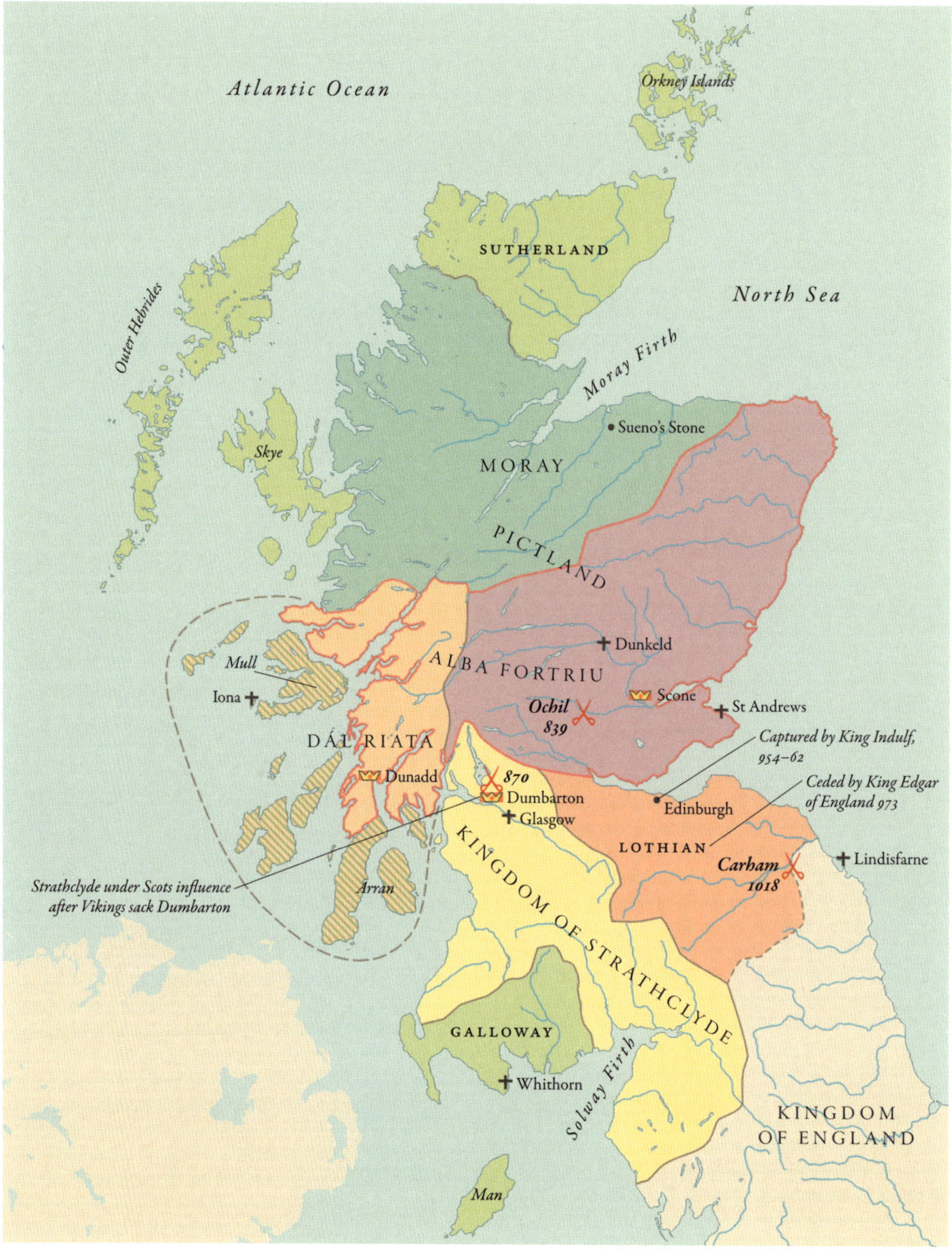

The foundation of Scotland

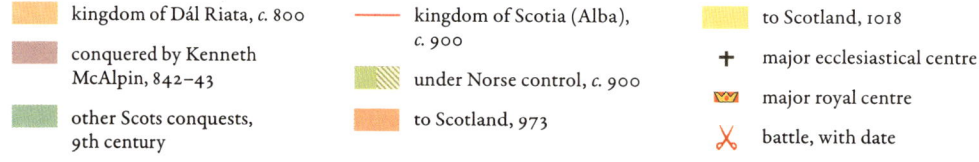

early Scotland remained a multi-ethnic kingdom. Though the Picts had probably been completely assimilated by the Scots before the early tenth century (they are not mentioned after 904), the Britons of Strathclyde and the English of Lothian still retained their original ethnic identities in the twelfth century.

As for the Scots, they did not see themselves as a people in their own right at all but considered themselves to be Irish. A true Scottish national identity was forged only in the wars of independence against England in 1296–1328.

Scandinavia beyond the Viking raids

The Viking raids began as a result of political developments within Scandinavia, as chiefdoms began to be forged into kingdoms. It was the completion of this process around the beginning of the eleventh century that also brought an end to them. With the consolidation of royal power, Scandinavian kings developed institutionalized means of gathering revenue from taxes and tolls, so there was no longer the same pressure to lead dangerous plundering raids. Kings came to see freelance Viking piracy as a threat to trade (which could be taxed) and to good relations with neighbouring kingdoms, so they gradually suppressed it.

At the beginning of the Viking age, Denmark was the most advanced Scandinavian kingdom. Danish kings controlled an area much larger than modern Denmark, including large parts of southern Sweden and Norway. However, this outwardly impressive kingdom was highly unstable. Danish kings were chosen from an extended royal family – and any male member was eligible for kingship. Succession disputes were very common. Unsuccessful claimants frequently went into exile and became Viking leaders in the hopes of winning wealth, reputation and a loyal following of warriors to help make a fresh attempt on the throne. This destabilized the Danish monarchy and the kingdom collapsed in the second half of the ninth century.

Around 900 Harald Fairhair (or Finehair, d. c. 930), king or chief of Vestfold, took advantage of the collapse of Danish power to make himself ruler of most of Norway by defeating a coalition of chiefs and petty kings at the Battle of Hafrsfjord. Harald's victory is traditionally seen as marking the foundation of the kingdom of Norway, but

The Scandinavian kingdoms to 1000

Area under Danish control:

- c. 800
- c. 995
- no permanent settlement
- royal or aristocratic centre
- site of regional assembly
- round fort built by Harald Bluetooth
- bishopric, with foundation date
- other important church
- defended settlement
- other fort
- trading place

his authority over the powerful jarls (or earls) of Hlaðir was purely nominal. The jarls valued their independence and generally did whatever they could to retard the growth of royal power in Norway.

The Danish kingdom recovered in the mid-tenth century under King Gorm (d. 958) and his son Harald Bluetooth (r. 958–87). Earlier Danish kings had exercised authority indirectly through local chieftains: Harald greatly advanced royal power by building and garrisoning a series of forts so that he could control his kingdom directly. Harald also restored Danish control of Norway. In 965 he was baptized by Poppo, a German missionary, and became the first Scandinavian king actively to promote Christianity. Harald's son Svein Forkbeard (r. 987–1014) further advanced the monarchy's wealth and authority by leading well-organized raids on England to raise tribute. Lacking effective revenue-raising institutions at home, Svein became a parasite on England's precociously efficient administration.

By leading these raids in person, Svein prevented any other Viking winning sufficient wealth and prestige to make a bid for the throne. However, Olaf Tryggvasson, a Norwegian Viking raiding England around the same time, established himself as king of Norway in 995. Olaf ruled for only five years before he was killed in battle against an alliance of Svein and Jarl Erik of Hlaðir. In his brief reign he used brutal methods to convert the Norwegians to Christianity. It was not until the 1040s that Norway finally emerged from Denmark's shadow.

The climax of Svein's career was his conquest of England in 1013 but he died within weeks of his victory. Under Svein's able son Cnut (r. 1016–35) Denmark was briefly the centre of a North Sea empire that comprised England, Norway and the earldom of Orkney. Much influenced by English institutions and Christian ideology, Cnut brought Denmark into the European cultural and political mainstream.

Little is known about the history of Sweden in this period. The Svear, after whom Sweden is named, had a close relationship with the neighbouring Götar. By 1000 both peoples were united under the rule of Olof Skötkonung ('the tax-gatherer', r. c. 995–1021), but this union was insecure, and it was only in the twelfth century that Sweden became a strongly united kingdom. Olof was a Christian but did not pursue a policy of forced conversion and paganism still flourished at the end of the eleventh century.

A silver crucifix, made to be worn as a pendant, found at Aunslev in Denmark. Dated to c. 900, it is the oldest known crucifix to have been found in Scandinavia.

The Reconquista begins

The dominant theme of Spanish medieval history is the Reconquista, the Christian reconquest of the Iberian peninsula from the Moors. Centuries of struggle against the Muslims (the reconquest was not completed until 1492) bred the spirit of militant Catholicism that, until recent times, was a characteristic of Spanish identity.

The Reconquista is traditionally said to have begun with the victory of Pelayo (r. 718–37) over the Moors at Covadonga, high in the Cantabrian mountains of Asturias in 718. Following his victory, Pelayo, a refugee Visigoth noble, founded the principality of Asturias,

A romanticized 19th-century painting of King Pelayo celebrating his victory over the Moors at Covadonga in 718. In Spanish historical tradition, this marked the beginning of the Christian Reconquista.

The Reconquista of Iberia begins, c. 750–c. 1000

- Christian state, c. 1000
- Muslim state, c. 1000
- northern limit of Muslim conquest, c. 750
- southern limit of Christian reconquest by 814
- ✠ town founded or resettled by Christians, with date
- town sacked by al-Mansur's armies
- boundary of Muslim state
- ⚔ battle, with date

which controlled the narrow strip of northern Spain between the Cantabrian mountains and the sea. After Garcia I (r. 909–14) moved his capital from Oviedo to León, Asturias became known as the kingdom of León.

The Abbasid revolution, which overthrew the Umayyad caliphate in 751, was a decisive event in the Christian recovery. As we have seen (p. 185), the sole surviving Umayyad, Abd al-Rahman I (d. 788), fled to Spain, seized Córdoba in 756 and spent the next thirty years securing control of Muslim Spain. Exploiting dissension among the Muslims, Pelayo's successors – son-in-law Alfonso I (r. 737–57) and grandson Fruela I (r. 757–69) – systematically ravaged the region between the Cantabrian mountains and the River Douro, forcing its inhabitant to resettle in Asturias and Galicia. This also increased resources of manpower and created a depopulated buffer zone between them and the Moors.

This frontier zone, the *tierras despobladas*, fluctuated according to the changing fortunes of the Christian and Muslim states but the general movement was south. Once control over part of the zone had been secured, Christian settlers were brought in to repopulate it. Many of these were *caballeros villanos* (knight-serfs), a uniquely Spanish institution of non-noble cavalry soldiers who were expected to support themselves with farming or trade but maintain constant readiness for action in the event of Moorish raids.

Charlemagne sought to profit from Abd al-Rahman's problem. Although his first expedition ended in disaster at Roncesvalles in 778, by the end of Charlemagne's reign he had established the county of Barcelona and extended Frankish power to the Ebro. When the power of the Frankish monarchy declined under Charlemagne's successors, the Moors won back much of the Ebro valley, while Navarre and Barcelona became independent Christian principalities.

Under Abd al-Rahman III (r. 912–61), who formally adopted the title of caliph in 929, the Moors began a determined counterattack. It was fortunate for the Christians that the Muslims' major objective was plunder and captives for ransom or slavery rather than the acquisition of territory, because Christian victories were rare in the tenth century. The raids attracted plenty of mercenary soldiers to supplement the levies who formed the bulk of the caliphate's armies: many of them came from North Africa but others were Christians from northern Spain itself. The raids also attracted jihadis from

Overleaf: The *mihrab* of the Great Mosque of Córdoba, built in the 10th century under the Caliph al-Hakam II, indicates the correct direction for Muslim prayer.

across the Muslim world – Spain became known as Dar Djihad, the 'Land of Jihad'.

The Moorish offensive reached its greatest intensity from 978 to 1002 under the leadership of the vizier al-Mansur (also known as Almanzor, 914–1002), the real power behind the throne of the feeble caliph Hisham II (r. 976–1008 and 1010–12). Al-Mansur led over fifty successful raids against León and Navarre, culminating in the 997 sack of the pilgrimage centre of Santiago de Compostela in the far northwest of Galicia. The Christians were so relieved when al-Mansur died that one chronicler wrote that he 'had been seized by the Devil and buried in hell'.

With al-Mansur's passing, the Moors never again posed a serious threat to the survival of the Christian states. Al-Mansur's domination of the caliph had fatally undermined the authority of the office: his death created a power vacuum and the caliphate was ripped apart by civil war as rival generals fought to fill it.

Byzantine recovery

After centuries of fighting retreat, in the tenth century the Byzantine Empire began to reassert itself as the dominant power of the eastern Mediterranean. It expanded its borders at the expense of its Christian and Muslim neighbours. The Byzantine recovery was partly a result of the decline of its greatest adversary, the Abbasid caliphate. Political disintegration began at the end of the eighth century during the reign of Harun al-Rashid when the Maghrib and Ifriqiya (Tunisia) became independent, and continued steadily until by 945 the caliphate was a purely spiritual office, its legitimacy contested by rival caliphs in Spain and Egypt.

Anatolia had borne the brunt of Arab jihadist invasions and, as its themes were the main source of troops for the Byzantine army, its defence had to be a priority. With the Muslim world riven, the empire's resources could now be redeployed to win back lost territory in Europe and the Middle East. The Byzantines' Macedonian dynasty produced a succession of able rulers who took advantage of the opportunities that the caliphate's decline offered. The founder of the Macedonian dynasty, Basil I, was known as 'the Macedonian' but came from Armenia and rose to power in 867

BYZANTINE RECOVERY

Gold *solidus* of the Byzantine emperor Basil II 'the Bulgar Slayer', and his brother and successor Constantine VIII.

by murdering his predecessor and supposed friend, the drunken Michael III.

Though illiterate, Basil was an able administrator who reformed Byzantine law and rebuilt the navy so that it could once again challenge the Muslims on the high seas. Basil failed to drive the Muslims from Sicily and Crete, but by conquering much of southern Italy and re-establishing an eastern frontier on the Euphrates he brought the empire its first territorial gains for over 200 years. Under Basil's immediate successors, the empire suffered further setbacks at the hands of the Bulgars, but expansion began anew during the reign of Romanus II when a naval expedition in 961 ended 150 years of Arab occupation in Crete. The general of that expedition, Nicephorus II Phocas, became emperor in 963 on the death of Romanus – probably poisoned by his wife Theophano, who then married Nicephorus.

Nicephorus enjoyed further victories over the Arabs in Cilicia and Syria, but the cost of his wars led to him being overthrown and murdered in 969 by John I Tzimisces. Again, Theophano married the new emperor. John was another capable general who won back substantial territories from the Bulgars and Arabs during his short reign. John's successor was the greatest of all Byzantine emperors, Basil II (r. 976–1025), son of Romanus II and Theophano. With his younger brother Constantine, he had been crowned co-emperor shortly before his father's death. Being too young to reign, the boys had remained in the care of their mother during the reigns of Nicephorus and John I Tzimisces. On John's death the brothers became co-rulers. Constantine was a debauched slacker who was happy to live it up in the palace, leaving the conduct of policy to Basil. This seems to have suited Basil, who was as dedicated to war as his brother was to pleasure.

Basil's first challenge was a resurgent Bulgar khanate under Tsar Samuel (r. 976–1014). In the early years of his reign Basil II had to wrest power from his great-uncle, the chamberlain Basil Parakoimomenos. Samuel took advantage of the power struggle to start winning back Bulgar territories lost in John's reign. Basil's first campaign against Samuel, in 981, ended with a disastrous defeat when the still inexperienced emperor marched straight into a well-prepared ambush. Basil went back on the attack in 996 and in a brutal twenty-two-year-long war destroyed the Bulgar khanate

Revival of Byzantine fortunes, 867–1025

- Byzantine Empire at the accession of Basil I, 867
- boundary of Byzantine Empire, 867
- expansion of Byzantine Empire by 1025
- boundary of Byzantine Empire, 1025

	border of Byzantine themes, 1025	////	Bulgar khanate, 976
TARON	Byzantine theme	●	Byzantine enclave, 867–1025
	Kyivan Rus', 1025		
	Holy Roman Empire, 1025		

and restored Byzantine control over the entire Balkan region, earning him the nickname 'Bulgar Slayer'. Much of Syria was conquered and Armenia annexed during his reign, bringing the Byzantine Empire to its greatest territorial extent. At the time of Basil II's death in 1025 the empire was the greatest power in Europe and the Middle East – its future seemed assured but before the century was out it had entered its terminal decline.

Kyivan Rus'

By AD 1000 Kyivan Rus' was a strong and stable Orthodox Christian state. Its culture and politics were powerfully influenced by the Byzantine Empire its leaders sought to emulate. If the founders of the Kyivan Rus' state, Rurik and Oleg (Helgi), are semi-legendary characters, their successor Igor (Ingvar, r. 912–45) belongs firmly to history. He had a troubled reign. In 941 Igor attacked Constantinople, but his fleet was destroyed by Byzantine galleys equipped with Greek Fire projectors, and two years later a Rus' force operating in the Caspian Sea suffered heavy losses for little profit. Igor was killed in 945 on a tribute-gathering raid against a Slav tribe.

Igor's son and successor Svyatoslav (r. 945–78) was the last pagan ruler of the Rus' and the first to have a Slav name. Svyatoslav pursued an aggressive foreign policy. In 964–65 he conquered the Volga Bulgars and Khazars then, encouraged by the Byzantines, he attacked the Bulgar khanate on the Danube in 967. However, his success so alarmed the Byzantines that they turned on Svyatoslav, defeated him at the Battle of Pereyslavets in 971, and forced his withdrawal. Returning to Kyiv, he was ambushed by Pechenegs at the Dnieper rapids and killed: Svyatoslav became just one more barbarian ruler to have his skull made into a drinking cup. Most of Svyatoslav's conquests were lost soon after his death and his son Vladimir I (r. 978–1015) pursued a more cautious foreign policy aimed at alliance with the Byzantines.

In the tenth century the Rus' lost their Scandinavian identity as they became assimilated by their more numerous Slav subjects. The first signs were apparent in the reign of Igor. All of the Rus' signatories to the trade treaty negotiated between Oleg and the Byzantines in 911 had Scandinavian names, but many of the signatories

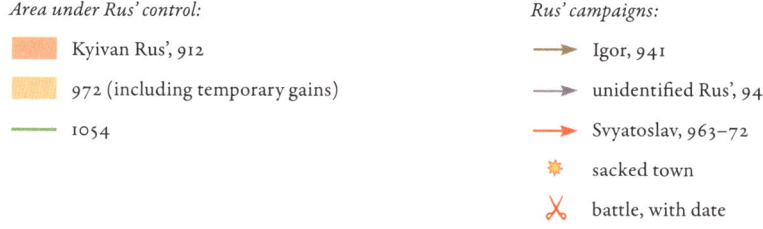

The Rus' state, 912–1054

Area under Rus' control:
- Kyivan Rus', 912
- 972 (including temporary gains)
- 1054

Rus' campaigns:
- Igor, 941
- unidentified Rus', 943
- Svyatoslav, 963–72
- sacked town
- battle, with date

to a similar treaty negotiated by Igor in 944 have Slavic names. The ruling dynasty all took Slavic appellations: Igor was the last Rus' ruler to have a Scandinavian name.

The Rus' ruling class probably also adopted Slavic religion, as Vladimir I worshipped the Slavic thunder god Perun before his conversion to Christianity in 988. By this date the majority of the ruling class must already have been Slavic-speaking because it was adopted as the language of the Church. A telling sign of the limited influence the Scandinavians had on their Slavic subjects is that there are only six Scandinavian loan words in the Russian language.

The most important influence on the Kyivan state was Byzantium, a result of Vladimir's decision to convert to Orthodox rather than Roman Catholic Christianity. Vladimir claimed that he was inspired by the beauty of Orthodox liturgy, but in reality it was probably Basil II's offer of marriage to his sister Anna that swayed Vladimir's decision. Anna was less than delighted by her union with a barbarian reputed to have taken part in human sacrifices and have hundreds of concubines, but it drew the Rus' firmly into the Byzantine cultural orbit. Kyivan Rus's alphabet, architecture, art, law, music and political ideologies were all Byzantine in origin.

In the later eleventh century, the Kyivan state began to break up into independent principalities, although all recognized the nominal superiority of Kyiv. The Kyivan state was finally swept away

A Byzantine warship using a 'Greek Fire' projector to defeat the Rus' attack on Constantinople in 941, from a manuscript of the chronicle of John Skylitzes.

by the Mongol and Tatar conquerors in the 1240s, but its heritage is foundational to both the modern Russian and Ukrainian national identities which began to develop only after the conquest.

EPILOGUE

The Birth of the West

Christianity – the social glue

In the year 1000, the young Holy Roman Emperor Otto III (r. 983–1002) made a pilgrimage to Aachen, where he opened the tomb of Charlemagne. He found the former emperor seated on a throne, sceptre in hand, looking, it was claimed, as if he was still alive. After paying his humble respects to the great man, Otto ordered that Charlemagne's nails be cut, for they had grown through his gloves, and had him dressed in fresh white clothes before resealing the tomb. A year earlier, Otto had appointed his French tutor Gerbert of Aurillac as pope, who took the name Sylvester II, after the pope who was believed to have baptized Constantine the Great. If Gerbert was a new Sylvester, the implication was clear: Otto was a new Constantine, the divinely appointed head of Christian society.

Otto made Rome his imperial residence and used a seal bearing on one side the legend *Renovatio Imperii Romanorum* (Renewal of the Roman Empire), and on the other, a portrait of Charlemagne, who had used the same legend on his own seal after his imperial coronation 200 years before. Otto's empire was the most powerful state in western Europe and few in 1000 would not have predicted a great future for it. The same would have been true of its eastern counterpart, the Byzantine Empire, which could more aptly claim to be the successor of Rome than could the Holy Roman Empire. It even seemed possible that, in the person of Otto, whose mother was the

The Holy Roman Emperor Otto III is shown seated in majesty in this illustration from the 11th-century Gospels of Otto III. Otto idealistically presented himself as a restorer of the Roman Empire.

Byzantine princess Theophano, the eastern and western empires might be reunited to bring all Christians under a single state and a divinely appointed emperor.

Harking back to an idealized Roman past was typical of the early Middle Ages but disguises the reality that Europe was on the brink of a profound transformation. Within a century, both of these mighty theocratic 'Roman' empires would have their best years behind them. The Byzantine Empire, which had done so much to protect Christendom from the Arabs, would have its power broken by a new Muslim enemy, the Seljuq Turks. The authority of the Holy Roman emperors would be fatally undermined by the papacy rebuking their claim to be the leaders of Christian society.

It may only be with the benefit of hindsight that we can see the early Middle Ages as the 'birth of Europe', but by 1000 the outlines of the modern Europe of nation states were already emerging. France, England, Scotland, Germany, Italy, Denmark, Poland and Hungary existed within close approximations of their modern borders, even if modern ideas of nationalism and the nation state did not yet exist. English identity was virtually coterminous with the kingdom of England, but in France the Frankish or French identity was still confined north of the Loire. In Germany, tribal identities were more important than a shared sense of German-ness. Italy was a kingdom but Italians were simply the people who lived there; though they shared the same language and culture, they had no sense of a common identity. The Scots still thought of themselves as being Irish. Loyalties everywhere were personal ones, to lord or king or town, not to an abstract notion of the state.

Overriding all local identities was Christendom. In theory, all Christians were still united in a single Church in 1000. In practice, doctrinal differences had strained relations between the western Roman Catholic Church and the eastern Orthodox Church almost to breaking point. The final breach lay only half a century into the future. The consequences of the split were profound and to this day western and eastern Europe are defined as much by culture as geography.

Compared to its Muslim neighbours, Europe in 1000 was economically and culturally backward. Muslims still found Byzantium impressive, but when they looked at western Europe they did not see beyond the unhygienic squalor of its small but now rapidly growing towns, to its steadily rising populations and expanding economies, which were the result of agricultural improvements in Carolingian times. These changes had already begun to shift the balance of power in favour of western Europe. In 700 it seemed a distinct possibility that Europe would be conquered and Islamized by the Arabs. In 1000 that was unlikely – the area under Christian domination was increasing rapidly. Economic growth also led to cultural expansion.

In the eleventh century literacy ceased to be the preserve of the Church: demand for secular education grew steadily as trade and government expanded. Urban cathedral schools and, later, universities replaced rural monasteries as the main centres of learning. The search for new intellectual tools to deal with an increasingly complex society led to the application of Classical philosophy to Christian theology and the revival of the study of Roman law. A new, distinctively western European civilization, with a triple Classical, Christian and Germanic inheritance, was being born.

Select Bibliography

Burns, Thomas, *A History of the Ostrogoths* (Indiana University Press, 1984).

Byock, Jesse, *Viking Age Iceland* (Penguin, 2001).

Christie, Neil, *The Lombards* (Blackwell, 1995).

Collins, Roger, *Early Medieval Europe 300–1000* (Macmillan, 2010).

Cunliffe, Barry, *Bretons and Britons* (Oxford University Press, 2021).

Fleming, Robert, *Britain after Rome: the Fall and Rise 400–1070* (Penguin, 2011).

Fletcher, Richard, *Moorish Spain* (Weidenfeld & Nicolson, 2001).

Halsall, Guy, *Barbarian Migrations and the Roman West 376–568* (Cambridge University Press, 2007).

Haywood, John, *The Historical Atlas of the Celtic World* (Thames & Hudson, 2001).

Haywood, John, *Northmen: The Viking Saga AD 793–1241* (Head of Zeus, 2015).

Haywood, John, *The Penguin Historical Atlas of the Vikings* (Penguin, 1995).

Heather, Peter, *Empires and Barbarians: Migration, Development and the Birth of Europe* (Macmillan, 2009).

Heather, Peter, *The Fall of the Roman Empire* (Macmillan, 2005).

Higham, Nicholas J. and Ryan, Martin J., *The Anglo-Saxon World* (Yale University Press, 2013).

Hill, David, *An Atlas of Anglo-Saxon England* (Blackwell, 1981).

Hodges, Richard, *Dark Age Economics: A New Audit* (Duckworth, 2012).

Holland, Tom, *In the Shadow of the Sword* (Little, Brown, 2012).

Hoyland, Robert G., *In God's Path: The Arab Conquests and the Creation of an Islamic Empire* (Oxford University Press, 2017).

James, Edward, *The Franks* (Blackwell, 1988).

James, Edward, *The Origins of France: from Clovis to the Capetians 500–1000* (Macmillan, 1982).

Jarman, Cat, *River Kings: The Vikings from Scandinavia to the Silk Roads* (Collins, 2021).

King, P. D., *Charlemagne* (Methuen, 1986).

Manco, Jean, *Ancestral Journeys: The Peopling of Europe from the First Venturers to the Vikings* (Thames & Hudson, 2015).

Mango, Cyril, *The Oxford History of the Byzantine Empire* (Oxford University Press, 2002).

Marozzi, Justin, *The Arab Conquests: The Spread of Islam and the First Caliphates* (Apollo, 2021).

McKitterick, Rosamund, *The Frankish Kingdoms under the Carolingians 751–987* (Longman, 1983).

Ó Cróinín, Dáibhí, *Early Medieval Ireland 400–1200* (Longman, 1995).

Price, Neil, *The Children of Ash and Elm: A History of the Vikings* (Allen Lane, 2020).

Raffensperger, Christian, *The Kingdom of Rus'* (Arc Humanities Press, 2017).

Reuter, Timothy, *Germany in the Early Middle Ages* (Longman, 1991).

Smyth, Alfred P., *Warlords and Holy Men: Scotland AD 80–1000* (Arnold, 1984)

Snyder, Christopher A., *An Age of Tyrants: Britain and the Britons AD 400–600* (Sutton Publishing Ltd, 1998).

Snyder, Christopher A., *Exploring the World of King Arthur* (Thames & Hudson, 2011).

Wolfram, Herwig, *A History of the Goths* (University of California Press, 1979).

Wood, Ian, *The Merovingian Kingdoms 450–751* (Longman, 1994).

Wood, Michael, *In Search of the Dark Ages* (BBC Books, 2023).

Sources of Illustrations

Maps and plans created by Roger Kean and designed by Alice C. Woodward.

2 Francis G. Mayer/Corbis/VCG via Getty Images

10 Roberto Fortuna/The National Museum, Copenhagen

13 Ali Meyer/Corbis/VCG via Getty Images

16 Museum of Vojvodina, Novi Sad, Serbia

20 Musei Capitolini, Rome. Marie-Lan Nguyen/Wikimedia Commons

21 Flavijus Piliponis/Adobe Stock

22–23 stocksolutions/Adobe Stock

25 Transfer from the Yale University Library, Numismatic Collection, 2001, Yale-French Excavations at Dura-Europos. Yale University Art Gallery, New Haven, CT (1938.6000.47)

28 Ms VectorPlus/Adobe Stock

32 Stig Alenäs/Alamy

38 Real Academia de la Historia, Madrid. WHPics/Alamy

42 DeAgostini/Getty Images

46 Acquired by Henry Walters, 1927. The Walters Art Museum, Baltimore (57.482)

47 Kunsthistorisches Museum, Vienna (Münzkabinett, RÖ 32482). Sandstein/Wikimedia Commons

49 enesdigital/Adobe Stock

50 Purchase, Joseph Pulitzer Bequest, 1987. The Metropolitan Museum of Art, New York (1987.90.30, 1987.90.1, 1987.90.2)

54 Archiv Gerstenberg/ullstein bild via Getty Images

55 Ashmolean Museum/Heritage Images/Getty Images

58, 63 Acquired by Henry Walters, 1930. The Walters Art Museum, Baltimore (54.422, 57.558)

68 DEA Picture Library/De Agostini via Getty Images

70 Funds given by Mr. Henry B. Pflager. Saint Louis Art Museum (65:1952)

74 Biblioteca Nacional de España, Madrid

78 Heritage Image Partnership Ltd/Alamy

83 Ruth Elizabeth White Fund. Yale University Art Gallery, New Haven (2016.75.3)

92 Renáta Sedmáková/Adobe Stock

97 Purchase from the J. H. Wade Fund. The Cleveland Museum of Art (2000.119)

98 Gift of Joe Hatzenbuehler. The Cleveland Museum of Art (2007.225)

100 Werner Forman/Universal Images Group/Getty Images

103 Peter Horree/Alamy

107 Musée Condé, Chantilly (Ms 869/522 fol.33v)/Bridgeman Images

110–11 Muhammed Enes Yildirim/Anadolu Agency via Getty Images

112 Gift of Darius Ogden Mills, 1904. The Metropolitan Museum of Art, New York (04.35.3357)

113, 119 Gift of J. Pierpont Morgan, 1917. The Metropolitan Museum of Art, New York (17.191.5, 17.190.1686)

121 Raffaello Bencini/Bridgeman Images

125 Gift of Martin A. Ryerson. Art Institute of Chicago (1922.4903)

130 Universal History Archive/Universal Images Group via Getty Images

132 The Trustees of the British Museum, London (1938,0202.1)

136 The British Library, London (Yates Thompson MS 26 f.50v, f.26r)

144 Valerie2000/Adobe Stock

146 PjrStatues/Alamy

148–49 Stephen Power/Alamy

151 National Museum of Scotland, Edinburgh (X.IB 189). Image © National Museums Scotland

157 Werner Forman/Universal Images Group/Getty Images

160 National Archaeological Museum, Madrid. Prisma Archivo/Alamy

164 From The Siyar-I-Nabi of Mustafa Dharir, copied by Mustafa Bin Vali, Turkey, 1594–95. Private Collection

169 Bibliothèque nationale de France. Département des Manuscrits. Français 22495

178 CNG, www.cngcoins.com

180–81 Victor/Adobe Stock

SOURCES OF ILLUSTRATIONS

182 Bibliothèque nationale de France. Département des Manuscrits. Arabe 5847

186 Bibliothèque nationale de France. Département des Manuscrits. Français 13502

188 CNG, www.cngcoins.com

191 Gift of J. Pierpont Morgan, 1917. The Metropolitan Museum of Art, New York (17.191.175)

196 Musée Condé, Chantilly (Ms. 867). Luisa Ricciarini/Bridgeman Images

199 Purchase, Gift of Dr. Mortimer D. Sackler, Theresa Sackler and Family, and John W. Byington Trust Gift, 2001. The Metropolitan Museum of Art, New York (2001.583)

202 The British Library, London (Royal 16 G. VI, f.117v)

207 Bibliothèque Sainte-Geneviève. Paris. Ms 782

208 engel.ac/Adobe Stock

219 Gift of J. Pierpont Morgan, 1917. The Metropolitan Museum of Art, New York (17.190.1710)

225 Frank/Adobe Stock

232 Harald Tittel/dpa/Alamy

235 Bibliothèque nationale de France, Département des Manuscrits, Français 6465

242 Bibliothèque nationale de France, Département Monnaies, médailles et antiques, CAR-1557

244 Bayerische Staatsbibliothek, Munich (BV035204406)

250 Purchase, Anonymous Gift, 1972. The Metropolitan Museum of Art, New York (1972.58)

254 Renáta Sedmáková/Adobe Stock

256–57 Özgür Güvenç/Adobe Stock

260 Manuscripts & Archives Research Library, Trinity College Dublin (IE TCD MS 58)

262 Bequest of Thomas Whittemore. Harvard Art Museums/Arthur M. Sackler Museum, Cambridge, MA (1951.31.4.1073)

265 Bibliothèque nationale de France. Département des Manuscrits. Latin 1118

268 Armands Pharyos/Alamy

271 Miscellany on the life of St. Edmund, *c.* 1130. The Morgan Library & Museum, New York (MS M.736)

276 Geography Photos/Universal Images Group via Getty Images

280 National Museum of Iceland, Reykjavík. Danuta Hyniewska/Adobe Stock

285 Aachen Cathedral Treasury. Sailko/ Wikimedia Commons

291 Danuta Hyniewska/Adobe Stock

294 Rogers Fund, 1955. The Metropolitan Museum of Art, New York (55.46.1)

299 Takashi Images/Adobe Stock

302 Biblioteca Nacional de España, Madrid (VITR/26/2)

304 Peter Barritt/Alamy

308 Imperial Treasury, Vienna. Imagno/Getty Images

310 Bibliothèque municipale de Besançon (Ms. 854)

313 Bibliotheca Palatina, Heidelberg University Library (Cod. Pal. germ. 345, Bl. 066v, 067v)

316 Ashmolean Museum/Heritage Images/ Getty Images

324 Gabriel Hildebrand/The Swedish History Museum, Stockholm (108914_HST)

325 Luis de Madrazo y Kuntz, Pelagius of Asturias in Covadonga, 1855. Museo del Prado, Madrid (P006272)

328–29 gob/Adobe Stock

331 Bequest of Thomas Whittemore. Harvard Art Museums/Arthur M. Sackler Museum, Cambridge, MA (1951.31.4.1422)

336 Biblioteca Nacional de España, Madrid (VITR/26/2)

338 Bayerische Staatsbibliothek, Munich (BSB-Hss Clm 4453)

Index

Bold page numbers refer to maps; *italic* page numbers indicate illustrations

Aachen 7, 209, 224, 239, 339; Cathedral 224, *225*; Charlemagne's palace *228*, 229
Abbasid dynasty and caliphate 172–83, **174–5**, **177**, *178*, 185, 276, 327, 330
Abd al-Malik, Caliph 179
Abd al-Rahman I, Emir of Córdoba 173, 185, 218, 327
Abd er-Rahman, Governor of Spain 202–3
Abraham (biblical figure) 161, 162
Abu al-Abbas, Caliph 173, *178*
Abu Bakr, Caliph 162, **163**, 165
Abu Muslim (Persian slave) 173
Ada Gospels 232, *232*
Adelaide of Italy, Holy Roman Empress 313
Adrianople, battle of (378) 49, 99
Adrianople, battle of (718) 172
Aegidius (Roman general) 95–6
Aethelfrith, King of Northumbria 137, 146
Aëtius, Flavius (Roman commander) 61, 62–3, 66, 95, 96
Aghlabid emirate **266**, 295
Agri Decumates 25, 42, 97
agriculture and farming 20, 42, 47, 61, 93, 176, 239, 242, 280, 341
Aidan, St 144, **145**
Aistulf, King of the Lombards 204, 207
al-Abbas (uncle of Muhammad) 173
Alain Barbetorte, Duke of Brittany **289**, 290
Alamanni (Germanic peoples) 25, 42, 54, 63, 96, 97, *97*, 188
Alamannia (Frankish kingdom) **234**, 235
Alans 43, **44–5**, 52–4, **53**, 55, 59, **60**, 61, 97
Alaric I, King of the Visigoths 58–9, 82, 86–7
Alboin, King of the Lombards 118
Alcuin of York 7–8, 9, 229, 232

Alexandria 33, 169, 218, *219*, 248, 250
Alfred the Great, King of the Anglo-Saxons 274, **275**, 315, *316*
Ali, Caliph 165
al-Mahdi, Caliph 176, **177**
al-Ma'mun, Caliph 178, 179
al-Mansur, Caliph 173, 176, **177**
al-Mansur, Vizier (Almanzor) **326**, 330
Alsace 97, 236
Althing (Icelandic assembly) 280, 284
Amalasuntha, Queen of the Ostrogoths 106, 107–8
Ambrosius Aurelianus (British war leader) 132, 138
Anastasius I, Eastern Roman Emperor 102, 188
Anastasius II, Eastern Roman Emperor 188, *188*
Anatolia 107, 108, 121, 124, 168–9, 172, 188, 302, 330
Angilbert (Frankish poet) 232
Angles 134, 136, 147, 191, 199
Anglo-Saxon Chronicle 137
Anglo-Saxons: origins 14, 132; artefacts *50*, *55*, *130*, *132*; conquest and settlement of Britain 14, 132–7, **133**, **135**, 138, 143, 144, 154, 159; Anglo-Saxon kingdoms 146–7, 154, 195, 242, 274, **275**, 294; Anglo-Saxon Church and missionaries 144, 204, *207*, 215, 229, 245, **246**, 248–50, 260, *260*, 261; Anglo-Saxon merchants 242
Angrarians 215, **217**
Anna, Princess consort of Kyiv 336
Anthemius, Western Roman Emperor 68
Antioch 33, 248, 250
anti-Semitism 82, 264–5
Aquitaine 61, 79, 81, 188, 202–3, 207, 211, 218, **234**, 235, 236, 238, 310
Arab merchants 276–7
Arabs 125, 161–85; establishment of caliphate 162, **163**; expeditions and conquests 165–72, **166–7**, **170–1**, 183–5, **184**, 202–3, 233, 250, 254–5, 259, 262, 265, 269, 295–8, **296–7**, 330–1; *see also* Abbasid dynasty and caliphate; Islam; Islamic civilization

and culture; Spain, Islamic; Umayyad dynasty and caliphate
Arbogast (Roman general) 58, **94**, 96
Arcadius, Eastern Roman Emperor *38*, 39, 55
Argyll 150
Arianism 33, 78, 79, 81, 83, 87, 89, 96, 98, 106, 113, 116, 119, 188
Armagh 142, 247
Armenia 25, 121, 330, 334
Arminius (Germanic chieftain) 39
Armorica 95, 159; *see also* Brittany
Arnulf, King of East Francia 288, 303, 312
Árpád (Magyar ruler) 303–4
Arthurian legends 137–40, **139**, 209
Asding Vandals 52, **53**, 59
Asparuh, Bulgar Khan 299
astronomy 178, 179, 209, 259
Asturias 183, 325–7
Athalaric, King of the Ostrogoths 107
Athaulf, King of the Visigoths 59
Athelstan, King of the English 9, 290, 315–16
Attila, King of the Huns 46, 62–6, **64–5**, 81, 128
Audoin, King of the Lombards 116, 118
Augsburg, battle of (910) 305
Augustine of Canterbury, St 146, 245, 247
Augustine of Hippo, St 70, *70*; *City of God* 70, 233
Augustus, Roman Emperor 17, 28, 39, 102
Austrasia 192, **193**, **194**, 198, 201, 211
Authari, King of the Lombards 118
Auvergne 75, 81
Auxerre 8–9
Avars 113, 116, 118, 119–21, *119*, **122–3**, 218, 219–21, *219*, **220**, 299, 304
Avitus, Western Roman Emperor 66

Badon, battle of *see* Mount Badon, battle of (*c.* 500)
Badr, battle of (624) 162, *164*, 165
Baetica (Roman province) 61, 81, 98
Baghdad 173, 176–8, **177**
Balearic Islands 89, 295
Ballon, battle of (845) 288, **289**

INDEX

Banu Qurayza (Jewish tribe) 162
Barcelona 59, 327
Bari 297, 298
Barmekids (Persian family) **177**, 178
Basil I, Byzantine Emperor 330–1
Basil II, Byzantine Emperor 331–4, *331*, 336
Basiliscus (Roman commander) **67**, 68, 71, 81, 89, 106
Basques 81, 183, 191, 218
Bavaria and Bavarians 96, 202, 218, **234**, 235, 236, 238, 312, **314**
Bede 8, 12, 144, 146; *Ecclesiastical History of the English People* 134; *Life of St Cuthbert* 136, *136*
Belgica (Roman province) 50, 187
Belgrade 120
Belisarius, Flavius (Eastern Roman military commander) 103, **104–5**, *107*, 108, **109**, 112, 118, 251
Benedict of Aniane, St 255, 258
Benedict of Nursia, St, Rule of 233–5, 255, 258
Benedictines 144, 255, 258, *258*
Berbers 93, 183, **184**, 185
Berchar, Mayor of Neustria 201
Bernicia **135**, 146
Bertha, Queen consort of Kent 146
Bjarni Herjolfsson 284
Bleda (Hunnish ruler) 62
Boethius 7, 86
Boniface, St (Wynfrith) 198, 204, *207*, 250
Boniface III, Pope 120
Boniface IV, Pope 254
Book of Kells *260*, 260, 261
Bordeaux, battle of (732) 202–3
Boris I, Bulgar Khan 303
Borre 201
Boulgarophygon, battle of (896) 302, *302*
Brissarthe, battle of (866) **289**, 290
Britain 131–59; Roman province *see* Britannia; end of Roman rule 6, 59, 131–4, *133*; Anglo-Saxon conquest and settlement 132–7, **133**, **135**, 138, 143, *144*; Anglo-Saxon kingdoms 146–7, 154, 195, 242, 247–8, 274, **275**, 294, 315, **317**; Viking raids and settlements 269, 270, **271**, 273–4, **275**, 294, 315–19, 324; unification of England 274, 315–18, **317**; *see also* Anglo-Saxons; Scotland and Scots; Wales

Britannia (Roman province) 12, 17, 25, 28, 50–2, **51**, 59, 131, 132, **133**
Brittany and Bretons 156, 157–9, *157*, 191, 218, 288–90, **289**; Britons in Brittany 95, 134, 138, 143, 144, 157–9, **158**
brooches 50, *63*; *see also* fibulae
Brunanburh, battle of (937) 316, **317**
Bulgars and Bulgar Khanate 102, 172, 276, **278–9**, 298–303, **300–1**, 331–4, **332–3**
Burgundy and Burgundians 42, 55, 63, 68, 75, 79, 96, 191, **193**, **194**, 199, 202, 288, 298, 305, 309
Buwayhid emirates **174–5**, 176
Byzacena (Roman province) 61
Byzantine Empire (Eastern Roman Empire) 15, 101–29; early emperors 68–9, 83, 101–2, 188, 199; under Justinian I 87, 102–16, 118, 119–20, 125, **129**, 191, 195; under Phocas 120–1, **122–3**, 265; under Heraclius 101, 121–5, **126–7**, 168; Arab campaigns and conquests 165–7, **166–7**, **170–1**, 183, 265, 295, **296–7**, 298; Lombard campaigns and conquests 204; Frankish campaigns and conquests **212–13**, 215, 218, 223, 295; Viking campaigns and conquests 276–7, 298; Bulgar campaigns and conquests 298–303, **300–1**, 331–4; Magyar raids 305; Byzantine recovery 330–4, **332–3**, 339–40; fall of 70, 128, 340
Byzantine culture and civilization 255, **256–7**, 262–4, 265, 331, 336
Byzantium 33, 101, 125; *see also* Constantinople

Caen 291, 294
Cairo 165, 178
Canterbury cathedral *146*
Capetian dynasty 309, 310–12
Cappadocia 17, 124, 255, **256–7**
Caracalla, Roman Emperor 24
Caradoc *see* Cerdic, King of Wessex
Carham, battle of (1018) 319, **320**
Carloman (son of Charles Martel) 203–4, 207
Carloman (son of Louis the German) 286, **287**
Carloman I, King of the Franks 207, 210, **210**, 211, 214, 215
Carolingian dynasty and empire

209–43; Carolingian takeover of Frankish kingdom 201–7, **206**, 209–11, **210**, 250; Charlemagne's early conquests 211–15, **212–13**; conquest of Saxony 214, 215–18, **217**; Charlemagne's continued campaigns 218–21, **220**, 265, 288, 295, 299, 327; Charlemagne's rule as emperor 221–33, **222**, **226–7**, **230–1**, 247, 254, 261, 269, 270; under Louis the Pious 233–6, *235*, 258; division and rule of empire after Louis the Pious 97, 198, 236–9, **237**, 284–8, **287**, 290, **296–7**, 298, 309–10, 312, 327; breakup of empire 284–8, **287**, 291, **292–3**, 309–10
Carolingian culture and civilization 247, 258, 259, 261, 262; Carolingian Renaissance 229–33, **230–1**, 263
Carthage 61, 62, 89, 92, 93, 106, 121, 183, 259
Carus, Roman Emperor 25
Catalaunian Plains, battle of (451) 63, **64**, 81, 95
Catholicism, Roman 79, 81–2, 87, 89, 96, 102, 106, 113, 119, 143, 187–8, 245, 305, 325, 340; *see also* papacy
Catterick, battle of (c. 600) 137
Celestine I, Pope 140
Celtic Church 141, 143–5, *144*, **145**, 147, 159, 255, 260, *260*
Celts 24, 132, 134, 136, 137, 157
Cerdic, King of Wessex 137
Chalcedon 172
Charibert I (Merovingian king) 192, **194**
Charlemagne *208*, 209–33, *235*, *242*; origins and early years 207, 209–11, **210**; early conquests 211–15, **212–13**; conquest of Saxony 214, 215–18, **217**; continued campaigns 218–21, **220**, 288, 295, 299, 327; coronation and rule as emperor 211, 215, 221–9, **222**, **226–7**, 242, 254, 261, 265, 269, 270; Carolingian Renaissance 229–33, **230–1**; reputation and importance 8, 147, 209, 233, 312, 339
Charles (son of Charlemagne) **222**
Charles III the Simple, King of West Francia 291, **292–3**, 309
Charles Martel 185, 198, 202–3
Charles the Bald, Carolingian Emperor **234**, 235–6, **237**, 238, 286, **287**, 288, 290

INDEX

Charles the Fat, Carolingian Emperor 239, 286–8, **287**, 309
Chester, battle of (616) 137, 154
Childebert I, Merovingian king 190, 191, **193**
Childebert II, Merovingian king **194**
Childeric I, King of the Salian Franks 95, 96, 187
Childeric III, King of the Franks 203–4
Chilperic I, Merovingian king 191–2, **194**
China 7, 12, 128
Chloderic, King of the Ripurian Franks 188
Chlodomer, Merovingian king 190, 191, **193**
Chlothar I, Merovingian king 190, 191, **193**
Chlothar II, Merovingian king 193, **194**, 195, 201
Chlothild, Queen consort of the Franks 187, 190
Christianity 245–8, **246**, 259–62, 339–41; in Britain 133, 134, 143–5, **145**, 146, 148, 150, 154, 245, 247–8, 260, *260*, 261, 273, 318; in Brittany 156, *157*, 159; in Bulgar Khanate 303; in Byzantine Empire 87, *100*, 102, 113, 120, 124, 125, 168, 221, 250, 262–3, 295; in Frankish territories 187–8, 198, 216, 221, 225, 229, 233–5, 245, 247, 250, 258, 259, 261; in Germanic kingdoms 33, 78, 79, 81–2, 83, 87, 89, *92*, 96, 97, 98, 106, 116, 119; in Holy Roman Empire 313–15; in Hungary 305, 313; in Ireland 134, 140–3, **142**, 144, *144*, 245, 247, 258–9; in Islamic caliphates and territories 161, 172, 173, **184**, 185, 325–30, *325*, **326**; in Kyivan state 247, 336; in Normandy 291, 294; in Roman Empire 28, 29–36, **34–5**, 70, 245; in Scandinavia 247, 318, 324; *see also* Arianism; Catholicism, Roman; Celtic Church; missionaries; monasteries and monasticism; Monophysitism; Orthodox Church; papacy; Reconquista; True Cross
Cimbri (tribe) 39, **40–1**
Cleph, King of the Lombards 118
Clovis I, King of the Franks 96, 97, *186*, 187–90, **189**, 202, 224

Cluny monastery 259, 298
Cnut, King of Denmark, Norway and England 318, 324
Codex Aureus (Golden Book) 244, 245, 261
Coenwulf, King of Mercia 147
Cologne 95, 198
Columba, St 144, **145**, 154
Columbanus (Irish missionary) 144, **145**
Commodus, Roman Emperor 20, 24
Conan Meriadec (legendary founder of Brittany) 159
Conrad I, King of Germany 312
Constantine I the Great, Roman Emperor 15, 29–36, *32*, *125*, 245, 250
Constantine III, Western Roman Emperor 49, 55, 59, 131
Constantine IV, Byzantine Emperor 169, 299
Constantine VIII, Byzantine Emperor 331, *331*
Constantinople: foundation 33–6, 101, *125*; construction and development 108, *109–10*, 116, **129**; blockaded by Persians and Avars 124; besieged by Arabs 168–71, **170–1**, 295; attacked by Vikings 276, 277; besieged by Bulgars 302, 303; Magyar raids 305; attacked by Rus' 334, *336*; sack of 1204 29, 101; captured by Ottoman Turks (1453) 70, 108, 128
Constantinople (characteristics): circus factions 103, 106, 120; impregnability 71, 125, 168, 169, 303; location and strategic importance 33, *125*; personification of *2*, *219*; population totals 128; seat of Christianity 33, 36, *125*, 248, 250; seat of learning 264
Constantinople (landmarks & places): churches *125*, 128, **129**; Hagia Sophia *32*, *32*, 108, *109–10*, 116; Obelisk of Theodosius *49*, *49*; walls 71, *125*, 128, 169
Constantius I Chlorus, Roman Emperor 28, *28*, 29, **30–1**
Constantius III Flavius, Western Roman Emperor 59, 61
Córdoba 183, 185, **326**, 327, *328–9*
Cornwall 138, **139**, 140, 157, 159

Corsica 89, 295
Covadonga, battle of (718) 325, *325*, **326**
Crete 295, 331
Crusades 101, 124, 168, *169*, 218
Culdee **142**, 143
Cuthbert, St 136, *136*
Cyprus 218, *219*, 295
Cyzicus 169

Dacia 17, *21*, 25, 42
Dagobert I, King of the Franks 159, 196, *196*
Dál Riata dynasty 150, **153**, 318, **320**
Dalmatia 68, 69
Damascus 165, 173, 176, 179, 182, 185; Great Mosque 182
Danelaw 273–4, **275**, 316–18, **317**
Danes 11, 191, 199, 273–4, 294, 315–18, 321–4, **322–3**, *324*; *see also* Vikings
'Dark Ages', use of term 11–12
David, King (biblical figure) 264, *265*
Deira **135**, 146
Desiderius, King of the Lombards 211, 214–15
Diocletian, Roman Emperor 25, 28–9, *28*, **30–1**, 33, 37, 124
divisio regni (Charlemagne; 806) **222**, 223
Dol 288, 290
Donation of Constantine 250
Dorestad 196, 198, 239–42, **240**, 270
Dublin 270, 273, 294, 316
Dumbarton 140, 319
Dumnonia 132, 154, 159
Dunadd 150, 318
Dyrham, battle of (577) 137, 154

East Anglia (Anglo-Saxon settlement and kingdom) *130*, 131, 134, 137, 146, 270, *271*, 274, 315, **317**
East Francia **237**, 238, 288, **300–1**, 303, 305, **306–7**, 312; *see also* Germany (post-Carolingian kingdom)
Easter, calculating date of 143, 144
Eastern Roman Empire *see* Byzantine Empire
Eastphalians 215, **217**
Ecgberht, King of Wessex 147
Ecgfrith, King of Mercia 147
Ecgfrith, King of Northumbria 146–7

Ecija, battle of (1711) 183, **184**
Edgar, King of England 318, 319, **320**
Edington, battle of (878) 274, **275**
Edmund the Martyr, St 270, *271*
Edward the Elder, King of the Anglo-Saxons 315
Edwin, King of Northumbria 146, 147
Egypt 47, 113, 121, 165, 168, 169, 176, 255, 265, 330
Einhard (Frankish scholar) 209, 215, 221, 232
Ellendun, battle of (825) 147, **275**
Erik Bloodaxe, King of Norway 316, **317**
Erik the Red (Norse explorer) 284
Erispöe, King of Brittany **289**, 290
Eriugena, John Scotus 8–9, 232–3, 261
Essex (Anglo-Saxon settlement and kingdom) 134, 146, **275**
Ethelbert, King of Kent 146, *146*
Ethelflaed, Lady of the Mercians 315
Ethelred, Lord of the Mercians 315
Eudes, Count of Blois 310
Eudes, King of West Francia 286, 288, 309, 310
Eudo, Duke of Aquitaine 202–3
Eudocia (daughter of Valentinian III) 89, 106
Eugenius, Western Roman Emperor **56**–**7**, 58
Euric, King of the Visigoths 81

Faroe Islands 144, 280
Fergus MacErc, King of Dál Riata 150
fibulae (brooches) *42*, *46*, *58*, *97*, *98*, *191*
Finns 276, 303, **322**
Flanders 291, 294
Floki Vilgerdarson (Viking explorer) 280
Fontenoy, battle of (841) 238
Fortriu (Pictish kingdom) 150, **153**, 154, 318, **320**
France (post-Carolingian kingdom) 305, 309–12, **311**
Francia 216, 229, 290; Muslim raids **296**–**7**, 298; Viking raids 269, 270, 274, 286, 288; *see also* East Francia; West Francia
Franconia 312, **314**

Franks 25, 42, 50, 52, 54, 63, 68, 81, 97, 98–9, 118, 146, 159, 199, 288, 295; early kingdoms 93–6, **94**, **114**, 187–8, 224; *see also* Carolingian dynasty and empire; Francia; Merovingian dynasty
Fraxinetum 297, 298
Frigidus, battle of (394) 58
Frisians 191, 195–8, **197**, 201, 202, 247
Fursa (Irish missionary) 144, *145*

Gaiseric, King of the Vandals 61–2, 66, 68, 89
Galerius, Roman Emperor 28, *28*, 29, **30**–**1**
Galicia 143, 144, **326**, 327, 330
Galla Placidia 59, 88
Gallaecia (Roman province) 59–61, 81, 97–8
Gallic Empire 25, **26**–**7**, 52
Gallienus, Roman Emperor 25, **26**–**7**
Gascony 190, 211
Gaul 25, 28, 47, 50, 52, **53**, 55, 59, 63, 66, 68, 81, 93, 95–6, 140–1, 187, 245
Gautbertus 8–9
Gelimer, King of the Vandals **104**, 106–7
Geoffrey of Monmouth 159
Gepids 42, 82, 96, **114**, 116, 118
Gerbert of Aurillac 339
German Empire *see* Holy Roman Empire
Germani (Germanic tribal peoples) 6, 9, 21–4, 39–42, **44**–**5**, 71, **76**–**7**, 93; origins 39, 199; raids and migrations 20–1, 39, **40**–**1**, 42, 50, 75, 93, 96, 97, 195, 199; religion 33, 78, 79, 81–2, 83, 87, 89, *92*, 96, 97, 98; social organization and administration 9, 21, 42, 75–9, 96; troops and warriors 37, 42, 58, 98–9; *see also* Alamanni; Anglo-Saxons; Bavarians; Burgundians; Franks; Gepids; Goths; Heruls; Lombards; Marcomanni; Rugii; Sarmatians; Scirians; Suevi; Vandals
Germany (post-Carolingian kingdom) 305, 309, 312–15, **314**
Geta, Roman Emperor 24
Géza I, King of Hungary 304, *304*, 305
Gibbon, Edward, *Decline and Fall of the Roman Empire* 70
Gildas 159; *On the Ruin of Britain* 132, 134, 138

Glaber, Ralph 6
Göreme (Cappadocia), 'Dark Church' 255, *256*–*7*
Götar 199, **322**, 324
Goths 25, 42, 47–9, **48**, 79, 99, 131, 199; *see also* Greuthungi; Ostrogoths; Tervingi; Visigoths
Greek Fire (weapon) 169, 172, 334, 336, *336*
Greenland **282**–**3**, 284
Gregory I the Great, Pope 8, 12, *13*, 146, 247–8
Gregory II, Pope 263
Gregory IV, Pope 236
Gregory VII, Pope 315
Gregory of Tours 188, 191–2, 199
Greuthungi (Gothic tribe) 42, 43, 47, 82
Guadalette, battle of (711) 183, **184**
Guntram, Merovingian king 192, **194**
Guthrum, King of East Anglia 274, **275**, 315

Hadrian, Roman Emperor 17, 20, *20*, 254
Hadrian I, Pope 214, 215
Hadrian the African, Abbot 8
Hadrian's Wall 20, *22*–*3*, 52, 140
Hafrsfjord, battle of (c. 900) 32, 321, **322**
Hajj (pilgrimage) 182, *182*
Harald Bluetooth, King of Denmark and Norway *10*, *11*, 247, **322**–**3**
Harald Fairhair, King of Norway 321–4
Harun al-Rashid, Caliph 176, 178, 265, 330
Hebrides 273, 280, 319
Heiric of Auxerre 8–9
helmets *16*, *17*, 99, *130*, 131
Hengist (legendary figure) 134, 136, 146
Henry I the Fowler, King of Germany 305, 312, *313*
Heraclius, Byzantine Emperor 101, 121, *121*, 124–5, **126**–**7**, 168
Heruls (Germanic peoples) 96, 199
Hildebad, King of the Ostrogoths 109
Hildegard (wife of Charlemagne) 211
Hippo Regius (Annaba) 61, 70, 107
Hispania (Roman province) 25, 28, **34**, **53**, 55, 59, 66, 81
Holy Roman Empire 15, 223, *308*, 309, 310, 312–15, **314**, 339–40

Honorius, Western Roman Emperor 54, 55, 58–9, 71, 86
Horsa (legendary figure) 134, 136, 146
Hugh Capet, King of the Franks 309, 310
Hugh the Great, Duke of the Franks 309, 310, *310*
Huneric, King of the Vandals 89
Hungary, Kingdom of 303–5, *304*, **306–7**
Huns 24, 43–6, **44–5**, 61, 62–6, *63*, **64–5**, 68, *68*, 71, 82, 95, 96, 97, 128, 298, 303, 304
Hygelac, King of the Geats 199

Ibn al-Arabi, Governor of Zaragoza 218
Iceland 144, 273, 280, **281**, **282–3**, 284
iconoclasm 221, 262–3, 265, 295, 302
Ifriqiya 176, 183, 330
Igor, Prince of Kyiv 334–6, **335**
Illyria 25, 58
India 12, 179, 201
Indulf, King of Alba 319, **320**
Ireland and Irish 6, 52, 132, **133**, 146, 150, 280; Early Christian Ireland 134, 140–3, **142**, 144, *144*, 154, 245, 247, 258–9; Viking raids and settlements 269, 270, 273–4, **275**, 294
Irene, Byzantine Empress 223, 263
Iron Age 132, 134, 156, *157*, 198
Islam 161–2, 165, 168, 172–3, 179, 182, 183, 262
Islamic civilization and culture 178–83, *180–1*, *328–9*
Isle of Man 132, 146
Italy (post-Carolingian kingdom) 309, 313
Ivan, St 299

Jelling Stone *10*, 11
Jengland-Beslé, battle of (851) **289**, 290
Jerusalem 33, 124, 125, 248, 250; Dome of the Rock *180–1*, 182
Jews 161, 162, **163**, 172, 173, **184**, 185, 264–7, **266–7**; *see also* anti-Semitism
John I Tzimisces, Byzantine Emperor 331

John Skylitzes 302, 336
Judaism 161, 173, 265
Judith of Bavaria 235–6
Julian, Roman Emperor 93
Julius Nepos, Western Roman Emperor 68–9, **72–3**, 81
Justin I, Eastern Roman Emperor 102
Justin II, Eastern Roman Emperor 102, 118, 120
Justinian I, Eastern Roman Emperor 32, 83, 87, 102–16, *103*, *107*, **114–15**, 118, 119–20, 125, **129**, 191, 195
Jutes 134, 136, 191, 199
Jutland 11, 39, 134, 195, 199, 201, **323**

Karbala, battle of (680) 165, **167**
Kavad II, Sasanian King of Kings 124–5
Kenneth MacAlpin, King of Dál Riata and the Picts 154, 318
Kent (Anglo-Saxon settlement and kingdom) 8, *50*, 134, 136, 146, *146*, 147, 274, **275**
Khazar khanate 265, **266–7**, 276, **278–9**, 334
Khusrau II, Sasanian King of Kings 120, 121, *121*, 124
Khwarazmians 178
Krum, Bulgar Khan 299, 302
Kubrat, Bulgar Khan 298
Kyivan Rus' **266–7**, 277, **278–9**, 334–7, **335**, *336*

law 79, 81, 137, 341; *Corpus Juris Civilis* (Byzantine Body of Civil Law) 113; *Lex Visigothorum* (Law of the Visigoths) 75; Salic code 224
Le Mans 188, 290
Lechfeld, battle of (955) 305, **306**, 313
Leif Erikson (Norse explorer) 284
Leo I, Eastern Roman Emperor 68
Leo III, Pope 221, 223, 264
Leo III the Isaurian, Byzantine Emperor 172, 262, *262*, 263, 265
Leo V the Armenian, Byzantine Emperor 302
León, Kingdom of **326**, 327, 330
Lex Visigothorum (Law of the Visigoths) 74, 75
Libius Severus, Western Roman Emperor 66
Libya 8, 165
Lindisfarne 269; Gospels 146, 261

Lindsey (Anglo-Saxon kingdom) 146, **275**
Lombards 79, 87, 97, **98**, 114, 116–19, **117**, **122–3**, 199, 204, 207, 211–15, **212–13**, 216, 218, 250, 251
London 52, 147, 315
Lothar I, Carolingian Emperor **234**, 235–6, **237**, 238, 284
Lothar II, Carolingian king 284–6, *285*
Lotharingia 284, 286
Lothian 319, **320**, 321
Louis II, Carolingian king 284, 298
Louis II the Stammerer, King of West Francia 310
Louis III the Child, King of East Francia 305, 312
Louis V, King of West Francia 309, 310
Louis the German, Carolingian king **234**, 235–6, **237**, 238, 284, 286
Louis the Pious, Carolingian Emperor 8, 219, **222**, 223, 233–6, **234**, *235*, 258, 284, 288
Luxeuil monastery 259, 297

Macedonia 58
Macedonian dynasty 330–1
Maghrib 176, 330
Magnus Maximus, Western Roman Emperor 58, 159
Magyars 233, 259, 269, 303–5, **306–7**, 313, *313*
Mainz 52, 54, 55, 93, 96, 250
Majorian, Western Roman Emperor 66, 251
Marcomanni (Germanic people) 20–4, 97
Marcus Aurelius, Roman Emperor 20–4
Marseille 298
Martianus Capella, *Philologia* 259–60
Masts, battle of the (655) **166**, 169
mathematics 179, 259, 261
Matthew the Evangelist, St 232, *232*
Mauretania 17, 61, 89, 92
Maurice, Eastern Roman Emperor 120
Maxentius, Roman Emperor 29, 32
Maximian, Roman Emperor 28, 29, **30–1**, 37
Mecca 161, 162, 179, 182
Medina 162, 165
Meginfred (Frankish chamberlain) 219, **220**

INDEX

Mercia (Anglo-Saxon settlement and kingdom) 146, 147, 154, 156–7, 242, 274, **275**, 315, **317**
Merovech (founder of Merovingian dynasty) 95, 190
Merovingian dynasty 93, 95, 159, 187–207, **189**, **193**, **194**, **205**, 223, 238, 239, 241, 250, 288, 309
Mersen, Treaty (870) 286, **287**
Mesembria, battle of (817) **301**, 302
Mesopotamia 17, 25, 121, 124, 176
Michael I, Byzantine Emperor 302
Michael II, Byzantine Emperor 295
Michael III, Byzantine Emperor 302–3, 331
Migration Period (c. 400–600) 195, 198–9, **200**
Milan 86
Milan, Edict of (313) 32
Milvian Bridge, battle of (312) 32
missionaries 134, 140–1, 144, **145**, 146, 198, 201, 204, 215, 229, 245–8, **246**, 250, 313, 324
monasteries and monasticism 143–4, **145**, 146–7, **148–9**, 154, 157–9, 235, 255–9, *258*, 261, 269–70, 298, 299, *299*
Mongols 298, 337
Monophysitism 102, 103, 113, 120, 161, **163**, 168
Monte Cassino monastery 204, 255, 259
Moravia **278**, 303, 312
Moray 319, **320**
Mount Badon, battle of (c. 500) 132, 137–8, **139**, 140
Mozarabs **184**, 185, 203
Muawiya, Caliph 165, 169
Muhammad, Prophet 161–2, **163**, *164*, 165, 168, 172, 173
Muirdach's High Cross 144, *144*
Muslims *see* Arabs; Islam; Islamic civilization and culture
Mu'tazilism 179

Nantes 288, **289**, 290
Naples 8, 108
Narbonne 59, 202
Narses (Byzantine general) **109**, 112, 118, 191
Navarre **326**, 327, 330
Nechtansmere, battle of (685) 147, **153**
Nennius, *History of the Britons* 138
Nero, Roman Emperor 20
Nerva, Roman Emperor 20

Nestorians 161, **163**
Neustria 187, 192, **193**, **194**, 201, 202
New World, discovery of **282–3**, 284
Newfoundland **282–3**, 284
Niall, King of Ireland 140
Nicaea: first council of (325) 33; second council (786) 263
Nicephorus I, Byzantine Emperor 302
Nicephorus II, Byzantine Emperor 331
Nika riots (532) 103, 106, 125
Nineveh, battle of (627) 124
Nomenoë, Duke of Brittany 288–90, **289**
Nordliudi 215, **217**
Noricum (Roman province) 58, 59, 69
Normandy and Normans 290, 291–5, *291*, **292–3**, 310; conquest of England 218, 294, 318
North America **282–3**, 284
Northumbria (Anglo-Saxon settlement and kingdom) 134, **135**, 136, 137, 143, 144, 146–7, 154, 269, 274, **275**, 315, **317**
Norway, Kingdom of 321–4, **322**
Novgorod 277
Numidia (Roman province) 61, 92
Nydam archaeological site 199

Odin (Norse god) *199*
Odo *see* Eudes, King of West Francia
Odoacer (Hunnic-Germanic soldier) 69, 75, 83, 87, 102
Offa, King of Mercia 147, 156, 242, 243
Offa's Dyke 147, 156–7
Olaf Tryggvasson, King of Norway 324
Oleg, Prince of Kyiv 277, **278–9**, 334
Olof Skötkonung, King of Sweden 324
On-Ogur (Magyar confederation) 303
Orestes (Roman general) 68–9
Orkney Islands 273, 324
Orléans 233, 310
Orthodox Church 245, **246**, 255, 262–3, 299, *299*, 303, 336, 340
Ostrogoths 7, 75, 82, 102, 106, 116; Ostrogothic kingdom 82–8, **84–5**, 88, 107–12, **109**, 191, 251
Otto I, Holy Roman Emperor 9, 305, *308*, 309, 312–15

Otto III, Holy Roman Emperor 284, 310, *338*, 339–40
Ottoman Turks 70, 108, 128, *164*

Paderborn 216, 221
paganism 29, 70, 95, 96, 113, 116, 125, 140, 187, 201, 215, 216, 233, 245, 247–8, 265, 294
Palestine 113, 121, 165, 168, 265
Pannonia 82, 116, 219
papacy 7, 120, 204, 214, 215, 221, 245, 248–50, 255
Papal State 207, **234**, 248–50, **249**
Paris 187, 191, 202, **241**, 286, 288, 310
Parthians 17, 20, 24
Patrick, St 140–1
Paul, Count (Roman general) 95–6
Pavia 108, 118, 191, 214, 215
Pechenegs (Turkic people) 276, 303
Pelayo, King of Asturias 325–7, *325*
Pepin the Short *see* Pippin III
Pereyslavets, battle of (971) 334, **335**
Persia 17, 47, 93, 103, 108, 112, 118, 120, 121–5, 165, **166–7**, 176, 182–3; *see also* Sasanian Empire
Persian army 36, 43, 121
Peter (apostle) 248
Petrarch 11
Petronius Maximus, Western Roman Emperor 66
Phocas, Eastern Roman Emperor 120–1, **122–3**, 265
Picts 52, 132, **133**, 134, 144, 147–54, *151*, **152–3**, 245, 273, 318, 321
Piero della Francesca *121*
Pillar of Eliseg 157
Pippin (son of Charlemagne) 219–21, **220**, **222**, 232
Pippin I, King of Aquitaine **234**, 235–6, 238
Pippin I, Mayor of Austrasia 201
Pippin II, King of Aquitaine 238
Pippin II, Mayor of Austrasia 198, 201–2
Pippin III, King of the Franks 87, 97, 203–5, **206**, 207, *207*, 209, 211, 250
Pippin of Herstal *see* Pippin II, Mayor of Austrasia
piracy 50, 61–2, 89, 93, 150, 190, 199, 233, 259, 269, 286, 295, 298, 321
Plato 6, 179, 232, 264
Pliska 299, 302
Poitiers, battle of (732) 185, 202–3, *202*

Postumus, Gallic Emperor 25
Proconsularis (Roman province) 61
Provence 81, 191, 286, 309

Quentovic 196, 242
quernstones 196, 239, **243**
Quraysh (tribe) 161–2, 165

Radagaisus (Gothic king) **56**, 58
Radanites (Jewish merchants) 265, **266–7**
Radbod, King of Frisia 198
Ravenna 7, 59, 83, 86–7, **88**, 92, *103*, 108, 116, 118, 204, 207, 250
Reccared I, King of the Visigoths 81, *160*
Recceswinth, King of the Visigoths 75, 161
Reconquista 325–30, *325*, **326**
Remigius, St, Bishop of Reims 8–9, *186*, 187, 188
Rheged (British kingdom) 156
Rhine frontier, collapse of (406–7) 52–5, **53**, 58, 95, 96, 97
Rhodri Mawr, King of Gwynedd **155**, 156
Riade, battle of (933) 305, **306**, 312, *313*
Ribe 201
Richard the Fearless, Count of Rouen 294
Richard the Good, Duke of Normandy 294
Ricimer (general) 66, 68, **72–3**, 89, **90**
'Ring' (Avar fortress) 219, **220**, 221
Riothamus, King of the Britons 95, 159
Ripuarian Franks **94**, 95, 188
Robert II, King of the Franks 310–12
Rollo, Count of Rouen 290, 291, *291*, **292–3**
Roman army and military defences 24, 25, 36–7, 43, 50–2, **51**, 58, 95, 98, 99, 112, 124
Roman Empire 15, 101–29; first century AD 17, 20; under Trajan 17, **18–19**, 20; under Hadrian 17, 20, *22–3*; reign of Marcus Aurelius 20–4; third-century crisis 24–5, **26–7**, 36; reign of Diocletian 25, 28–9, **30–1**, 33, 37; under Constantine I 29–36; under Theodosius I 28, 29, 39, **48**, 49, 55–8, **56–7**, 128; last of

the western emperors 66–70, **72–3**, 81; fall of western empire 11, 39–73, 93, 101–2, 195, 239; *see also* Byzantine Empire
Romanus II, Byzantine Emperor 331
Rome 250–5, **252–3**; third century 28, **30–1**; sack of 410 55–9, **56–7**, 62, 70, 71, 250, 251; sack of 455 62, 66, 89, 251; in Ostrogothic kingdom 108, 112, 251; siege of 537–8 108, **109**, 251; siege of 544 **109**, 112; in Byzantine Empire 204, 254; in Carolingian Empire 215, 221, 254, 297, 298; late-ninth century 255
Rome (characteristics): location and communications 86; papacy 204, 207, 248–50, 255; patriarchate 33; population totals 250–1, 255; symbolism and personification 2, 55, *219*
Rome (landmarks & places): aqueducts 251; Castel Sant' Angelo 254; Circus Maximus 83, 251; Forum 251, 254; Lateran Palace 251, 254, *254*; Leonine City 255; Pantheon 254; San Lorenzo Church 254; St Peter's Church 221, 254–5; Trajan's Column 21, *21*; Vatican 255
Romulus Augustulus, Western Roman Emperor 68–9, 101
Roncesvalles Pass, battle of (778) 218, **326**, 327
Rosamund (daughter of Cunimund) 118
Rouen 294; Cathedral *291*
Rugii (Germanic peoples) **40–1**, 64, 69, 96
Rurik (ruler of Novgorod) 277, 334
Rus' people 247, **266–7**, 274–9, **278–9**, 334–7, **335**, *336*

Saffarid emirate 176
Salian Franks **94**, 95, 187
Salomon, King of Brittany **289**, 290
Samanid emirate 176
Samuel, Bulgar Tsar 331
Santiago de Compostela 330
Sardinia 89, 106, 295
Sarmatians 43, 96
Sasanian Empire 24, 25, *25*, **114**, 120, 121–5, **122–3**, 163, 165, 168, 176

Saxo Grammaticus 199
Saxon Shore (Roman military command) 50–2, **51**
Saxony and Saxons 50, *50*, 52, *55*, 95, 132, 134, 137, 191, 199, 201, 202, 312; Carolingian conquest and rule 214, 215–18, **217**, 219, 225, 247, 286; *see also* Anglo-Saxons
Scandinavia 321–4, **322**, **323**; pre-Viking 196, 198–201, **200**, 242
Scirians (Germanic peoples) 65, 96
Scotland and Scots 132, 134, 138, 146, 150–4, **152–3**, 270, **275**, 316, 318–21, **320**
Seljuq Turks 340
Septimania 190, 202, 203, 218
Serena (wife of Stilicho) 54
Sergius I, Patriarch of Constantinople 124
Severus, Septimius, Roman Emperor 24
Shapur I, Sasanian King of Kings 25, *25*
Shetland Islands 273, *276*
Sicily 62, 89, 106, 108, 169, 295, 331
Sigibert I, Merovingian king 192, **194**
Sigibert the Lame, King of the Ripuarian Franks 188
Sigismund of Burgundy, St 191
Siling Vandals 52, **53**, 59–61, **60**
Simeon I, Emperor of Bulgaria 302, *302*, 303
Sisebut, King of the Visigoths 81
Skellig Michael monastery 147, *148–9*
Slavs 112, 116, 119–21, **122–3**, 218, 276, 277, 299, 303, 312, 334
Soissons 187, 191, 204
South Cadbury hillfort 132, 140
Spain: Visigothic kingdom 79–82, **80**, **114**, 183; Vandals in 89, 97–8; Islamic Spain 82, 173, 183–5, **184**, 202, 245, 295, **296–7**, 298, 325–30, *328–9*; Frankish campaigns 218–19; Reconquista 325–30, *325*, **326**; *see also* Hispania
Spoleto 118
St Clair-sur-Epte, Treaty of (911) 291
St Emmeram's monastery 261
St Ivan's monastery 299, *299*
Stephen II, Pope 204, 250
Stephen III, Pope 211
Stilicho (military commander) 54, 55, 58, 59, 131

INDEX

Stora Hammars stones *268*, 269
Strasbourg 96, 238
Strathclyde 156, 316, 319, **320**, 321
Suevi (Germanic peoples) 52, 54, 55, **60**, 66, 79, **80**, 81, 96, 97–8, **114**
Sussex (Anglo-Saxon settlement and kingdom) 134, 137, 146, **275**
Sutton Hoo ship burial *130*, 131
Svear (Swedish people) **200**, 201, **322**, 324
Svein Forkbeard, King of Denmark 294, 324
Svyatoslav I, Prince of Kyiv 334, **335**
Swabia 211, 286, 312, **314**
Sylvester I, Pope 250, 339
Sylvester II, Pope 339
Syria 25, 113, 121, 162, 165, 168, 169, 265, 331

Tariq (Arab general) 183
Tassilo III, Duke of Bavaria 211
Teia, King of the Ostrogoths 112
Tertry, battle of (687) 201
Tervingi (Gothic tribe) 42, 46–7
Teutones (tribe) 39, **40–1**
Theodahad, King of the Ostrogoths 107–8
Theodomire of Alicante (Visigothic noble) **184**, 185
Theodora (wife of Justinian I) 87, 102, 106, 116
Theodore of Tarsus, Archbishop of Canterbury 8
Theodoric (Frankish count) 219, **220**
Theodoric II, King of the Visigoths 66, 81
Theodoric the Great, King of the Ostrogoths 82–6, *83*, **84–5**, 87, 102, 107, 188, 251
Theodosius I, Roman Emperor 28, 29, *38*, 39, 48, 49, 55, **56–7**, 101, 128
Theodosius II, Eastern Roman Emperor 75, 128
Theodulf, Bishop of Orléans 232, 233
Theophano, Byzantine Empress 331, 340
Theudebald, Merovingian king 190
Theudebert I, Merovingian king 190, 191
Theuderic I, Merovingian king 190, **193**
Thiudimir, King of the Ostrogoths 82
Thor (Norse god) 247, 280, *280*
Thrace 47, 82

Thuringians 187
Tingitana (Roman province) 61
Toledo 81, 161, 183
Toledo, Council of 78, *78*
Totila, King of the Ostrogoths **109**, 112
Toulouse 81, 188
Tournai 95
Tours 203
Tours, battle of *see* Poitiers, battle of (732)
Trajan, Roman Emperor 17, **18–19**, 20, 21, *21*
Trans, battle of (939) **289**, 290
Trinity, doctrine of the 33, 173
Tripolitania 89, 165
True Cross 101, 121, 124, 125
Tulunid dynasty 176, 183
Tunisia 183, 295, 298, 330

Uí Néill dynasty 141
Umar I, Caliph 165
Umar II, Caliph 172
Umayyad dynasty and caliphate 165–72, **166–7**, 173, 179, *180–1*, 182, 183–5, **184**, 327
Uthman, Caliph 165
Utrecht 198, 250

Valamir, King of the Ostrogoths 82
Valens, Eastern Roman Emperor 47, *47*, 49
Valentinian II, Western Roman Emperor *38*, 39
Valentinian III, Western Roman Emperor 66, 89, 106
Valerian, Roman Emperor 25
Valsgärde 201
Vandals: conquest and rule in Africa 59–62, **60**, 63–8, **67**, 71, 75, 81, 89–93, 97, 102–7, **104–5**, 259; crossing of Rhine frontier 52–5, **53**, **56**, 97; sack of Rome (455) 62, 66, 89, 251; Vandal kingdom 89–93, **90–1**, 102–7, **104–5**
Vannes 288, **289**
Vendel 201
Venice and Venetians 29, 218, 295, 298
Verbitza, battle of (811) **301**, 302
Verdun, Treaty of (843) 236–9, **237**, 241, 284
Verona 108, 112, 215
Vestfold 201, 321
Vikings 154, 199, 233, 236, 242, 247, 259, *268*, 269–84, **272**, 276, 286, 288, **289**, 290, 291, **293**, 294–5, 298, 315–19, 321, 324

Visigoths 49, 59–61, **60**, 63, 66, 68, 74, 75, 78, 95, 159, **160**, 161, 188; sack of Rome (410) 55–9, **56–7**, 62, 70, 71, 250, 251; Visigothic kingdom 79–82, **80**, **114**, 183, 185, 190, 264–5
Vithim, King of Greuthungi 43
Vivarium (Calabria) 7, 8
Vladimir I, Prince of Kyiv 247, 334
Volga Bulgars 276, 334
Vortigern, 'King of the Britons' 132, 134
Vouillé, battle of (507) 81, 188

Waifar, Duke of Aquitaine 207
Wales 6, 132, 138, 140, 147, 154–7, **155**
Wallia, King of the Visigoths 59
Waroc (Breton chieftain) 159
Wattonids 201
Wedmore, Treaty of (878) 274
Wessex (Anglo-Saxon settlement and kingdom) 134, 137, 146, 147, **237**, 274, **275**, 315, 316–18, **317**
West Francia 236, **237**, 238, 286, 291, **306–7**, 309–10; *see also* France (post-Carolingian kingdom)
Westphalians 215, **217**
Whitby, synod of (664) 144
Widukind, Duke of Saxony 216
Wilfrid, St, Bishop of York 198
William Longsword, Count of Normandy 294
William the Conqueror, King of England 294, 318
Willibrord, St 198, 201
Witigis, King of the Ostrogoths 108, **109**, 191, 251
Worms 96, 224
Wroxeter 132, 156
Wynfrith *see* Boniface, St

Xiongnu (nomad confederation) 43, **44–5**

Year of the Four Emperors (69) 20
York 132, 229, 274, 294, 315, 316, **317**

Zab, battle of (750) 173
Zacharias, Pope 204
Zaragoza 218
Zeno, Eastern Roman Emperor 68–9, 83, 102
Zoroastrianism 124, 161, 172

352